The Amazing Collection

Paul's Letters to the Churches Teaching Curriculum

Romans Through 2 Thessalonians

© 2017 by Big Dream Ministries, Inc.

No part of *The Amazing Collection*, whether audio, video, or print may be reproduced in any form without written permission from Big Dream Ministries, Inc. P.O. Box 324, 12460 Crabapple Road, Suite 202, Alpharetta, Georgia 30004
1-678-366-3460
www.theamazingcollection.org

ISBN-13: 978-1-932199-66-6
ISBN-10: 1-932199-66-7

By Big Dream Ministries

Cover design by Melissa Swanson

Some of the anecdotal illustrations in this book are true to life and are included with the permission of the persons involved. All other illustrations are composites of real situations, and any resemblance to people living or dead is coincidental.

Unless otherwise identified, all Scripture quotations in this publication are taken from the *New American Standard Bible (NASB)*.
© The Lockman Foundation 1960, 1962, 1968, 1971, 1972, 1973, 1975, 1977, 1995

Printed in the United States

INTRODUCTION TO PAUL'S LETTERS TO THE CHURCHES
Set Nine: Romans through Second Thessalonians

As we move on in our study of the New Testament books, we will begin an exploration of an entirely different form of literature. As we saw in Set Eight, the first five books of the New Testament are a historical narrative or story. They focus on people, places, and events. Beginning with Romans and ending with Revelation, we will study twenty-two books that make up the epistolary section of the New Testament—letters written from one person to another person or group of people.

The first thirteen of these letters were written by the apostle Paul, nine of them to local churches and four of them to men leading local churches. The books of Romans through Second Thessalonians were written by Paul over a period of fourteen years to seven churches scattered throughout Asia Minor, Greece, and Rome. These churches were in different stages of maturity and all needed instruction from the great apostle. Though Paul did not found all of them, he was looked to for leadership as these churches moved through various seasons of growth and challenge.

The names of the letters are derived from the city that the church was in, such as Romans was written to the church that was in Rome, and so on. These letters fit historically into the Book of Acts.

- ~ **Romans:** develops church doctrine and shows clearly the righteousness of God.
- ~ **First Corinthians:** addresses the serious problems that were occurring in the church in Corinth and it speaks to the correction of church problems.
- ~ **Second Corinthians:** Paul defends his ministry, his apostleship, and his actions and authority.
- ~ **Galatians**: clearly teaches that we have incredible liberty in Christ, incredible freedom.
- ~ **Ephesians:** calls for believers to walk worthy of the gospel of Christ.
- ~ **Philippians:** expresses the great joy we have in Christ.
- ~ **Colossians:** portrays the supremacy of Christ or the completeness of Christ.
- ~ **First Thessalonians:** points to the coming of the Lord.
- ~ **Second Thessalonians:** points to the day of the Lord.

Though these letters were written about 2,000 years ago, Pauls' words are just as important and applicable to churches and Christians today as they were in his time.

© 2018 Big Dream Ministries, Inc.

THE TEACHING GUIDE BULLETS/BOXES

Below is a reference guide explaining the bullet points. Do not let these become a stumbling block — they were designed to make the teaching outline easier to follow. Please note that the material presented in the boxes for "Teaching Tip," "Note," and "Application" may be used as time allows or you feel appropriate for your particular class.

Remember: your main goal is to share God's story!

▪	***Teaching Outline Points***	These are the teaching notes that come directly from the lessons taught by Pat Harley, Eleanor Lewis, Margie Ruether, and Linda Sweeney. They follow the student workbook's outline.
~	***Additional Teaching Notes***	
∗	***Further Detail***	These are additional teaching notes that bring greater detail to each lesson.
★	***Teaching Tip***	The information contained in these boxes is designed to give you more information — whether on background or culture or context.
♦	***Note***	
❋	***Illustration***	These "stories" are designed to directly support the points being made in the lesson. If you would prefer to use personal illustrations and/or applications, please be very sure that your personal story directly supports the lesson being taught in the workbook. Don't, however, fall prey to simply sharing a good story! Text may also emphasize a point by presenting a thought-provoking question.
❖	***Application***	
✝	***Scripture References***	These are specific scriptures being cited. We have used the New American Standard Bible (NASB).
⇨	***Summary Points***	These summarize an important "take-away" from the section being taught.
⌑	***Reviewing What We've Learned and Final Thoughts***	Repetition is a great teaching tool. These bullet points reiterate important topics with the goal to help those in your Bible study to "remember to remember." They will be used within the lesson and at the end in "Final Thoughts."

ROMANS

God's Righteousness Described

"For I am not ashamed of the gospel ...

For in it the righteousness of God is revealed.

Romans 1:16–17

SESSION FORTY-FIVE: ROMANS
God's Righteousness Described

✝ **Memory verse:** *"For I am not ashamed of the gospel ... For in it the righteousness of God is revealed." (Romans 1:16–17)*

Introduction: The book of Acts tells of the great expansion of the church as the good news began to spread throughout the Roman Empire and beyond. Increasingly there came a need for Christian doctrine to be set forth to protect churches from being led astray by false teachers or by those who wanted to return to the Mosaic Law. The book of Romans, one of the most important books in Scripture, is a masterful presentation and interpretation of what Jesus Christ' redemption accomplished through His life, death, and resurrection. Paul explains the important themes of church doctrine: the condemnation of God against sin, the sinfulness of man and his great need for righteousness before God, the righteousness given to man through the death of Christ the perfect sacrifice, the justification of man before God, and the glorification of man to follow. He gives clarity to the sinful nature of man, the salvation offered to him, and the lifestyle possible for him after his salvation. The entire picture is given from salvation (freedom from the penalty of sin) to sanctification (freedom from the power of sin) to glorification (freedom from the presence of sin).

- **Oral Review:** Please refer to the **REVIEW Section** in the following Teaching Guide Outline.

- **Homework:** Because this is the beginning of a new set, homework review may not be appropriate if time has passed since completion of the last set and students may not have their workbooks with them. The following questions, however, are good for review.
    The growth of the church in questions on the bottom of page 125 and all of 126
    The teaching about the Holy Spirit on pages 128–129
    Last question on page 132
    Middle question on page 138 asking: "Who is the last person you encouraged?"

- **Review Helps:** Written review is provided at the end of the teacher presentation. (Optional and time permitting.)

- **Teacher Presentation on the Book of Romans**

- **Learning for Life:** You may choose to discuss all or just one or two of the questions on page 32.

- **Closing prayer:** Pray that the truths in this profound theological book would reach both the minds and hearts of each person in the class and that they would not be ashamed of the Gospel—understanding that in it the righteousness of God is revealed.

ROMANS
Theme: God's Righteousness Described

OUTLINE AID FOR TEACHERS:

I. **MAN'S SIN: THE NEED FOR GOD'S RIGHTEOUSNESS (Romans 1–3:20)**

- **Romans 1:1–16**

    A. The gospel reveals the <u>RIGHTEOUSNESS of God.</u>

- **Romans 1:18**

    B. The gospel also reveals the <u>WRATH</u> of God against sin.

- **Romans 1:20–32**

    C. God revealed Himself to man through <u>CREATION</u>. (Gentiles are without excuse.)

    1. Man exchanged the <u>GLORY</u> of God for the glory of man.
    2. Man exchanged <u>TRUTH</u> for a lie.
    3. Man exchanged <u>NATURAL</u> sex for unnatural.

- **Romans 2**

    D. God revealed Himself in the <u>LAW</u>, but man broke it. (Jews are without excuse.)

- **Romans 3:1–20**

    E. God's conclusion is that <u>NO ONE</u> is righteous.

II. **GOD'S SALVATION: THE EXPLANATION OF RIGHTEOUSNESS (ROMANS 3:21–8)**

- **Romans 3:21–24**

    A. Justification is a legal term meaning "to <u>DECLARE</u> righteous."

- **Romans 3:25**

    B. We are justified by <u>FAITH</u> in Jesus apart from works.

- **Romans 4**

    C. Abraham was justified when he <u>BELIEVED</u> God, and God added righteousness to his account.

- **Romans 5–6**

    D. Justification means to make <u>PEACE</u> with God (past).
    E. Glorification means to be <u>PRESENT</u> with God (future).
    F. Sanctification means to develop the <u>CHARACTER</u> of God (present).
    G. Justification requires the <u>DEATH</u> of Jesus. Sanctification requires the <u>LIFE</u> of Jesus.

© 2018 Big Dream Ministries, Inc.

ROMANS
Theme: God's Righteousness Described

- **Romans 7–8**

    H. Paul said there are three laws:

    1. The law of <u>GOD</u>.
    2. The law of <u>SIN</u>.
    3. The law of the <u>SPIRIT</u>.

III. **MAN'S RESPONSIBILITY: THE JEWS' RELATIONSHIP TO RIGHTEOUSNESS (ROMANS 9–11)**

- **Romans 9**

    A. God chose Israel, but only a remnant of Israel <u>CHOSE</u> God.

    B. Israel pursued righteousness by <u>WORKS</u> and stumbled.

- **Romans 10–11**

    C. There is no distinction between Jew and Gentile. Whoever will <u>CALL</u> on the name of the Lord will be saved.

    D. God is not finished with Israel, for His <u>CALLING</u> is irrevocable.

IV. **GOD'S WILL: THE APPLICATION OF RIGHTEOUSNESS (ROMANS 12–16)**

- **Romans 12**

    A. Present your <u>BODY</u> to God as a living sacrifice.

    B. Be at <u>PEACE</u> with all men.

- **Romans 13**

    C. Be in <u>SUBJECTION</u> to authorities.

    D. Make no provision for the <u>FLESH</u> in regard to its lusts.

- **Romans 14**

    E. Don't <u>JUDGE</u> your brother.

- **Romans 15**

    F. <u>SERVE</u> and love your brother.

© 2018 Big Dream Ministries, Inc.

Romans
[God's Righteousness Described]

ROMANS

ROMANS
Theme: God's Righteousness Described

THE BASICS:
- **Who: The Author:** Paul
  - **Main Characters:** Believers in Rome
- **What:** Paul's discourse on God's gift of righteousness, which is received by faith and results in right living
- **When:** Written in A.D. 57, near the end of Paul's third missionary journey
- **Where:** Written to Rome from Corinth
- **Why:** To combat false teaching regarding righteousness

MEMORY VERSE: *"For I am not ashamed of the gospel ... For in it the righteousness of God is revealed." Romans 1:16–17*

****

REVIEW:

- The *Old Testament History* books showed the problem of disobedience and its consequences.
  - Disobedience caused Adam and Eve to be sent out of the garden—and the nation of Israel to be divided and exiled from God.
- The Old Testament prophets repeatedly warned that disobedience would bring God's judgment, but promised a Messiah who would come to make things right.
- It is interesting to note that none of the Old Testament books were written as letters.

- The *New Testament History* books show that the Messiah has come.
- The first four, the gospels, dealt with the history of Jesus. Each writer approached the life of Christ from a different perspective:
  - **Matthew:** addressed a Jewish audience and showed Jesus as the long-awaited King of the Jews.
  - **Mark:** addressed a Roman audience and presented Jesus as a suffering servant—a servant to all men and women.
  - **Luke:** addressed a Greek audience and presented Jesus as the Perfect Man.
  - **John:** addressed all people and revealed Jesus as God. He also wrote that everyone must make an individual decision about Jesus Christ.
- All four Gospels end with the death and the resurrection of Christ.
- Luke followed up with a history book, taking up God's story where the gospels ended.
  - **Acts:** begins with Christ ascending into heaven, followed by the Day of Pentecost when the Spirit of God came dramatically upon believers.
    - The Church of Jesus Christ was born on the Day of Pentecost.

ROMANS
Theme: God's Righteousness Described

- ⋆ The remainder of Acts shares the history of the spread of Christianity and the growth of the Church.
- ⋆ It is also in Acts that we are introduced to an extraordinary man: Paul.

OVERVIEW:

Background on Paul
- He probably received a Greek education in Tarsus, his hometown.
- He later moved to Jerusalem and received an excellent religious education under the great Jewish scholar Gamaliel.
  - ~ It was probably during this time that he learned the skill of tent-making.
- Paul was brilliant—zealous for the Jewish faith—very dangerous to Christians.
- It was while he was on his way to Damascus to arrest and persecute Christians that he had a dramatic encounter with the risen Lord.
- Paul's encounter with Jesus Christ was the second most significant event in the New Testament. Through the Holy Spirit, Paul:
  1. Devoted himself to spreading the gospel.
     - ⋆ Extending the influence of Christianity throughout most of the known world at that time.
  2. Planted churches.
  3. Shaped the doctrine of the church.
  4. Corrected false thinking.
  5. Encouraged Christians.

⇨ **Paul wrote thirteen letters that have had universal significance.**

- The first nine letters written by Paul are to churches. They are placed in the Bible in the order of their size, not the date they were written.
- Romans is the longest, but it was actually the sixth book that Paul wrote.
- It was probably written in 57 A.D.
- It is believed that Paul was in Corinth as he wrote the believers back in Rome.

****

❊ **ILLUSTRATION:** Romans is a book that changes lives. Three hundred years after it was written, Augustine, a Roman citizen, was sitting in the garden of a friend. He was lamenting his notoriously immoral, wicked, ungodly lifestyle—he had a mistress and an illegitimate child. But Augustine also had a Christian mother who prayed for him and who had given him a copy of a book (actually a scroll). It was the Book of Romans. As he sat in the garden, he had placed the scroll on his lap. It slid to the ground and he became aware

ROMANS
Theme: God's Righteousness Described

of a young child chanting, "Take up and read, take up and read." Augustine took up that scroll and this is what he read:

"Let us behave properly as in the day,
not in carousing and drunkenness, not in sexual promiscuity and sensuality,
not in strife and jealousy,
but put on the Lord Jesus Christ and make no provision for the flesh."

Augustine stated that he didn't read any further—he didn't have to. The light came on and he knew immediately what he had to do with Jesus Christ: he had to put on Jesus and make Him Lord of his life. Augustine's life changed—radically.

****

⇨ **The purpose of Romans is to describe the righteousness of God.**

I. MAN'S SIN: THE NEED FOR GOD'S RIGHTEOUSNESS (ROMANS 1–3:20)

✞ **Romans 1:1b-4a** "… set apart for the gospel of God, which He promised beforehand through His prophets in the holy Scriptures, concerning His Son, who was born of a descendant of David according to the flesh, who was declared the Son of God with power by the resurrection from the dead…"

- Paul began his letter by relating facts about the gospel:
  ~ The gospel message was not new.
  ~ The Old Testament prophets had presented the gospel.
    * They had said the Messiah (Jesus) would come from the line of David in the flesh—that He would be God. And, Jesus proved He was God by His resurrection.

A. The gospel reveals the <u>RIGHTEOUSNESS</u> of God.

✞ **Romans 1:16** "For I am not ashamed of the gospel, for it is the power of God for salvation to everyone who believes, to the Jew first and also to the Greek."

- The gospel is the power of God for salvation to everyone who *believes*.
- It was presented to the Jew first and then also to the Greek.

⇨ **The gospel reveals the very character of God—His righteousness.**

- Paul stated that, when we look at the gospel, we see the righteousness of God and the reality that man is a sinner.

B. The gospel also reveals the <u>WRATH</u> of God against sin.

© 2018 Big Dream Ministries, Inc.

ROMANS
Theme: God's Righteousness Described

- **Romans 1:18** "For the wrath of God is revealed from heaven against all ungodliness and unrighteousness of men who suppress the truth in unrighteousness …"
  - God's wrath was displayed on the cross—as Jesus died for each one of us, for our sin.

C. God revealed Himself to man through <u>CREATION</u>. (Gentiles are without excuse.)

Romans 1:20–23
- God revealed Himself in a number of ways, beginning with His creation, so men (and women) are without any excuse.

****

- **ILLUSTRATION:** There is a story of Napoleon that illustrates this fact. He was on the deck of a ship in the Mediterranean on a starry night. He passed some of his officers who were derisively debating the existence of God. Napoleon pointed to the stars and said, "Gentlemen, you will have to do away with those first."

****

- **Creation proves that there is a God.**
- **Romans 1:22-23** "Professing to be wise, they became fools, and exchanged the glory of the incorruptible God for an image in the form of corruptible man and of birds and four-footed animals and crawling creatures."
  - God revealed Himself, yet man rejected the Creator for the created.
  - Instead of worshipping the glorious God Who could create all things out of nothing and could speak words and make everything come into being, men worshipped the glory of man—not the glory of God!
  - Every time they exchanged something for God, He gave them over to it.

1. Man exchanged the <u>GLORY</u> of God for the glory of man.

Romans 1:24
- God gave them over to the lusts of their hearts.

2. Man exchanged <u>TRUTH</u> for a lie.

Romans 1:25–26a
- Again, instead of worshipping and serving the Creator, they worshipped and served the creation.
- As a result, God turned them over to degrading passions.

ROMANS
Theme: God's Righteousness Described

3. Man exchanged <u>NATURAL</u> sex for unnatural.

<u>Romans 1:26b–28</u>
- This third exchange immediately followed their exchanging truth for a lie.
- Women and men, in effect, abandoned how they had been created for sex.
- As a result, God gave them over to a depraved mind.

⇨ **These "exchanges" represented men's rejection of what God had made evident to them—resulting in a downward spiral that led to a depraved mind (all the while professing themselves to be "wise").**

> ★ **TEACHING TIP:**
> *You may have students that will struggle with this teaching. Let God's Word speak for itself. Remember: God's Word is the plumb line that a Christian should always use to determine how we are to live and conduct our lives.*

> **NOTE:** It is important to understand what "righteousness" means:
> ♦ Righteousness speaks to "holiness" or "purity."

⇨ **Man has a problem—we are not pure. Instead, we have depraved minds.**

✝ **Romans 1:29–32** "… being filled with all unrighteousness, wickedness, greed, evil; full of envy, murder, strife, deceit, malice; they are gossips, slanderers, haters of God, insolent, arrogant, boastful, inventors of evil, disobedient to parents, without understanding, untrustworthy, unloving, unmerciful; and although they know the ordinance of God, that those who practice such things are worthy of death, they not only do the same, but also give hearty approval to those who practice them."

- God gives a very clear picture of unrighteousness. It, in fact, includes descriptions that we may very well gloss over in our own lives:

  ~ Greedy
  ~ Haters of God
  ~ Untrustworthy

  ~ Envious
  ~ Arrogant
  ~ Unloving

  ~ Contentious
  ~ Disobedient to parents
  ~ Unmerciful

  ~ Gossip

ROMANS
Theme: God's Righteousness Described

- Don't miss the last line in Romans 1:32! It speaks to those who give "hearty approval" to such actions or lifestyles—they are just as culpable!
- This is what happens when we reject God's revelation about Himself.

> ★ **TEACHING TIP:**
> "Men love everything but righteousness and fear everything but God."
> ~ Vance Havner

D. God revealed Himself in the LAW, but man broke it. (Jews are without excuse.)

- While creation was given to all people as a witness to God, the law was given to the Jews as a witness to the holiness of God.
- Paul turned his attention to the Jews.

Romans 2
- Paul accused the Jews of boasting in God's law—all the while breaking it!
- Having the law given to them by God Himself made the Jews without excuse in understanding God's righteousness.

E. God's conclusion is that NO ONE is righteous.

Romans 3:1–19

✞ **Romans 3:9b** "…for we have already charged that both Jews and Greeks are all under sin …"

- Paul concluded that all men—Jews and Gentiles—are under the penalty of sin.
- God has made it clear that no one is innately righteous, not even one. (Romans 3:10)

⇨ **God has made a declaration as a Judge. He has declared us (each one of us) "guilty" of unrighteousness.**

REVIEW:
- For three chapters, Paul has presented the case against man—man (we) are not righteous.
- Paul has made it clear that we need God's righteousness.

- In Romans 3:20, Paul explained how man is not made righteous.
  - NOT by "works" of the law—rather, the law gave man the knowledge of sin.
    * The law convinces us of our sin.
    * The law is a witness to how we fall short of ever being righteous by something we may "do."

> ★ **TEACHING TIP:**
> "God has nothing to say to the self-righteous."
> ~ Dwight L. Moody

ROMANS
Theme: God's Righteousness Described

II. GOD'S SALVATION: THE EXPLANATION OF RIGHTEOUSNESS (ROMANS 3:21-8)

- This is the second division of Romans.
- God's salvation is presented and righteousness is explained.

✞ **Romans 3:23-24** "… for all have sinned and fall short of the glory of God, being justified as a gift by His grace through the redemption which is in Christ Jesus; …"

> ★ **TEACHING TIP:**
> *It is important to note that this book contains "big" words: righteousness, justification, and propitiation. The goal is to help your students not only understand these words, but to apply them.*

A. Justification is a legal term meaning "to <u>DECLARE</u> righteous."

<u>Romans 3:21-24</u>
- God, who declares us guilty, is also the One who can declare us righteous.
- Our righteousness is linked directly to Jesus Christ.
- We are justified (made righteous) through Jesus as a gift by His grace.

⇨ **A simple way to remember the definition of "justification" or "justified":** *He made me just as if I'd never sinned.*

B. We are justified by <u>FAITH</u> in Jesus apart from works.

- We are not made righteous by works or by the law.
- We are made righteous through the work of Jesus.

✞ **Romans 3:25** "… whom [Jesus] God displayed publicly as a propitiation in His blood through faith…"

> **NOTE:** It is important to understand what "propitiation" means:
> - Propitiation means "covering, placation or reconciliation."

- Let's understand how this relates to Jesus and a believer:
  - The blood that Jesus shed on the cross covers the one who has faith in Him.
  - When God looks down and sees you or me, He sees the atoning blood of Jesus and, thus, sees us "as if we had never sinned." (Justified!)

> **NOTE:** Why is a blood "covering" needed?
> - In the book of Hebrews, we are told that there can be no forgiveness without the shedding of blood—and sinners need God's forgiveness!

ROMANS
Theme: God's Righteousness Described

REVIEW:
- We are justified by grace.
- This is a gift of God.

C. Abraham was justified when he BELIEVED God, and God added righteousness to his account.

- Paul wanted the people to understand that this teaching was not a new idea, so he used Abraham as an illustration.

Romans 4
- Paul stated that if Abraham was justified by his "works," then he would have had something to boast about—but that is not what Scripture (God's Word) says.

✝ **Romans 4:3** "For what does the Scripture say? "ABRAHAM BELIEVED GOD, AND IT WAS CREDITED TO HIM AS RIGHTEOUSNESS."

> **NOTE:** Justification is a legal term meaning "to declare righteous." In Romans 4:3, your Bible translation may use the words "credited" or "reckoned"—this is an accounting term and means "to add to your account."

- What happened with Abraham? What was Paul teaching those in Rome?
  - Abraham believed God.
  - God subtracted sin and added righteousness to Abraham's account.
- Was Abraham saved by the works of the law? NO!
  - The law had not been given during Abraham's time and would not be for six hundred more years.
  - Abraham was not circumcised, which was a requirement of the law.
- What did Abraham do? He believed God!
  - And God put righteousness (holiness or purity) in his account.

D. Justification means to make PEACE with God (past).

✝ **Romans 5:1** "Therefore, having been justified by faith, we have peace with God through our Lord Jesus Christ, …"

Romans 5
- Justification is something that happens in the believer's past.

ROMANS
Theme: God's Righteousness Described

- In one point in time:
  1. We must each recognize and admit that we are sinners—that God is right that we <u>all</u> have sinned. (Essentially agreeing with God that not one of us is righteous on our own.)
  2. We must each acknowledge the blood covering provided by Jesus as our propitiation for sin.
  3. We must each accept Jesus' blood as our personal propitiation.
  4. At that moment of faith in Jesus, God declares us as "justified."

> ✶ **TEACHING TIP:**
> *Note that this is a personal, individual decision that takes God at His Word and acts upon it in belief.*

E. Glorification means to be <u>PRESENT</u> with God (future).

- God also promised us "the hope of the glory of God," which speaks to a future "glorification."
  ~ When we are justified, we can know that someday we will be in the presence of God.

F. Sanctification means to develop the <u>CHARACTER</u> of God (present).

- But there is "time" between the past and future—the present!
- We are not to simply wait until the future comes. Right now, we need to be sanctified.

> **NOTE:** What does it mean to be "sanctified?"
> - Sanctification involves developing the character of God in our lives—this will take a lifetime.
> - Some in your class may have heard it explained as being "set apart *to* God," which indicates that a believer is to be set apart *from* the world.
>
> ⇨ **Sanctification leads the believer to becoming more and more like Jesus.**

- How do we develop and take on the character of Christ?

✞ **Romans 5:3–4** "And not only this, but we also exult in our tribulations, knowing that tribulation brings about perseverance; and perseverance, proven character; and proven character, hope; …"

⇨ **God uses tribulations in our lives to bring about perseverance that develops His character within us!**

ROMANS
Theme: God's Righteousness Described

- How can tribulations lead us to hope?
- **Romans 5:5** "... and hope does not disappoint, because the love of God has been poured out within our hearts through the Holy Spirit who was given to us."
    - ~ In those difficult circumstances, we experience the love of God— poured into our hearts—through the Holy Spirit.

> ★ **TEACHING TIP:**
> *In Romans 15:16, Paul explained that the believer is sanctified by the Holy Spirit.*

> ❖ **APPLICATION:** Can you relate to this? Have some of the hardest times in your life resulted in being some of the best times in your life spiritually? Times when you have deeply experienced the presence of God—His strength and His love?

G. Justification requires the <u>DEATH</u> of Jesus. Sanctification requires the <u>LIFE</u> of Jesus.

- **Romans 5:10** "For if while we were enemies we were reconciled to God through the death of His Son, much more, having been reconciled, we shall be saved by His life."

> ❖ **APPLICATION:** Do you see that your salvation is more than just Jesus dying for you? It also involves Jesus living for you—within you—because this is how we take on or develop the character of God. We need His life within!

⇨ **Justification happens at one point in time. You only need to ask Jesus Christ into your life once! But sanctification is ongoing as we grow to be more like Him.**

Romans 6
- Before Christ, we had a sin problem.
    - ~ No matter how hard we may have tried "to be good," our tendency to sin won out.
- But having been justified in Christ, we are no longer to be "slaves" to sin—Jesus bought us out of this slavery in order that we may live a "new" life. (Romans 6:6)
- **Romans 6:22** "But now having been freed from sin and enslaved to God, you derive your benefit, resulting in sanctification, and the outcome, eternal life."

> ★ **TEACHING TIP:**
> *The believer was once a slave to sin and had no righteousness.*

- How are we sanctified?
    - ~ We present our body to Christ, to the Spirit, as a slave of righteousness, which results in sanctification.

ROMANS
Theme: God's Righteousness Described

- ~ As we present ourselves to Him, He will develop the character of God within us and the outcome is eternal life: glorification.
- Paul turned to the subject of the law because Christ has called believers to obey it.

H. Paul said there are three laws:

<u>Romans 7</u>

   1. The law of <u>GOD</u>.
   * It defines sin. (Romans 7:7–11)
   * It is holy. (Romans 7:12)
   * It is righteous. (Romans 7:12)
   * It is good. (Romans 7:12)

   2. The law of <u>SIN</u>.

- Paul also explained that there is a real struggle that happens within the man or woman seeking to live a sanctified life:

✝ **Romans 7:19–20** "For the good that I want, I do not do, but I practice the very evil that I do not want. But if I am doing the very thing I do not want, I am no longer the one doing it, but sin which dwells in me."

> ❖ **APPLICATION:** Have you struggled with knowing how Jesus would have you respond to a situation—such as forgiving someone who has hurt you deeply—but instead you have been pulled to respond "in the flesh"—with bitterness and no forgiveness?

- Paul explained that there is a principle that we must acknowledge: the desire to do the wrong thing (sin) is present in the one who wants to do good (obedience to Christ).

⇨ **There is an inner conflict in man between the law of God and the law of sin.**
   ~ Paul asked a question: "Who will set me free from this problem?"

> **NOTE:** There is a problem presented in Romans 7:
> - Paul mentioned the law twenty-four times.
> - He used the pronoun "I" thirty-eight times.
> ⇨ **Paul clearly established the precept that <u>"I" alone</u> can never obey the law.**
> ⇨ **We cannot be holy, live holy, without the Holy Spirit … that is the struggle.**

ROMANS
Theme: God's Righteousness Described

3. The law of the SPIRIT.

Romans 8
- In Chapter 7, Paul posed the question as to who could help him with his inner struggle to be and do good.
- In Chapter 8, he gave the answer: the Holy Spirit.

✝ **Romans 8:2** "For the law of the Spirit of life in Christ Jesus has set you free from the law of sin and of death."

- Paul mentioned the Holy Spirit seventeen times in Chapter 8.

⇨ **The law of God is good. I can't obey it because of the law of sin. But the answer is the law of the Spirit.**

****

❈ **ILLUSTRATION:** As we noted before, Augustine struggled with his flesh. But even after he accepted Christ in faith and was forgiven for all the immorality he had committed in his life, do you know what he prayed? It went something like this: "Lord, give me chastity ... but not yet." We all struggle with our flesh, don't we?

****

- It all comes back to Jesus.

✝ **Romans 8:3-4** "For what the Law could not do, weak as it was through the flesh, God did: sending His own Son in the likeness of sinful flesh and as an offering for sin, He condemned sin in the flesh, so that the requirement of the Law might be fulfilled in us, who do not walk according to the flesh but according to the Spirit."
  ~ The law could (and does) reveal sin, but it cannot help us to stop sinning (that was never its purpose).
  ~ God sent His own son, Jesus, in the likeness of sinful flesh, so that the requirement of the law (an atoning sacrifice) might be fulfilled in us who no longer walk according to the flesh but according to the Spirit.

⇨ **The believer needs to walk after the Spirit.**

> **NOTE:** In the homework for Romans, the students will learn several things about the Holy Spirit:
> - He assures us that we are children of God.
> - Without Him, we cannot please God.
> - He will help us when we pray, even in those times when we do not know how to pray.

ROMANS
Theme: God's Righteousness Described

- At the end of Chapter 8, Paul gives a rich explanation of the security the believer has in Jesus. Paul was convinced that nothing could ever separate him from the love of God in Christ Jesus, our Lord.

- This thought—the security and love that was found in Jesus Christ—reminded Paul of the nation of Israel.
    ~ Weren't they also "separated?"
    ~ Was God being unjust or unrighteous in His dealings with Israel?

III. MAN'S RESPONSBILITY: THE JEWS' RELATIONSHIP TO RIGHTEOUSNESS (ROMANS 9–11)

Romans 9
- Paul expressed his great grief over the nation of Israel's rejection of Jesus as their Messiah.
- Paul's love for Israel was such that he was even willing to be separated from God if it would help the nation of Israel to be united with Jesus Christ. (Romans 9:5a)

A. God chose Israel, but only a remnant of Israel <u>CHOSE</u> God.

- Paul's grief over the nation of Israel's response to Christ was due to the fact of who they were and what they had been given from God Himself:

✞ **Romans 9:3b–5** " … my kinsmen according to the flesh, who are Israelites, to whom belongs the adoption as sons, and the glory and the covenants and the giving of the Law and the temple service and the promises, whose are the fathers, and from whom is the Christ according to the flesh, who is over all, God blessed forever. Amen."

> ★ **TEACHING TIP:**
> *The Gentiles did not have this rich heritage of faith. In fact, they had not been pursuers of righteousness, but attained it through faith in Jesus Christ. (Romans 9:30)*

  ~ They had been chosen by God.
  ~ They had been adopted as sons.
  ~ They had been given the covenants.
  ~ They had been given the law and the temple.
  ~ They had been given the promises (from prophets).
  ~ They had been given God's Son, Jesus Christ.

B. Israel pursued righteousness by <u>WORKS</u> and stumbled.

- What was the problem with the Jews? What were they missing?

ROMANS
Theme: God's Righteousness Described

- **Romans 9:31–32** "… but Israel, pursuing a law of righteousness, did not arrive at that law. Why? Because they did not pursue it by faith, but as though it were by works. They stumbled over the stumbling stone, …"
    - Paul explained that the Jews had tried to attain righteousness through the law via "works"—not through Jesus Christ.
    - And because of this approach to righteousness (through works), the Jews continued to stumble in their efforts—no matter how hard they "worked," righteousness would never be achieved.

REVIEW:

- Here was the problem for the Jews:
    - God had chosen Israel, but Israel had not chosen God (except for a remnant).
    - The Jews tried to find righteousness through works of the law (their own efforts), and they stumbled.
    - They continued to stumble and stumble because of the stone of stumbling, which could not and can never be circumvented through man's efforts.

- **Romans 9:33** "BEHOLD, I LAY IN ZION A STONE OF STUMBLING AND A ROCK OF OFFENSE, AND HE WHO BELIEVES IN HIM WILL NOT BE DISAPPOINTED."

⇨ **The stone of stumbling and rock of offense was Jesus Christ Himself—the very one in whom they needed to believe—to attain the righteousness they worked for!**

- Left in this situation, the news was only bad for the Jews. But Paul followed up this sobering message with good news—a choice for the Jews.

C. There is no distinction between Jew and Gentile. Whoever will <u>CALL</u> on the name of the Lord will be saved.

Romans 10

- **Romans 10:9–10** "… that if you confess with your mouth Jesus as Lord, and believe in your heart that God raised Him from the dead, you will be saved; for with the heart a person believes, resulting in righteousness, and with the mouth he confesses, resulting in salvation."

    - Righteousness comes through:
        - Confessing with your mouth Jesus as Lord.
        - Believing in your heart that God raised Him from the dead.

> ★ **TEACHING TIP:**
>
> *Salvation and righteousness walk hand-in-hand—righteousness only comes from believing (faith) in Christ Jesus.*

ROMANS
Theme: God's Righteousness Described

- Whoever calls upon the name of the Lord—whether Jew or Gentile—will be saved. (Romans 10:12)
- In Romans 3, Paul explained that there was no distinction between Jews and Gentiles when it came to sin—all have sinned. Here he brought that same truth in regards to salvation—all can be saved by calling on the name of the Lord.

⇨ **Whether Jew or Gentile, we are all saved the same way—through faith in Christ Jesus.**

D. God is not finished with Israel, for His <u>CALLING</u> is irrevocable.

- Paul then asked a question that the Jews were certain to pose. (Romans 10:14)
    - ~ How can they (the Jews) call unless they have heard?
- Had Israel heard "the call" regarding the Messiah? YES!!
    - ~ Through the prophets.
    - ~ Through the law.
    - ~ Through Jesus Himself.

> ★ **TEACHING TIP:**
> *There is a vast difference between "hearing" and "responding" to what you have heard.*

Romans 11
- Paul posed a second question: "Israel did not stumble so as to fall, did they?" (Romans 11:11a)
- The answer: "May it never be!" (Romans 11:11b)
- Paul then explained what had happened:

☩ **Romans 11:11b–12** "But by their transgression salvation has come to the Gentiles, to make them jealous. Now if their transgression is riches for the world and their failure is riches for the Gentiles, how much more will their fulfillment be!

- Paul's message was and is clear:
    - ~ Salvation has come to the Gentiles to make the Jews jealous.
    - ~ God is not through with Israel.
    - ~ In other words, Israel has not stumbled so as to fall.
- Paul ended this teaching with words of encouragement to the Israel:

☩ **Romans 11:29** "... for the gifts and the calling of God are irrevocable."
- ~ God does not call somebody and then "uncall" them.
- ~ God does not give a gift and take it back.

ROMANS
Theme: God's Righteousness Described

****

* **ILLUSTRATION:** Paul's life is actually an illustration of the nation of Israel. He was zealous for God, but self-righteous (through works). He was temporarily blinded, and then given sight to know Jesus. This is true for Israel. They are zealous, but self-righteous (through works). They are temporarily blinded, but will be given sight.

****

IV. GOD'S WILL: THE APPLICATION OF RIGHTEOUSNESS (ROMANS 12–16)

- In the last five chapters of Romans, Paul makes practical applications in regards to righteousness—how it is to be lived out in the believer's life.

A. Present your **BODY** to God as a living sacrifice.

✝ **Roman 12:1** "Therefore I urge you, brethren, by the mercies of God, to present your bodies a living and holy sacrifice, acceptable to God, which is your spiritual service of worship."

- Paul has spoken before about "presenting" ourselves to God.
  ~ Back in Romans 6:13, he encouraged believers to present themselves to God as instruments of righteousness.
- Here Paul stated that we were to present ourselves as a "living sacrifice" to God.

****

* **ILLUSTRATION:** The problem with a living sacrifice is the tendency to crawl off the altar! There was a medical doctor, Dr. Walton Wilson, who had a life-changing conversation with a missionary:
  ~ The missionary asked him, "Who is the Holy Spirit to you?"
  ~ Dr. Wilson answered, "He is one of the persons of the Godhead."
  ~ The missionary then asked, "But what is the Holy Spirit to you personally?"
  ~ Dr. Wilson confessed, "He is nothing to me. I have no contact with Him, no powerful relationship with Him, and could get along very well without Him."
  ~ The missionary responded that there was a reason Dr. Wilson's life seemed fruitless.

After this conversation, Dr. Wilson attended a medical convention. One of his office nurses slipped a tract into his briefcase. It expounded on Romans 12:1–2 and pointed out to whom we needed to present ourselves to:
  ~ Not to the Father ... He is on the throne.
  ~ Not to Jesus ... He has a body of His own.
  ~ It is the Holy Spirit that wants your body.

ROMANS
Theme: God's Righteousness Described

Upon reading this tract (and having been prompted by the missionary's questions), he prayed a prayer in which he offered his body (eyes, hands, and feet), where he would live, and his personal health to God to do with him what He wanted.

Dr. Wilson went on to write a number of Christian books, found a Christian college, and pioneered Christian radio.

****

> ❖ **APPLICATION:** What about you? Who reigns over your body? Have you given your life (body, mind, and spirit) fully over to the Holy Spirit to control?

- In being a "living sacrifice," Paul called the believers to not be conformed to this world (in which evil abounds) but to be transformed (to become more and more like Jesus) "… by the renewing of your mind, so that you may prove what the will of God is, that which is good and acceptable and perfect." (Romans 12:2)

- This approach to living—giving ourselves fully to the Holy Spirit's control—will impact every aspect of our lives, our relationships. Paul instructed the Roman believers (and us) on how to live this new life.

B. Be at **PEACE** with all men. (Romans 12:18)
~ We should not be known as being constantly disagreeable or as one who loves to begin and continue (without end) arguments.

C. Be in **SUBJECTION** to authorities. (Romans 13:1-7)
~ This does not mean that we will fully agree with those in authority (we may not agree with them at all). BUT the believer is called to respect their position and recognize that our sovereign God has allowed them to be in it.

D. Make no provision for the **FLESH** in regard to its lusts. (Romans 13:14)
~ The believer is to "put on Christ"—His character, His will, His ways.
~ As a "living sacrifice," we will need to daily (moment by moment) make the choice to refuse any activity that does not reflect Jesus.

E. Don't **JUDGE** your brother. (Romans 14)
~ The word "judge" used here carries the idea of "condemnation."
~ As Paul penned this letter, the Jewish believers were condemning the Gentile believers for not being like the Jewish believers in what they ate, etc..

ROMANS
Theme: God's Righteousness Described

- ~ The church today can fall into this trap—"Feel what I feel, think what I think, eat what I eat, drink what I drink, look as I look, do as I do—and then, only then, will I have fellowship with you."

> ★ **TEACHING TIP:**
> An early 17th century theologian said, "In essentials unity, in non-essentials liberty, in all things charity."

- **F. <u>SERVE</u> and love your brother. (Romans 15)**
  - ~ As a "living sacrifice," we are to exhibit brotherly love, kindness, and patience.
  - ~ This is an exhortation to "deny self" if it would promote the betterment of a brother or sister in Christ.
- In Romans 16, Paul ended his letter by listing names of those who were living out their faith in Christ.
  - ~ He tells of twenty-six people who were serving the Lord—nine were women.

FINAL THOUGHTS AND APPLICATION

- ⌑ The book of Romans is a book that can change people's lives.
- ⌑ Paul made the case that we need God's righteousness and explained how to obtain it.
- ⌑ Our salvation involves the past, the present, and the future. One easy way to remember:
  - ~ Justification (past): Freed from the *penalty* of sin.
  - ~ Sanctification (present): Freed from the *power* of sin.
  - ~ Glorification (future): Freed from the *presence* of sin.

- ❖ **APPLICATION:** The book of Romans calls the reader to self-examination.
  1. **Have I been justified?**
  - ~ Can I look back to my past and note the point in time when I agreed with God that I was a sinner?
  - ~ Did I ask Him to cover my sins with His atoning blood so that God the Father could look at me just as if I had never sinned?
  2. **Am I striving to live a sanctified life?**
  - ~ Do I live in obedience to God's Word—is it my plumb line on how to live?
  - ~ Do my actions, reactions, mindset, and words reflect the character of Christ?
  3. **Am I confident that one day I will be glorified?**
  - ~ Do I rest in the truth that this present life is not all there is?
  - ~ Do I have full security in my faith that one day I will live with God?

- ❖ **FINAL APPLICATION:** Is God's righteousness evident in your life? By His Spirit do you live in peace with, serve, and love others?

ROMANS REVIEW HELPS

✧ **Ask the class if they can reconstruct the history of the Old Testament giving the main ideas for the following sets. Have the class work as a team, and if they get stumped, allow them to use their Bibles if necessary. Allow about fifteen minutes.**

They are in order below:

1. Pentateuch
2. Kingdom Books
3. Post-Exilic Books
4. Poetical Books
5. Major Prophets
6. Early Minor Prophets
7. Later Minor Prophets
8. New Testament History

ROMANS

FIRST CORINTHIANS

Church's Problems Corrected

But now faith, hope, love abide these three;

but the greatest of these is love.

1 Corinthians 13:13

SESSION FORTY-SIX: FIRST CORINTHIANS
Church's Problems Corrected

✝ **Memory verse:** *"But now faith, hope, love, abide these three; but the greatest of these is love." (1 Corinthians 13:13)*

Introduction: The church in Corinth had been founded in the early days of the spread of the gospel as recorded in the book of Acts. The church had been taught and experienced freedom from the penalty, power, and presence of sin, and yet they were wallowing in many serious sins that mimicked the corrupt culture around them. Paul minced no words with these believers as he addressed their sin corporately and individually. This letter is largely practical, as it deals with not only spiritual/doctrinal questions the church was having, but also moral issues that were finding their way into a church that was positioned in a highly immoral society. Divisions in the church, questions about marriage, food, worship, and the resurrection are some of the issues Paul firmly deals with in this letter. Many of these problems are the very same that churches today must face. Paul gives clear direction as to how a church should handle the problems and also lovingly answers the doctrinal questions with clarity.

- **Oral Review:** Please refer to the **REVIEW Section** in the following Teaching Guide Outline.

- **Homework:** Review the homework from the book of Romans.

    Question on page 37
    Questions at the top of page 40
    Questions at the bottom of page 43 and all of page 44
    First and last question on page 46

- **Review Helps:** Written review is provided at the end of the teacher presentation. (Optional and time permitting.)

- **Teacher Presentation on the Book of First Corinthians**

- **Learning for Life:** You may choose to discuss all or just one or two of the questions on page 56.

- **Closing prayer:** Pray for the church and the people in it—that God would unify believers and they would be a living testimony to the greatness of God and the power of Jesus Christ. Pray that the church would have a great influence in the community and represent Christ well as it shows the world Christ's love.

FIRST CORINTHIANS
Theme: Church's Problems Corrected

OUTLINE AID FOR TEACHERS:

I. **PAUL AND THE CORINTHIAN CHURCH**

   A. The History of Corinth

      1. The Corinthians worshiped Aphrodite, the goddess of <u>LOVE</u>.

      2. The temple boasted <u>ONE THOUSAND</u> consecrated prostitutes.

      3. "To act like a Corinthian" symbolized gross <u>IMMORALITY</u>.

   B. Paul and the Church in Corinth

      1. Paul established the church on his <u>SECOND</u> missionary journey (see Acts 18:1–18).

      2. He wrote this letter to the church on his <u>THIRD</u> missionary journey when he was in Ephesus.

II. **PAUL'S ANSWER TO CHLOE'S PEOPLE'S REPORT (1 CORINTHIANS 1:10–4:21)**

   - **1 Corinthians 1:10–17**

   A. There were divisions caused by <u>SELF-EXALTATION</u>.

      1. They did not understand the work of the <u>CROSS</u>.

   - **1 Corinthians 2**

      2. They did not understand the work of the <u>HOLY SPIRIT</u>.

   - **1 Corinthians 3–4**

   B. There were consequences for their lack of understanding.

   - **1 Corinthians 3:1–9**

      1. They would not grow <u>SPIRITUALLY</u>.

   - **1 Corinthians 3:10–15**

      2. They would lose eternal <u>REWARDS</u>.

III. **PAUL'S ANSWER TO AN ANONYMOUS REPORT (1 CORINTHIANS 5–6)**

   - **1 Corinthians 5**

   A. Gross sexual <u>IMMORALITY</u> should not be tolerated.

      1. Remove the offender from the <u>CHURCH</u>.

      2. Do not associate with immoral <u>BELIEVERS</u>.

FIRST CORINTHIANS
Theme: Church's Problems Corrected

- **1 Corinthians 6:1-8**

    B. Christians should not SUE Christians.

- **1 Corinthians 6:9**

    C. Sexually immoral people will not inherit the KINGDOM of God.

- **1 Corinthians 6:12-20**

    1. Our bodies are temples of the HOLY SPIRIT.

    2. Our bodies are to bring GLORY to God.

IV. **PAUL'S ANSWERS TO QUESTIONS RAISED IN A LETTER (1 CORINTHIANS 7-16)**

- **1 Corinthians 7:1-7**

    A. Paul addressed confusion concerning MARRIAGE.

    1. Married couples should not DENY one another sexually.

- **1 Corinthians 7:12-16**

    2. A believing spouse should not DIVORCE because of his or her mate's unbelief.

- **1 Corinthians 7:32-35, 39**

    3. Singleness allows greater freedom for Christian SERVICE.

- **1 Corinthians 8-9:27**

    B. Paul addressed confusion concerning FOODS consecrated to pagan gods.

    1. Do nothing that causes your weaker brother to STUMBLE.

    2. Exercise SELF-CONTROL in all things.

- **1 Corinthians 12-14**

    C. Paul addressed confusion concerning SPIRITUAL GIFTS.

    1. Spiritual gifts are for the common GOOD of the church.

    2. LOVE is superior to all gifts.

    3. God's definition of LOVE is found in 1 Corinthians 13:4-7.

- **1 Corinthians 15**

    D. Paul addressed confusion concerning the RESURRECTION.

    1. If Christ has not been raised, then our faith is WORTHLESS.

    2. We will have bodies that are IMPERISHABLE.

FIRST CORINTHIANS
Theme: Church's Problems Corrected

3. Christ's resurrection was witnessed by <u>FIVE HUNDRED</u> people.
4. At the last trumpet, the dead will be raised, and the living in Christ will be <u>CHANGED</u>.

I Corinthians
[Church's Problems Corrected]

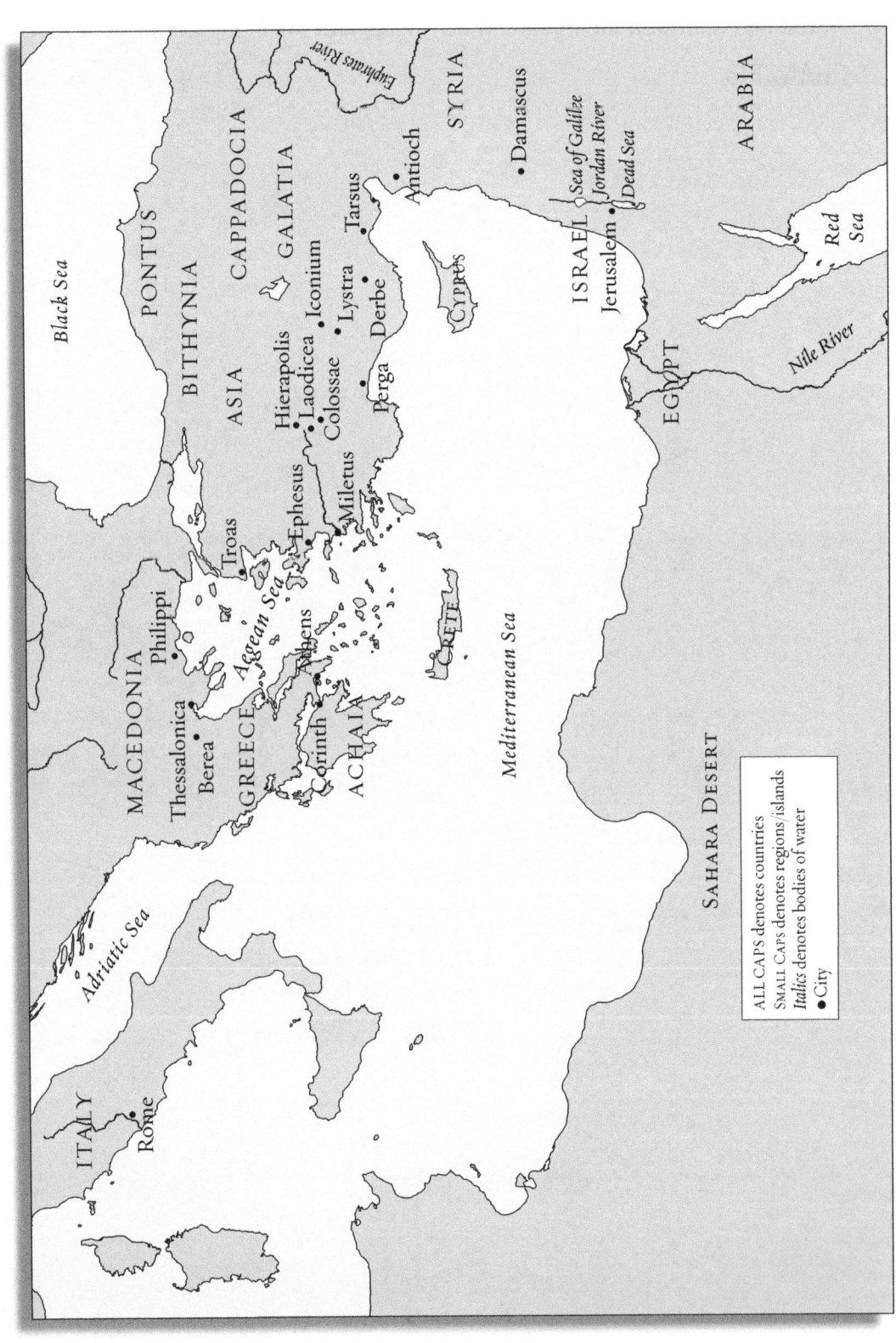

FIRST CORINTHIANS
Theme: Church's Problems Corrected

THE BASICS:
- ⇨ **Who: The Author:** Paul
  - **Main Characters:** Believers in Corinth
- ⇨ **What:** A letter addressing problems within the church
- ⇨ **When:** Written in A.D. 56
- ⇨ **Where:** Written to Rome from Ephesus
- ⇨ **Why:** To answer questions brought to Paul by some church members

MEMORY VERSE: *"But now faith, hope, love, abide these three; but the greatest of these is love."* 1 Corinthians 13:13

****

REVIEW:

- ⌑ The *Old Testament History* books showed the problem of disobedience and its consequences.
  - ~ Disobedience caused Adam and Eve to be sent out of the garden—and the nation of Israel to be divided and exiled from God.
  - ~ The prophets repeatedly warned of the consequences of disobedience—God's judgment.
- ⌑ The *New Testament History* books show that the Messiah has come.
  - ~ **Matthew:** showed Jesus as the long-awaited King of the Jews.
  - ~ **Mark:** presented Jesus as a suffering servant—a servant to all men and women.
  - ~ **Luke:** presented Jesus as the Perfect Man.
  - ~ **John:** revealed Jesus as God and that everyone must make an individual decision about Jesus Christ.
  - ~ **Acts:** began with Christ ascending into heaven, followed by the Day of Pentecost when the Spirit of God came dramatically upon believers and the church of Christ was born. It gave insight into how Christianity spread and the church grew. And Paul was introduced.
- ⌑ In *Paul's Letters to the Churches*, we are given a glimpse into the needs of the churches that Paul was invested in as he taught, instructed, exhorted, and encouraged them—pouring out God's wisdom into them in love.
  - ~ **Romans:** a letter in which Paul presented God's righteousness. In doing so, he presented the truth that all men are sinners (whether Jew or Gentile) and all are in need of God's salvation—Jesus is the answer.
- ⌑ Paul also made it clear in the book of Romans that man, though saved by grace, will struggle with his tendency to sin—there will be a constant struggle regarding obedience to God versus pleasing self.

FIRST CORINTHIANS
Theme: Church's Problems Corrected

OVERVIEW:

****

* **ILLUSTRATION:** One of the most exciting and difficult days in an adult's life involves taking a child to begin his or her first year at college. As parents, we have invested at least eighteen years into that child—we have tried to shape them spiritually and morally. But as you look at them in the rearview mirror, you wonder, "Are they really ready to fly solo?"

  Many of us follow that "drop off" day with a parental letter exhorting our child to "be and do good" (because Mom and Dad are watching!). As a parent, we want our children to succeed in life—but we also want to warn them of the pitfalls of bad choices—choices that can be made in a moment, choices that can have life-long consequences, good and bad.

  Why write a letter? Because when we write letters, we can better lay out what we want to say. It gives us space to organize our thoughts, consider the words we use—erase and start all over! The reality is, when we write letters, we can perfect the message that we want to communicate, so that our child can hear our "voice" through the pages. Written letters also allow the content to be read over and over again.

****

- As we open up the first letter to Corinth, Paul is writing to his children at the young church there.
  ~ Paul has left to continue his missionary journeys, but knows that the culture in which this church resides is very immoral.
  ~ Paul recognized that the believers in this church will have a struggle against this morally bankrupt city.
- Paul wrote this letter to address specific problems in this church.
- The book is divided into three parts:
  1. The history of this church.
  2. Division within this church.
  3. Church doctrine dealing with sin within this church.

I. PAUL AND THE CORINTHIAN CHURCH

A. The History of Corinth

- It had a population of about 700,000.
- It was a large and very important city.
  ~ Located on a trade route, it was bustling with commerce—a prosperous city.

FIRST CORINTHIANS
Theme: Church's Problems Corrected

1. **The Corinthians worshiped Aphrodite, the goddess of <u>LOVE</u>.**

    a. **The temple boasted <u>ONE THOUSAND</u> consecrated prostitutes.**
    * The worship of Aphrodite encouraged sexual immorality.
    * People flocked to Corinth because it was a city in which "anything goes."

    > ★ **TEACHING TIP:**
    >
    > *Important to Remember: This was the believers' environment—they struggled against the temptations that surrounded them every day in that culture.*

    b. **"To act like a Corinthian" symbolized gross <u>IMMORALITY</u>.**

B. **Paul and the Church in Corinth**

  1. **Paul established the church on his <u>SECOND</u> missionary journey (see Acts 18:1–18).**

  - In Corinth, he met Priscilla and Aquila, who were tentmakers.
  - He spent a year and a half in Corinth.
  - Every Sabbath, Paul would go to the synagogue to reason with the Jews.
    ~ He taught them that Jesus Christ was the Messiah they had longed for.
    ~ He taught that Jesus was crucified, died, was buried, and then was raised from the dead.
  - There were many who joined Paul while he was there, but many more did not.
  - Ultimately, Paul was thrown out of the synagogue.
  - The church in Corinth, though little, was strong in faith.

  2. **He wrote this letter to the church on his <u>THIRD</u> missionary journey when he was in Ephesus.**

  - It had been about four or five years since he had been in Corinth.
  - And now this church had problems that needed addressing.

⇨ **The purpose of 1 Corinthians is to address specific church problems and to instruct on how to correct them.**

II. PAUL'S ANSWER TO CHLOE'S PEOPLE'S REPORT (1 CORINTHIANS 1:10–4:21)

- As the book opened, it is clear that Paul had received a report that there were problems in the church.

FIRST CORINTHIANS
Theme: Church's Problems Corrected

✝ **1 Corinthians 1:11** "For I have been informed concerning you, my brethren, by Chloe's people, that there are quarrels among you. "

> **NOTE:** Who was Chloe?
> - There is little known about her—only this one verse mentions her.
> - We do know that she must have been a Christian woman living in Corinth and that she, at least, was an acquaintance of Paul's. (Because he refers to her by her first name.)
> - It also seems likely that she was well known to believers of that area.

- The *reported* problem? Quarrels—disputes, disagreements, and divisions—among themselves.

> ❖ **APPLICATION:** Have you experienced this in your local church?
> ~ It is clear that there are churches today experiencing the same problems as the early church.
> ~ It's as if things haven't changed in 2,000 years!

A. There were divisions caused by <u>SELF-EXALTATION</u>.

1 Corinthians 1:10–17
- The basis of the quarrel involved church leadership—who should they follow?
    ~ Some wanted to follow Paul—he had actually founded the church.
    ~ Others thought Peter was the better choice—he had actually walked with Jesus while He ministered on earth.
    ~ Others voted for Apollos—he was a skilled orator, a great speaker.

> ★ **TEACHING TIP:**
> *Can you imagine Paul's reaction to hearing this report? It had to break his heart because Paul was not about exalting Paul.*

- The *real* problem? They were following different <u>people</u>, which resulted in a form of self-exaltation.
    ~ "**I** am following the *right* one because I am following Paul. No, **I** am following the *right* one because I am following Peter … or Apollos."
- Paul's heart and ministry was single-focused: exalting Jesus Christ and Jesus Christ only.

1. They did not understand the work of the <u>CROSS</u>.

First Corinthians

FIRST CORINTHIANS
Theme: Church's Problems Corrected

- Paul questioned their understanding:

✝ **1 Corinthians 1:13** "Has Christ been divided? Paul was not crucified for you, was he? Or were you baptized in the name of Paul?"
  - ~ No one went to the cross for these people other than Jesus.
  - ~ If they were going to follow someone, it must only be Jesus.

> ❖ **APPLICATION:** This is an important lesson for us today.
>   - ~ Men and women can teach you. They, in fact, can be great teachers of the Word.
>   - ~ BUT your heart is to be solely devoted to Jesus Christ—not to a teacher of His Word.

✝ **1 Corinthians 1:15, 17** "… so that no one would say you were baptized in my name … For Christ did not send me to baptize, but to preach the gospel, not in cleverness of speech, so that the cross of Christ would not be made void."
  - ~ Paul's purpose (as was Peter's and Apollo's) was to preach the gospel.
  - ~ His purpose was to properly and fully exalt Jesus Christ alone.

2. They did not understand the work of the HOLY SPIRIT.

1 Corinthians 2

- Paul explained that the people did not understand the source—the power behind—his teaching. His teaching was not based on his own wisdom (the wisdom of men).
- The source of Paul's wise teaching was the Holy Spirit Himself, Who through His power imparted God's wisdom.

B. There were consequences for their lack of understanding.

1 Corinthians 3–4

- If the people did not understand clearly and fully the work of the cross and the work of the Holy Spirit, then they were in danger of their disagreements producing negative and destructive consequences.

1. They would not grow SPIRITUALLY.

1 Corinthians 3:1–9

- Arguing over which "mere man" to follow revealed that they were still "infants in Christ"—when they should have been growing. (1 Corinthians 3:1–4)

> ★ **TEACHING TIP:**
> *When believers follow a "mere man" (no matter how gifted a teacher) over first and foremost following Jesus Christ Himself, the end result will be jealousy and strife among the people.*

FIRST CORINTHIANS
Theme: Church's Problems Corrected

- They were walking "fleshly" (which includes all feelings that are not aimed at glorifying God, but instead are focused on gratifying self).

2. They would lose eternal **REWARDS**.

1 Corinthians 3:10–15
- Each believer serves the Lord in some manner.
  - Paul laid the foundation of the church in Corinth—in other words, he helped found the church there.
  - Others built upon it through teaching God's Word.
- Paul stated that the foundation upon which everyone was to serve is Jesus Christ.
- He then reminded them that a person's work (for the Lord) would be ultimately judged by Jesus (at the judgment seat of Christ—2 Corinthians 5:10).
  - Their work would be tested—by fire.
    * Gold, silver, and precious stones would stand the flame, being found accomplished in God's truth, holiness, and obedience.
    * Wood, hay, and stubble, however, would be easily burned up, being found accomplished from false doctrines and error, mistaken views.
  - The test would reveal that which had eternal value and that which was worthless.

> ❖ **APPLICATION:** Do not cause division in the church by self-exaltation (that does not glorify Jesus Christ, but maligns His work on the cross and the work of the Holy Spirit). To ignore this exhortation is very, very dangerous.

III. PAUL'S ANSWER TO QUESTIONS RAISED IN A LETTER (1 CORINTHIANS 7–16)

- The second report that Paul received from the church in Corinth was even worse than the first.

> ★ **TEACHING TIP:**
> *Sadly, don't we see sexual immorality being ignored and not addressed in many churches today?*

A. Gross sexual **IMMORALITY** should not be tolerated.

1 Corinthians 5
- It was shared that one of the men in the church was sleeping with his father's wife.
  - Some believe this might have been his step-mother. It still was gross sexual immorality.
- Paul shared that even the Gentiles would not participate in such lewd behavior.

FIRST CORINTHIANS
Theme: Church's Problems Corrected

- What made matters worse—the people in the church were not recognizing nor dealing with this sin in their midst!
- Paul, however, did not take this scenario lightly.
- In fact, he was very strong and specific as to how this situation was to be handled.

1. Remove the offender from the CHURCH.

2. Do not associate with immoral BELIEVERS.

> **NOTE:** Paul was NOT stating that believers were never to associate with immoral people—those who have never made a commitment to Christ. Paul was speaking to *immoral believers* who had chosen to knowingly and willingly continue in sin.

****

❋ **ILLUSTRATION:** There once was a deacon in a church who began to have an adulterous affair with a female co-worker. It came to the attention of the church leadership. First, two fellow deacons addressed this sin with their Christian brother, but he continued in the relationship. Then several deacons met with him to no avail. Finally, the elders of the church met with him and he still refused to leave this woman. His refusal to repent from his sin resulted into two church disciplinary actions: (1) He was told to leave the church; and (2) church members were instructed not to associate with him.

He ultimately divorced his wife and began "living it up." His wife stayed in the church and experienced love and support from the fellowship. Several years passed. One Sunday, the Senior Pastor stated that he wanted to introduce a special visitor—it was the deacon who had been removed from the church body. He stood at the pulpit and publicly confessed his very public sin of adultery. He then introduced his "beloved"—it was the wife of his youth! Through church discipline, God had worked on this man's heart—his relationships with God, his wife, and church family were restored. It was an incredible testimony!

Paul's teaching here may seem harsh—yet God's ways are always best for the sinner.

****

B. Christians should not SUE Christians.

1 Corinthians 6:1-8

- A second problem in this church involved the people suing one another.
- Paul instructed them that they should not do this—a believer should never sue another believer.

FIRST CORINTHIANS
Theme: Church's Problems Corrected

- Paul's basis for such teaching was simple:
    - The "plaintiff" in this case was a believer.
    - The "defendant" was another believer in the church.
    - He addressed the plaintiff who had the choice on whom would "hear" the matter (litigation)—fellow saints (believers) in the church or a worldly court (made up of unbelievers).
    - His conclusion: if as saints they would one day judge the world, then should they not be able to work out an issue among themselves and other Christians? Why would they, as believers, seek the world's input or judgment on a matter?
- Paul was not stating that there would never be differences among believers. Rather, he was instructing them in how they should address them.

> ★ **TEACHING TIP:**
>
> *You may have someone in your class who is in the midst of legal problems with another believer. You should never give "legal counsel"—let God's Word speak for itself through the Holy Spirit.*

C. **Sexually immoral people will not inherit the <u>KINGDOM</u> of God.**

✞ **1 Corinthians 6:9** "Or do you not know that the unrighteous will not inherit the kingdom of God? Do not be deceived; neither fornicators, nor idolaters, nor adulterers, nor effeminate, nor homosexuals, ..."

> ★ **TEACHING TIP:**
>
> *Note that Paul says here, "Don't be deceived." The culture in which we live will attempt to redefine sin as an acceptable "new normal."*

- We need to understand that sexual immorality is a sin.
- We need to teach our children this truth—and encourage them not to be "deceived."

> ❖ **APPLICATION:** God's Word is clear—if a person consistently and continually participates in sexual immorality, he/she will not inherit the kingdom of God.
>   - If you have participated in sexual immorality, can you repent? Can you be cleansed by the grace of God? Absolutely!
>   - However, Scripture is clear that a believer is not to participate in such acts.

<u>1 Corinthians 6:12-20</u>

1. **Our bodies are temples of the <u>HOLY SPIRIT</u>.**
    * The Holy Spirit dwells in us. We are His temple (His house).
    * Understanding that, we should not knowingly (choosing to disobey God's Word) taint it with sin.

FIRST CORINTHIANS
Theme: Church's Problems Corrected

2. Our bodies are to bring <u>GLORY</u> to God.

- Our bodies (and how we use them) have been given to us to bring glory to God.
- If we are sexually immoral, we bring no glory to God—only shame to Jesus Christ.

IV. PAUL'S ANSWERS TO QUESTIONS RAISED IN A LETTER (1 CORINTHIANS 7–16)

✟ **1 Corinthians 7:1a** " Now concerning the things about which you wrote, …"

- From this point on in his letter, Paul systematically answered questions that were posed to him—whether it was a problem, issue, or need for further understanding.

A. Paul addressed confusion concerning <u>MARRIAGE</u>.

<u>1 Corinthians 7:1–7</u>

1. Married couples should not <u>DENY</u> one another sexually.

* Why? So that the body does not become a manipulative tool in which games against one another can be played.
* It is important for couples to understand that, in marriage, a man no longer owns his own body, his wife does. Likewise, a wife does not own her own body, her husband does. (1 Corinthians 7:4)
* If prayer is needed, then to take time off from sex would be acceptable. (1 Corinthians 7:5)

<u>1 Corinthians 7:12–16</u>

2. A believing spouse should not <u>DIVORCE</u> because of his or her mate's unbelief.

- It is important to understand the context of this statement:
  - The believers in this church were now living a new life in Christ.
  - But they were married to a man or woman who were not believers—who had not accepted Christ.
  - They were feeling uncomfortable about being married to a non-believer.
- The believers in this situation had begun to question if they should divorce their spouse, so that they would not be in a partnership with an unbeliever.
- Paul's response: No!

> ★ **TEACHING TIP:**
> *Be sensitive to the fact that you may have people in your class that are in this very situation and have the same question.*

FIRST CORINTHIANS
Theme: Church's Problems Corrected

- ~ They were not to leave their unbelieving spouse.
- ~ They were to stay as they were—in their marriage covenant.
    - Paul's reasoning: Their "new life in Christ"—their new way of living (in actions and words)—may be the very thing that would lead that spouse to faith in Jesus Christ.
    - There was a caveat. If the unbelieving spouse chose to leave the marriage, then the believer was to let him or her go.
    - This was quite a problem in this little church at Paul's writing.

3. Singleness allows greater freedom for Christian <u>SERVICE</u>.

<u>1 Corinthians 7:32-35, 39</u>
- If a person was not married, then they shouldn't force the situation to be married—trying hard to find someone to marry.
- If they were content being single, then they were to see this as an opportunity to serve Christ in a more dynamic way because they were able to give all their service to Him.
    - ~ In marriage, spouses are called to serve each other, as well as the Lord.
- If widowed, then they were not to feel compelled to remarry. It may be better to stay single.
- In other words, if someone was single, they were to embrace it and give themselves in service to the Lord.

B. Paul addressed confusion concerning <u>FOODS</u> consecrated to pagan gods.

- This is a subject matter that we do not deal with today in our culture, but it was an issue in this early church.
- There are two principles, however, that we can apply to our lives today.

<u>1 Corinthians 8-9:23</u>

1. Do nothing that causes your weaker brother to <u>STUMBLE</u>.

****

✼ **ILLUSTRATION:** A young believer who was a recovering alcoholic (early in his journey into sobriety) wanted to become active in his Sunday school class. His goal was to surround himself with believers who knew his story—his thought was that their fellowship would undergird his commitment to Christ and support his struggle into sobriety. After a few class fellowships in various homes, he called someone in his church who was a mature Christian and had also dealt with alcoholism. He asked, "I want to follow Christ completely, but I still so often want to have a drink ... knowing full well that will send me back into a living hell. What should I do?" She responded, "You need to drop

FIRST CORINTHIANS
Theme: Church's Problems Corrected

all drinking buddies for the time being." He was quiet for a moment and then shared, "That would be my Sunday school class."

The members of that class had become a stumbling block for this young believer who needed their support. Were they free to drink? Absolutely! But they were doing it at the great cost of a weaker brother in Christ.

****

⇨ **As believers, we must live in an intentional awareness of our impact on others. Never do we want to cause a weaker believer to backslide or an unbeliever to reject Jesus because of our exerting our own "rights"—by putting ourselves "over" those the Lord brings upon our path.**

2. Exercise <u>SELF-CONTROL</u> in all things.

> ★ **TEACHING TIP:**
> *These athletes had to give up their "rights" to certain foods and activities in order to win in the games. As believers, we should be willing to do the same with the desire to "win" God's approval.*

<u>1 Corinthians 9:24–27</u>
- The people were very familiar with the Greek games.
  - ~ At that time, the Isthmian games were held near Corinth. These games were second only to the Olympics.
- Self-control was required by those who participated in the games. A commitment was made regarding a daily regimen of exercise and diet.
- Their goal was to "win"—self-control was required!

⇨ **As believers, we must use self-control in all we do.**

C. Paul addressed confusion concerning <u>SPIRITUAL GIFTS</u>.

> **NOTE:** It is important to understand that the subject of spiritual gifts is an area in which different denominations disagree—perspectives will not be the same. We are not to allow our disagreements, however, to divide the church. Be respectful and use only God's Word in your remarks.

<u>1 Corinthians 12–14</u>

1. Spiritual gifts are for the common <u>GOOD</u> of the church.

- In explaining spiritual gifts, Paul compared the church to the human body (a living organism).

FIRST CORINTHIANS
Theme: Church's Problems Corrected

- ~ The body has different parts to it—hands, feet, eyes, mouth, heart, liver, etc.
  - * All are necessary for the body to function.
  - * All must work as they were designed for the body to be healthy.

  - * If our body limbs or organs competed against one another or refused to do what they were created to do or tried to be what God did not create them to do, then the body would suffer greatly and debilitating illness would ensue.
- ~ In the same way, the church is a "living body" made up of people with different spiritual gifts—all are needed and necessary. All must work as they were designed (by God) for the church to be healthy.

- Spiritual gifts are mentioned in other books in the Bible. Some of the gifts that Paul mentioned are *(these descriptors are only for the teacher's better understanding)*:
  - ~ **Word of wisdom:** *ability to clearly explain the word of God in a manner that people understand.*
  - ~ **Word of knowledge:** *a clear, learned understanding of salvation, church doctrines, and responsibilities to one's faith.*
  - ~ **Faith:** *confidence in God, His Word.*
  - ~ **Healing:** *different kinds of disease need different kinds of healing. (Might be prompted by human skill in the course of time.) This was promised to and demonstrated by the disciples in the early church.*
  - ~ **Miracles:** *different from "healing," so refers probably to more "extraordinary" or "unusual" kinds of miracles.*
  - ~ **Prophecy:** *ability to interpret and convey the purposes or truth of God, particularly in regard to sin, dangers, or responsibilities of God's people.*
  - ~ **Distinguishing spirit:** *discernment.*
  - ~ **Tongues and Interpreting Tongues:** *power to speak in various languages and power to interpret the language that might be used.*
  - ~ **Helps or Service:** *those who render aid and assistance in a practical manner.*
  - ~ **Administration:** *ability in doing business, presiding over deliberations, and directing over the affairs of the church.*
  - ~ **Teaching:** *teaching, explaining, and applying God's Word in an edifying way (more emphasis on "growing up" believers).*
  - ~ **Preaching:** *announcing God's Word—the gospel, His kingdom (more focused on conversion of unbelievers).*
  - ~ **Exhortation:** *encourages others in the faith—building them up in Christ.*

FIRST CORINTHIANS
Theme: Church's Problems Corrected

- ~ **Leadership:** *closely related to the gift of administration. Leads, assists, protects, and cares for others in the body.*
- ~ **Mercy:** *ability to empathize with others with compassion in words and actions. Desires to provide relief to those experiencing difficult times, whether physical, emotional, or spiritual.*

> ★ **TEACHING TIP:**
> *We do a tremendous disservice to God when we think that we have nothing to offer because God has given you a gift to be used for good.*

- The Bible is clear that every believer is given a spiritual gift from Christ.
  - ~ It is not a gift to be hidden or used sparingly because it was not given for "just" you.
  - ~ It has been given to the believer to develop and support the church body.

> ❖ **APPLICATION:** We live in such a competitive culture that it is very easy to fall into a trap of comparing our abilities to others. Often we focus on those we perceive as truly "important" to the fellowship and find ourselves lacking.
> - ~ But behind that visible leader in your church are hundreds more using their "invisible, behind the scenes" gifts to build up the body.
> - ~ Consider these two spiritual gifts:
>   - * **Service:** these are the folks who put up and take down chairs for a church service while others are in their cars headed home—or have the coffee perking when people arrive for a church event.
>   - * **Hospitality:** These are the first to greet and welcome members and strangers as they arrive. They also are the ones who offer their homes for ministry and church fellowship (and we never see all the time or effort they took to prepare their homes for those coming).

⇨ **Every believer has been given a spiritual gift from God and each one is critical to the growth and health of the church.**

2. LOVE is superior to all gifts.

- God makes it clear that all of the spiritual gifts are important.
- But a spiritual gift can become worthless if it is not covered in the love of Christ.
- Every gift should be employed through the love of Jesus and out of love for Jesus and for one another.

3. God's definition of LOVE is found in 1 Corinthians 13:4–7.

- Our culture has all kinds of definitions for "love."

FIRST CORINTHIANS
Theme: Church's Problems Corrected

- God's definition of "love" is something the world could never author because:
  - It is self-sacrificial.
  - It can only be accomplished by the Spirit of God working through a person.

- The components of God's definition for "love" involve these characteristics ***(these descriptors are only for the teacher's better understanding)***:
  - **Patient:** *slow to anger even when provoked—not quick to become irritable with others.*
  - **Kind:** *gentle, tender, wishes well for others—not harsh or severe with others.*
  - **Not jealous:** *delights in the welfare of others (wealth, health, etc.)—not envious of it.*
  - **Does not brag:** *regards others with esteem—not a feeling of superiority over others.*
  - **Not arrogant:** *modest and unassuming—not "puffed up" with a conviction of self-importance.*
  - **Does not act unbecomingly:** *conducts life (words and actions) in a manner that honors Christ—not unprincipled or offensive or unseemly behavior.*
  - **Does not seek its own:** *seeks the things of God (what will honor Him most)—not "self"-seeking or selfish.*
  - **Is not provoked:** *restrains one's temper—not easily roused to anger.*
  - **Does not take into account a wrong suffered:** *does not keep a "record" or "ledger" of wrongs done, but instead forgives completely—not unforgiving and bitter.*
  - **Does not rejoice in unrighteousness:** *grieves over one's own sin and the sinful actions of others—does not take delight in others falling into sin.*
  - **Rejoices in truth:** *celebrates the virtue and goodness of others—not in their vices.*
  - **Bears all things:** *willing to freely forgive sins against them and cover them with the mantle of love—not publicly divulging the faults of others or seeking revenge.*
  - **Believes all things:** *willing to think the best of others when there is no evidence of the opposite—not given to accepting gossip as a "fact."*
  - **Hopes all things:** *optimistic expectation for the best for others (salvation, repentance, restoration)—not quickly concluding that someone is beyond hope.*
  - **Endures all things:** *remains steadfast for the sake of Christ, whether in illness, tribulations, persecution, or death.*
  - **Never fails:** *it offers permanent, unending grace.*

FIRST CORINTHIANS
Theme: Church's Problems Corrected

> ❖ **APPLICATION:** Can you begin to imagine the heart change you would experience if you committed to reading this one passage weekly? What if you:
> - Read these verses and prayed that the Lord would reveal areas in your life that needed changing?
> - Asked the Lord to help you *desire* to grow in His definition of "love?"
>
> ⇨ **Commit to practically applying these verses to those in your world—family, friends, co-workers, neighbors, church members, etc.**

D. Paul addressed confusion concerning the RESURRECTION.

1. If Christ has not been raised, then our faith is WORTHLESS.

✝ **1 Corinthians 15:12–14** "Now if Christ is preached, that He has been raised from the dead, how do some among you say that there is no resurrection of the dead? But if there is no resurrection of the dead, not even Christ has been raised; and if Christ has not been raised, then our preaching is vain, your faith also is vain."

- Paul was adamant that this was absolutely inaccurate thinking. In fact, it was very dangerous.
  - If Christ was not resurrected, then everyone was totally wasting their time and not pleasing God—beginning with Paul.
- Everything in the Christian faith hinges on the fact that Jesus died, was buried, and rose from the dead. (1Corinthians 15:15–19)

⇨ **Jesus literally conquered death (the consequence of sin). This is of utmost importance to the Christian faith.**

2. We will have bodies that are IMPERISHABLE.

1 Corinthians 15:35–49
- There were some in the Corinth church who wondered about what happened to their bodies after they died.
  - "If we are raised from the dead, are these bodies (that we now have) the bodies we are going to keep? Is this it?"
- Paul responded with a resounding, "No! The body you now have is not the body you will have in eternity." One day they would have bodies that would be raised:
  - An imperishable body
  - In glory
  - A spiritual body
  - Bearing the image of the heavenly

FIRST CORINTHIANS
Theme: Church's Problems Corrected

3. Christ's resurrection was witnessed by <u>FIVE HUNDRED</u> people.

<u>1 Corinthians 15:3-11</u>
- There were some in the church at Corinth who questioned whether the resurrection had even happened.
- Paul rebuffed these comments by reminding them of the many people who had seen Jesus after His death and burial. Jesus appeared to:
  - Peter
  - The disciples
  - 500 believers at one time—many of whom were still alive to testify to Christ's resurrection
  - James
  - All the apostles
  - Paul himself

4. At the last trumpet, the dead will be raised, and the living in Christ will be <u>CHANGED</u>.

<u>1 Corinthians 15:50-57</u>
- Paul further explained what would happen when the "trumpets sounded" at Christ's return:
  - The dead will be raised.
  - And those still alive will be changed in a moment!

> ❖ **APPLICATION:** Knowing this all to be true, such good news demands a response.
> ✝ **1 Corinthians 15:58** "Therefore, my beloved brethren, be steadfast, immovable, always abounding in the work of the Lord, knowing that your toil is not in vain in the Lord."

FINAL THOUGHTS AND APPLICATION

- This book was written to a church to help solve problems that had arisen within it.
- Paul was not interested in them continuing to live in the mire that surrounded them.
- He wanted these believers to know how to live righteously with Jesus Christ.
- Intermingled in Paul's responses is the voice of a father—a spiritual father—who loved the Corinth church deeply and wanted only the best for them ... even if it required church correction.

❖ **FINAL APPLICATION:** What areas of your life have you turned over to the control of Jesus Christ?

FIRST CORINTHIANS REVIEW HELPS

✧ **Match the person or phrase with the book.**

1. Genesis
2. Exodus
3. Joshua
4. David
5. Solomon
6. Prophet in the lions' den
7. Prophet in the well
8. Prophet who saw the Lord high and lifted up
9. The last writing prophet
10. Matthew
11. Mark
12. Luke
13. John
14. Acts
15. Romans
16. 1 Corinthians
17. 2 Kings
18. Esther
19. Nehemiah
20. Job
21. Jewish Hymnbook

Paul addressed church problems
Jesus the Suffering Servant
Isaiah
Explains righteousness
Jesus the King and Messiah
Conquered Jericho
Abraham
Second King of Israel
Moses
Jesus is God
The birth of the church
Built the first temple in Jerusalem
Daniel
Jesus the Perfect Man
Jeremiah
Malachi
Uncle Mordecai
Psalms
Suffering and sovereignty
Rebuilt wall
Judah exiled to Babylon

FIRST CORINTHIANS REVIEW HELPS
(Answers for Facilitators)

✧ **Match the person or phrase with the book.**

1.	Genesis	**Abraham**
2.	Exodus	**Moses**
3.	Joshua	**Conquered Jericho**
4.	David	**Second king of Israel**
5.	Solomon	**Built the temple in Jerusalem**
6.	Prophet in the lions' den	**Daniel**
7.	Prophet in the well	**Jeremiah**
8.	Prophet who saw the Lord high and lifted up	**Isaiah**
9.	The last writing prophet	**Malachi**
10.	Matthew	**Jesus the King and Messiah**
11.	Mark	**Jesus the Suffering Servant**
12.	Luke	**Jesus the Perfect Man**
13.	John	**Jesus is God**
14.	Acts	**The birth of the church**
15.	Romans	**Explains righteousness**
16.	1 Corinthians	**Paul addressed church problems**
17.	2 Kings	**Judah exiled to Babylon**
18.	Esther	**Uncle Mordecai**
19.	Nehemiah	**Rebuilt the wall**
20.	Job	**Suffering and sovereignty**
21.	Jewish Hymnbook	**Psalms**

First Corinthians

SECOND CORINTHIANS

Paul's Ministry Defended

For we do not preach ourselves but Christ Jesus as Lord,

and ourselves as your bond-servants for Jesus' sake.

2 Corinthians 4:5

SESSION FORTY-SEVEN: SECOND CORINTHIANS
Paul's Ministry Defended

☦ **Memory verse:** *"For we do not preach ourselves but Christ Jesus as Lord, and ourselves as your bond-servants for Jesus' sake." (2 Corinthians 4:5)*

Introduction: The book of 2 Corinthians is Paul's second letter to the Corinthians and is much different from the first. There were some in the church who had been spreading rumors about Paul and his authority over the church and his role as a spiritual guide and apostle. Where the first letter dealt with specific questions the church leaders had asked of Paul, this one is more personal and defensive. It is in this letter that he defends his apostleship, declares his authority, and describes to the church in no uncertain terms all he had gone through to spread the Gospel of Jesus Christ. In staggering confidence in God, he proclaims God's grace is sufficient. God has given him the strength to endure the suffering for Christ. Along with his defense, he also challenges believers to open their hearts and "pocketbooks" and give generously to the kingdom work for the glory of God and the benefit of the giver.

- **Oral Review:** Please refer to the **REVIEW Section** in the following Teaching Guide Outline.

- **Homework:** Review the homework from the book of 1 Corinthians.

    Question on page 59
    Questions at the end of page 62
    Questions on page 67
    Questions at the end of page 70

- **Review Helps:** Written review is provided at the end of the teacher presentation. (Optional and time permitting.)

- **Teacher Presentation on the Book of 2 Corinthians**

- **Learning for Life:** You may choose to discuss all or just one or two of the questions on page 79.

- **Closing prayer:** Pray for the pastor and leaders of the church—that God would protect them spiritually and from false accusations that could divide and destroy a church. Pray that each participant would see themselves as Christ's bondservant, wholly devoted to Him.

SECOND CORINTHIANS
Theme: Paul's Ministry Defended

OUTLINE AID FOR TEACHERS:

I. **PAUL DEFENDED HIS MINISTRY BY EXPLAINING HIS ACTIONS (2 CORINTHIANS 1–7)**

- **2 Corinthians 1:3-7**

   A. Believers were greeted with teaching on God's COMFORT. (2 Corinthians 1:3-7)
   1. STRENGTHEN, encourage, and teach them during trials.
   2. Help others who were suffering when SHARED.

- **2 Corinthians 1:12-2:13**

   B. Paul explained his itinerary CHANGES and sought their understanding.

- **2 Corinthians 2:14-7:16**

   C. Various important spiritual TRUTHS were shared.
   1. Believers were both a sweet FRAGRANCE of victory and a foul smell of death.
   2. Their changed HEARTS were proof of Paul's ministry.
   3. Paul preached God's GRACE and the Christ-like transformation that results.
   4. Believers are God's VESSELS used to preach Christ.
   5. Believers are told to "not lose HEART."
   6. NOW is the time for salvation, so conduct yourselves accordingly:
      a. Be equally YOKED.
      b. Be PURE (holy).
      c. Be REPENTANT rather than merely sorrowful.

II. **PAUL CHALLENGED THE CORINTHIANS TO GENEROUS GIVING (2 CORINTHIANS 8–9)**

- **2 Corinthians 8:1-6**

   A. The Philippians' COLLECTION for the Jerusalem saints was praised.

- **2 Corinthians 8:7-8:15**

   B. The Corinthian church should SUPPORT kingdom work by giving.

- **2 Corinthians 8:16-9:5**

   C. Paul shared principles and promises regarding GIVING.

SECOND CORINTHIANS
Theme: Paul's Ministry Defended

III. **ACCUSATIONS AGAINST PAUL'S AUTHORITY WERE ANSWERED (2 CORINTHIANS 10–13)**

- **2 Corinthians 10**

  A. Paul denied false <u>CHARGES</u>.

- **2 Corinthians 11:1–12:13**

  B. Paul defended his <u>APOSTLESHIP</u> with proof of his authority.

- **2 Corinthians 13:1–14**

  C. Paul announced his future plans to <u>VISIT</u> Corinth.

2 Corinthians
[Paul's Ministry Defended]

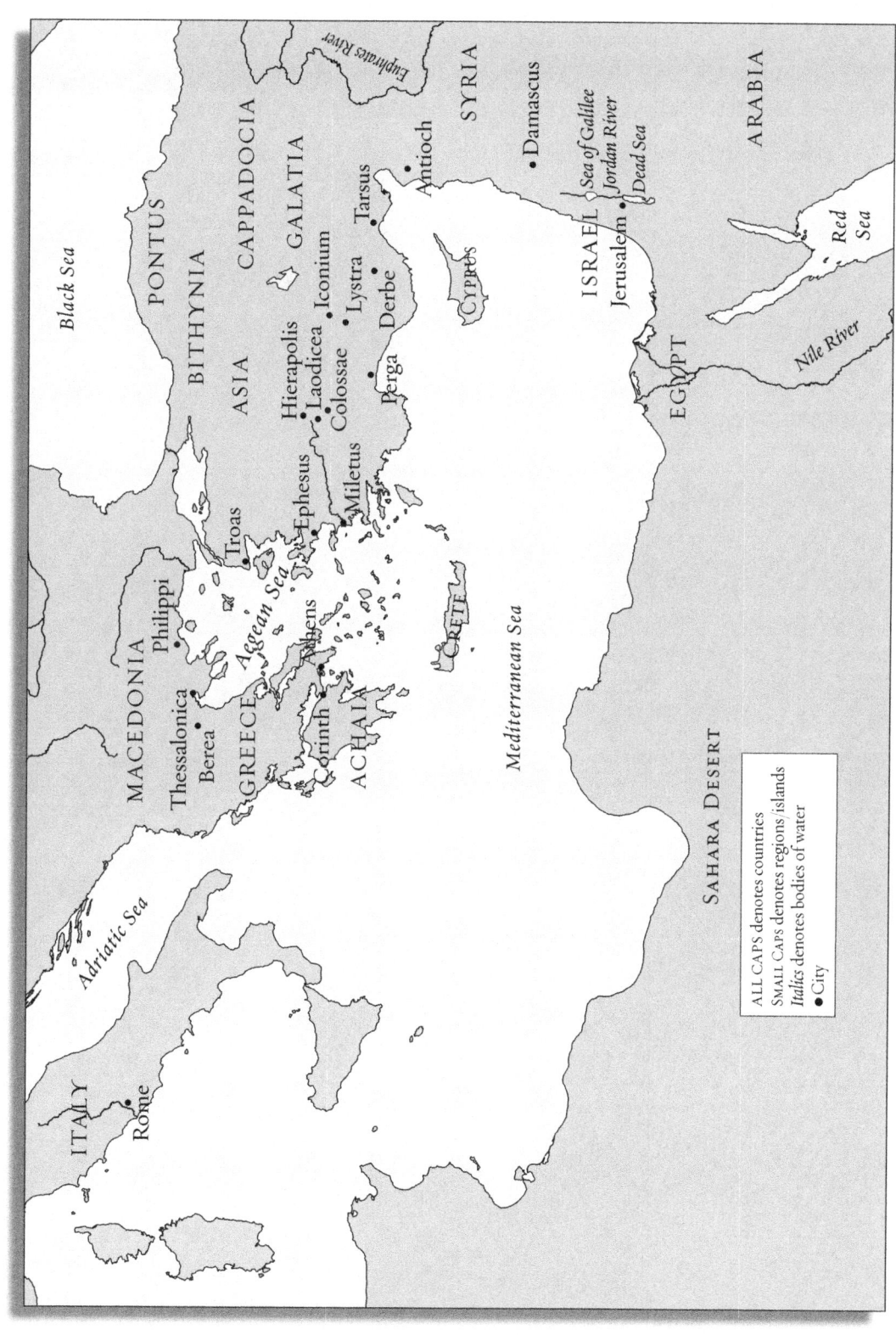

SECOND CORINTHIANS

SECOND CORINTHIANS
Theme: Paul's Ministry Defended

THE BASICS:
- **Who:** **The Author:** Paul
  - **Main Characters:** Believers in Corinth
- **What:** Paul's defense of himself against false charges and accusations
- **When:** Written in A.D. 56
- **Where:** Written to Corinth from Macedonia (possibly Philippi)
- **Why:** To defend himself against those in Corinth making false accusations regarding his authority and apostleship

MEMORY VERSE: *"For we do not preach ourselves but Christ Jesus as Lord, and ourselves as your bond-servants for Jesus' sake."* 2 Corinthians 4:5

****

REVIEW:
- The *Old Testament History* books showed the problem of disobedience (sin) and its consequences (slavery and death). The prophets foretold of judgment and the Messiah to come.
- The *New Testament History* books show that the Messiah has come and the church was born. Each gospel focused on a different aspect of Jesus:
  - **Matthew:** Jesus is the long-awaited King of the Jews.
  - **Mark:** Jesus is the suffering servant—a servant to all men and women.
  - **Luke:** Jesus is the Perfect Man.
  - **John:** Jesus is God.
  - **Acts:** the church was born.
- In Paul's letters to the Churches, we have seen him explain who we are in Christ and the struggle to live out a righteous life.
  - **Romans:** a letter in which Paul presented God's righteousness.
  - **First Corinthians:** a letter in which Paul wrote to help solve problems that had arisen within the church. It was not Paul's desire for them to continue to live in the sinful mire that surrounded them. He explained how to live righteously with Jesus Christ.

OVERVIEW:

****

- **ILLUSTRATION:** Have you ever been falsely accused of something? If you have, then you know how hurtful and hard such a situation is. But the real question is, "What do you do when this scenario occurs in your life?" Do you respond by spreading rumors about the

SECOND CORINTHIANS
Theme: Paul's Ministry Defended

person who has falsely accused you? Do you get angry? Do you get "your" people together to go against "their" people?

How you respond is very serious, especially if you are one who teaches God's Word. Why? Because your character is not the only one in question—God's character is also because you have represented Him as you have taught His truth.

****

- It would be good to remember a few facts about the church in Corinth:
  ~ Paul had founded it, yet this church seemed to have given him more problems to address than all the other churches combined.
  ~ This was basically a high-maintenance church!

- In 1 Corinthians, Paul had been direct and faithful to the Word of God as he addressed the sin in their midst and entreated them to demonstrate not only self-discipline, but church discipline on a specific offender.
  ~ The problems in the church, however, grew worse, so Paul sent Titus to ensure the people obeyed his instructions. (2 Corinthians 7:13–15)
  ~ Titus reported back that the majority of the people were behind his ministry and walking in obedience to God's Word. (2 Corinthians 7:5–6)

- The tone of 2 Corinthians is more personal as Paul responded to those who questioned and attempted to discredit his authority, actions, and motives.
- It was written from somewhere in Macedonia (many believe in Philippi) in the latter part of 56 A.D.

⇨ **The purpose of 2 Corinthians was to give a defense of Paul's ministry.**

I. PAUL DEFENDED HIS MINISTRY BY EXPLAINING HIS ACTIONS (2 CORINTHIANS 1–7)

A. Believers were greeted with teaching on God's <u>COMFORT</u>. (2 Corinthians 1:3–7)

✝ **2 Corinthians 1:3–7** "Blessed be the God and Father of our Lord Jesus Christ, the Father of mercies and God of all **comfort**, who **comforts** us in all our affliction so that we will be able to **comfort** those who are in any affliction with the **comfort** with which we ourselves are **comforted** by God. For just as the sufferings of Christ are ours in abundance, so also our **comfort** is abundant through Christ. But if we are afflicted, it is for your **comfort** and salvation; or if we are **comforted**, it is for **your comfort**, which is effective in the patient enduring of the same sufferings which we also suffer; and our hope for you is firmly

SECOND CORINTHIANS
Theme: Paul's Ministry Defended

grounded, knowing that as you are sharers of our sufferings, so also you are sharers of our **comfort**."

- The word "comfort" is used ten times in these seven verses.
- Paul wanted them to see the connection between trials and comfort because it would reveal the God of comfort that they served.

   1. **STRENGTHEN**, encourage, and teach them during trials.

   2. Help others who were suffering when **SHARED.**

> **NOTE:** God often allows trials in our lives in order to get our attention and teach us:
> - To draw nearer to Him.
> - To be dependent upon Him.
> - To share what we have learned through our own trials to those who are suffering.

- In Acts 9, God shared with Paul, through Ananias, that he would suffer many trials. (Acts 9:10–18)
- Paul was teaching what he had *lived*!
  - Paul had suffered great persecution and suffering as he shared the gospel of Christ and founded churches.
  - He had also experienced the comfort of God through those hard ordeals.

⇨ **Paul could comfort those who were suffering because he had experienced the real pain of trials and the absolute promise of God's comfort to the believer.**

> ❖ **APPLICATION:** What kind of comforter are you?
> - Do you bring hope to the hurting? Do you encourage others by sharing how you have come through a similar situation—how victory is possible, though the pain is real at present?
> - Or do you add to a person's despair by compounding the pain with judgmental sounding phrases or empty platitudes? Consider Job's friends!

****

ILLUSTRATION: A young woman stood at the open grave of her father. His casket had been lowered, people were leaving the cemetery, and she felt completely alone. As she stood there, she thought about her mother who had died four years earlier. She had been very close to her parents and now they were both gone. She felt as though her heart was physically breaking—

SECOND CORINTHIANS
Theme: Paul's Ministry Defended

and the sense of "aloneness" grew. An older woman walked up to comfort her with a hug and these words, "Oh, honey, you are an orphan now. That just hurts my heart." And then she walked away—pleased that she had had the opportunity to comfort the young woman. Anything but comfort, however, had taken place.

****

> ❖ **APPLICATION:** The truth of the matter is that we are all either coming out of a trial or entering into a trial. Don't waste your suffering! Use the experience and what God has taught you through it to comfort others.

B. Paul explained his itinerary **CHANGES** and sought their understanding. (2 Corinthians 1:12-2:13)

- Paul had promised the people that he would visit them and then did not.
  - ~ Some had begun to accuse him of being "wishy-washy."
- Paul explained that he had wanted to receive their response to his first letter before coming to them in order to determine how he would deal with them and the problems within the church.

C. Various important spiritual **TRUTHS** were shared. (2 Corinthians 2:14-7:16)

1. Believers are both a sweet **FRAGRANCE** of victory and a foul smell of death.

2 Corinthians 2:14-16
- This was an illustration that the people in Corinth would understand.
  - ~ When a victorious Roman general returned home from his conquests, a huge celebratory parade was given for him.
  - ~ Pots of incense would burn to honor the hero—a fragrant aroma of victory.
  - ~ The army would follow behind him and they would also enjoy the praise of the people.
  - ~ Slaves and captives followed next. They had been brought to fight in an arena against wild beasts—their certain demise carried the smell of death.
- Paul used this familiar illustration to remind the people that Christians (believers) are to be a sweet fragrance—of victory and life in Jesus Christ.
  - ~ And this fragrance should draw people to a Christian.

SECOND CORINTHIANS
Theme: Paul's Ministry Defended

- Paul recognized, however, that not all people will be drawn to the fragrance of Christ.
  - There will be those who will reject it—reject the truth.
  - To them this aroma is not sweet; it becomes a smell of death—and death will be their destiny if they do not turn to Christ.

> ★ **TEACHING TIP:**
> *Jesus was not what the Jewish people expected as their Messiah. They had been waiting for a king to ride in on a horse and liberate them, not a humble man who reached out in love and mercy to serve all people (including Gentiles).*

2. **Their changed <u>HEARTS</u> were proof of Paul's ministry.**

<u>2 Corinthians 3:1–3</u>
- Paul used a mirror to show the proof, the results, of his ministry. He told the people to look at themselves—they were the proof!
  - The believers in this church had changed hearts, which led to transformed lives.
- Paul stated that the people were a reflection of his teaching.
  - Christ was now written on their hearts by the Holy Spirit—not on tablets of stone.

> ★ **TEACHING TIP:**
> *Someone once said, "Christians read the Bible, but unbelievers read Christians." What are people reading in your life?*

3. **Paul preached God's <u>GRACE</u> and the Christ-like transformation that results.**

<u>2 Corinthians 3:4–18</u>
- Paul preached God's grace that led to Christ-like transformation.
- Jesus Christ brought a new covenant with Him—the covenant of grace.

> **NOTE:** What does "grace" mean?
> - God's unmerited favor—a kindness from God that we do not deserve.
>   - Not based on something we have done.
>   - Not based on something we will ever be able to do.
> - It is a gift from God.
> - It is witnessed in our salvation—impacting our new birth and our new life in Christ.

- Paul wanted the people to understand that those who held onto the Law of Moses as the way of salvation would die—the law defined sin, it did not give life.

SECOND CORINTHIANS
Theme: Paul's Ministry Defended

- ~ To take hold of such a wrong belief was like putting a veil over their faces that kept them from seeing the truth.
  This lack of understanding and holding on to the old covenant with a hardened heart would remain until they came to Jesus Christ. (2 Corinthians 3:14–16)
- Paul desired them to see that there was liberty—freedom—in Christ!

> ★ **TEACHING TIP:**
> *This is a wonderful reminder that we have Jesus living within us—the presence and power of the Holy Spirit within!*

4. Believers are God's <u>VESSELS</u> used to preach Christ.

<u>2 Corinthians 4:1–15</u>
- Paul explained that the gospel is hidden from those who reject it—thus, are perishing.
  - ~ These people are blinded by Satan.
  - ~ They cannot see and they cannot understand the truth.
  - ~ This impacts how they live—they live in the flesh.
- Paul exhorted the people in Corinth to understand that God would use them to draw those who were "blind" to see the truth.

5. Believers are told to "not lose <u>HEART</u>."

<u>2 Corinthians 4:1, 9, 16–18</u>
- If one loses heart, he typically becomes despondent and disheartened.
- To not lose heart means "to stay with something, to stay encouraged, to be emboldened."
- Paul explained to these church members why they should not lose heart:
  - ~ They now had a ministry, as they also had received mercy from God. (v.1)
    - ∗ God had entrusted this ministry to these people through His mercy and favor.
  - ~ They had been afflicted in every way, but not crushed. (v.8a)
    - ∗ In sharing the Gospel, they had experienced pressing trials—but they had overcome them.
  - ~ They had been perplexed, but not despairing. (v.8b)
    - ∗ They had experienced doubts and anxiety at times, not knowing what to do—but they had also experienced unexpected strength and resources to combat their fears and lack of understanding. (God's grace supplies this!)
  - ~ They had been persecuted, but not forsaken. (v.9a)
    - ∗ The book of Acts speaks to their persecution in all places—but God never deserted them. His presence, power, and provision sustained them.

© 2018 Big Dream Ministries, Inc.

SECOND CORINTHIANS
Theme: Paul's Ministry Defended

- ~ They had been struck down, but not destroyed. (v9b)
  - * This alluded to the contests of wrestlers or gladiators who would throw their opponents down to the ground.
  - * Paul and these believers had been thrown down by their enemies—but not killed because they got up from the fight, recovered their strength, and prepared to face new conflicts, new persecutions, and new trials.

2 Corinthians 4:16—5:20
- Paul wanted those in the Corinth church to adopt an "eternal" perspective—to <u>know</u> that their bodies were, indeed, aging, but inwardly their souls were being renewed.
- He consoled them by reminding them that their suffering for Christ paled in comparison to the glory that awaited them—again, an "eternal" perspective.
  - ~ Paul never denied that earthly life was hard.
- Paul focused on what was to come—what should be remembered as we persevere through this life.
  - ~ Heaven is our home, not this world—we are just passing through.
  - ~ When we arrive "home," we will receive brand new, glorified bodies.
  - ~ Yes, there are hardships in this life, but they are momentary—compared to eternity with Jesus Christ.
- Paul taught and lived out an intentional, eternal mindset:
  - ~ His earnest desire was to be with the Lord in heaven—free from the earthly hardships.
  - ~ However, until God called him home, he was devoted to living a life that was pleasing to Christ.

> ★ **TEACHING TIP:**
> *Yes, we are all getting older—but those in Christ are also being renewed from within and prepared for heaven!*

⇨ **Paul encouraged the people to live this life as "new creatures in Christ!"**

- Paul also wanted the Corinthian believers to understand that they would each stand before Jesus Christ:
- ✞ **2 Corinthians 5:10** "For we must all appear before the judgment seat of Christ, so that each one may be recompensed for his deeds in the body, according to what he has done, whether good or bad."
  - Their (our) behavior—how we conduct ourselves as Christians—matters.

> ★ **TEACHING TIP:**
> *A good visual here is one of a camcorder—taping every action and every word—running 24/7 with no "pauses."*

© 2018 Big Dream Ministries, Inc.

SECOND CORINTHIANS
Theme: Paul's Ministry Defended

⇨ **Believers will be answerable to Christ and appear before Him—their true character and works will be judged.**
- ~ There will be no "pretending" at this judgment—motives will be exposed, as well.

> **NOTE:** Be aware—this verse can cause confusion for some as it pertains to *"judgment."*
> - ♦ For believers, this will be an accounting of how they lived out their faith in Christ— a time when Christ will reward the fruit of their labor for Him.
> - ⇨ **Consider that Paul has gone to great lengths in exhorting the Corinthians on how they should conduct themselves as believers in Christ—no matter the immoral culture and influences of their day.**

6. NOW is the time for salvation, so conduct yourselves accordingly:

<u>2 Corinthians 6</u>
- Paul taught them that there was a behavior by which a Christian should live— including how they responded to trials and unavoidable times of duress and distress.
- Paul wanted these believers to fully understand that they represented the ministry of Jesus Christ in all they said and did.

a. Be equally <u>YOKED</u>.

<u>2 Corinthians 6:14–16</u>
- Paul taught on how they were to be bound together in partnerships.
- He used visuals to demonstrate the problem:
  - ~ What *partnership* did righteousness have with lawlessness? None.
    - * Honesty and dishonesty cannot partner together.
  - ~ What *fellowship* did light have with darkness? None.
    - * There is absolutely no similarity—they are totally separate.
  - ~ What *harmony* did Christ have with Belial? None.
    - * *Belial* literally means "wickedness" or "worthlessness"—this would refer to a pagan governed by Satan.
  - ~ What *commonality* did a believer have with an unbeliever? None.
    - * Belief in Jesus Christ and unbelief in Him are in total conflict with one another; there is no union of conviction.

SECOND CORINTHIANS
Theme: Paul's Ministry Defended

- ~ What *agreement* did the temple of God have with idols? None.
  - * Christians are themselves the temple of God and should make no pact with one who worships an image of a little "g" god.

> ★ **TEACHING TIP:**
> It is important to remember how sinful the city of Corinth was. These believers were surrounded and tempted by a pagan culture.

> ❖ **APPLICATION:** This is a lesson that should be taught early on to our children.
> - ~ Practically speaking, we should teach this principle *before* a daughter or son heads out on their first date because every "date" is a potential mate.
> - ~ We should pray for our child's future spouse and his or her salvation—early on, just as we have prayed for our own child's salvation.
> - ~ Share this prayer with your child and emphasize that God has someone very special for him or her—encourage and exhort them to wait for His best!

b. Be <u>PURE</u> (holy).

2 Corinthians 6:17
- To "be pure" means to come out from among or be separate from the world and its beliefs and things—all that which is not of God.
- Paul called them to separate from that which was unclean—the idolaters and unbelievers.
- As we have studied, Israel struggled with this concept.
  - ~ They constantly intermingled with the heathen nations.
  - ~ That mingling led many to marry heathen wives who would bring their idols into their new homes—resulting in Israel turning to idol worship.
  - ~ God called them "adulterers" because they were unfaithful to Him.
- Paul stressed the importance of being faithful to God by being separate from the world to Him.

c. Be <u>REPENTANT</u> rather than merely sorrowful.

2 Corinthians 7:8–13
- Paul's first letter had been direct and hard-hitting as he addressed sin in their midst and their compromising attitude toward it.
- Paul stated that he knew the letter had brought them sorrow but, more importantly, it had brought them to repentance.

SECOND CORINTHIANS
Theme: Paul's Ministry Defended

> **NOTE:** Godly sorrow (repentance) is not mere grief, but it is a sorrow that leads one to change, to reform. It involves agreeing with God about a sinful action or attitude, confessing it, and then turning from it to walk in obedience to God.

- They needed to change (their thoughts and actions) and Paul's letter had led them to see this truth about themselves.

> ❖ **APPLICATION:** If God has revealed an area in your life that is sin, do not simply be "sorry" about it, but turn to Him in obedience and make the appropriate changes in your life. This is not a call to take lightly—none of us know the number of our days so, while we have an opportunity, let us all be wise in taking our responses to the Lord and His word seriously.

II. PAUL CHALLENGED THE CORINTHIANS TO GENEROUS GIVING (2 CORINTHIANS 8–9)

NOTE: These chapters have great principles that we will skim for the sake of time, because our focus is Paul's defense of himself.

- Paul turned his attention toward giving. His desire was to raise awareness for them, so that they would support the impoverished saints.

A. The Philippians' COLLECTION for the Jerusalem saints was praised. (2 Corinthians 8:1–6)

> ★ **TEACHING TIP:**
> Sadly, many give out of their abundance or from their leftovers, but not these faithful and happy "givers!"

- He praised the Philippians for giving out of their poverty.
- They gave out of the difficulties—they begged to give! They wanted to help others!

B. The Corinthian church should SUPPORT kingdom work by giving. (2 Corinthians 8:7-9:15)

- Paul encouraged the Corinthians by reminding them of Christ and His example of sacrificial giving.
  ~ He gave up everything so that we might be made eternally rich.
- Kingdom work spreads this good news!

SECOND CORINTHIANS
Theme: Paul's Ministry Defended

C. Paul shared principles and promises regarding GIVING. (2 Corinthians 8:16-9:5)

- A few of the principles mentioned are:
  - A believer is not to give grudgingly or under compulsion—exuding a *"have to give"* spirit.
  - God loves a cheerful giver—one who radiates a *"want to give"* spirit.
  - Ultimately, a believer will receive in the same manner in which he or she gave. (This speaks to spiritual blessings, not necessarily to wealth or possessions.)

III. ACCUSATIONS AGAINST PAUL'S AUTHORITY WERE ANSWERED (2 CORINTHIANS 10-13)

A. Paul denied false CHARGES. (2 Corinthians 10)

- Earlier in this letter, Paul addressed the people's complaints regarding his being inconsistent or "wishy-washy"—based on the fact that he wrote to them instead of coming to see them as he had initially promised.
- Now they turned to his "style" of ministry—they had issues with his looks and how he communicated. To them, he was unimpressive.

> ★ **TEACHING TIP:**
> *As we read these verses, it is hard for us to fathom their complaints against Paul—certainly this is not our impression of this mighty apostle! But note: what he taught and wrote them was not in dispute because he faithfully and consistently taught Jesus Christ alone.*

✝ **2 Corinthians 10:1, 10** "Now I, Paul, myself urge you by the meekness and gentleness of Christ — I who am meek when face to face with you, but bold toward you when absent! ... For they say, 'His letters are weighty and strong, but his personal presence is unimpressive and his speech contemptible.'"

- The charge: Paul was uninspiring in person, his speech distasteful—he was not at all like his letters.
  - They expected him to be an impressively strong speaker, a powerhouse—instead he was meek. (Note: meekness is actually "strength under control" and, in Paul's case, God's control.)
  - They expected Paul to be "bigger than life," but he stated that no one was to be "bigger than Christ."
- Their struggle: how could he be in authority over them?

B. Paul defended his APOSTLESHIP with proof of his authority. (2 Corinthians 11:1-12:13)

SECOND CORINTHIANS
Theme: Paul's Ministry Defended

> **NOTE:** Paul was dealing with false teachers and apostles in the church (2 Corinthians 11:3-4). They were "smooth and crafty talkers" and were leading the people to stray from simple and pure devotion to Christ. These charismatic teachers were *not* teaching the truth of Jesus. In fact, they were offering up other versions of Him ("another Jesus") and a different gospel to accept. All of this put the people in danger.

- Paul made the case for his authority. With the false teacher/apostles in mind, he gave a striking contrast.
  1. Paul stated that he may not have been the most polished speaker (Greek was not his first language), but he had only spoken the truth to them—and he did so boldly and with understanding of God's Word.

  2. He loved the people and was jealous for their affections to be with Christ alone.
     - Paul could count the many times he had been in jail and beaten for the cause of Christ, whereas the false teachers counted their "own" converts.

  3. He preached the gospel and served the people without charging them a fee for both—he was not trying to make money off of them nor did he want to be a burden.
     - In fact, other churches had provided for his visit to Corinth.
     - Paul ministered with an attitude of giving, not one that focused on "how much can I get from you?"

  4. He enumerated a list of problems with the false teachers: they were deceitful, they disguised themselves as apostles of Christ (just as Satan disguised himself as an angel of light), and they pretended to be righteous but were not.

  5. He then related facts about himself: a descendant of Abraham; a servant of Christ who had experienced innumerable acts of persecution for the gospel of Jesus Christ—imprisonments, beatings, danger of death, stoning, along with the many dangers from robbers, countrymen, Gentiles, circumstances (city, wilderness, or sea); false brethren.

> ★ **TEACHING TIP:**
>
> *How did Paul keep going? How did he not give up on these people? He loved them, he cared for them, and he did not want them to be deceived. Paul knew they were in danger!*
> *He knew that the "false" teacher or apostle can present a crafty and compelling platform that can "hook" the unsuspecting.*

SECOND CORINTHIANS
Theme: Paul's Ministry Defended

6. He shared two revelations as evidence of his apostleship.
   a. He had been caught up in the heavens and taken to the third heaven (he had kept this secret for fourteen years).
      ~ Whether he was physically caught up in the heavens or whether this was a vision, we do not know. He shared this only to support his apostleship.
      ~ Whatever Paul experienced was so awesome that he could not repeat what he heard because he had no hope of doing it justice.

   > ★ **TEACHING TIP:**
   > *First heaven: where clouds are and airplanes fly.*
   > *Second heaven: our universe.*
   > *Third heaven: where God abides.*

   b. He was given a thorn in his flesh.
      ~ This "thorn" could have been physical (the constant persecution and beatings) or emotional (the rejection and false accusations he experienced)—many opinions abound, but no one knows for sure.
      ~ The purpose, however, was to keep him humble and reliant upon Christ Jesus—he had nothing to brag about, except Jesus and what He had done in Paul's life.
      ~ Three times he asked God to remove the thorn, but God responded, "No, My grace is sufficient for you, and my power is perfected in weakness."
      ~ God wanted Paul's life to testify to his dependence on Jesus, not self.

7. He told the people about the many signs and wonders and miracles he had performed, which alone proved his authority.

C. Paul announced his future plans to **VISIT** Corinth. (2 Corinthians 13:1–14)

- When he returned to them, he did not want to find them living a carnal life.
   ~ A carnal life speaks to living "like the world" and they had been changed to "new creatures" with a "new life."
- He challenged them to self-examination.
   ~ He called them to look carefully within and make sure that Jesus Christ, indeed, was in them.
- He closed with words of encouragement, instruction, blessing, and comfort.

FINAL THOUGHTS AND APPLICATION

¤ We, as believers, are called to be obedient to God and to know His Word.

SECOND CORINTHIANS
Theme: Paul's Ministry Defended

- ¤ If we are falsely accused of saying something that is incorrect or if the truth we are teaching is challenged, we must be able to stand up, stand firm, and confront such allegations with God's truth.
- ¤ This drives home the fact that each believer must know God's Word in order to discern the false and defend against it with truth alone.

⇨ **God's Word is our only authority. Upon it is where we are to stand so that we can counteract anything false that comes against it.**

❖ **FINAL APPLICATION: Do you know God's Word so that you can find comfort in times of affliction and can make a solid defense of your faith if accused?**

SECOND CORINTHIANS REVIEW HELPS

✧ **Match the phrase with one of the following books:**

Romans OR 1 Corinthians

1. All have sinned and fall short of the glory of God.

2. But now faith, hope, love, abide these three.

3. I have been informed...that there are quarrels among you.

4. I am not ashamed of the gospel for it is the power of God for salvation.

5. There is no condemnation for those who are in Christ Jesus.

6. Now concerning spiritual gifts, I do not want you to be unaware.

7. This is my body, which is for you; do this in remembrance of Me.

8. For God demonstrates His own love for us in that, while we were yet sinners, Christ died for us.

9. Who will separate us from the love of Christ?

10. If Christ has not been raised, your faith is worthless.

SECOND CORINTHIANS REVIEW HELPS
(Answers for Facilitators)

✧ **Match the phrase with one of the following books: Romans OR 1 Corinthians**

1. All have sinned and fall short of the glory of God.
   Romans 3:23

2. But now faith, hope, love, abide these three.
   1 Corinthians 13:13

3. I have been informed...that there are quarrels among you.
   1 Corinthians 1:11

4. I am not ashamed of the gospel, for it is the power of God for salvation.
   Romans 1:16

5. There is no condemnation for those who are in Christ Jesus.
   Romans 8:1

6. Now concerning spiritual gifts, I do not want you to be unaware.
   1 Corinthians 12:1

7. This is my body, which is for you; do this in remembrance of Me.
   1 Corinthians 11:24

8. For God demonstrates His own love toward us in that, while we were yet sinners, Christ died for us.
   Romans 5:8

9. Who will separate us from the love of Christ?
   Romans 8:35

10. If Christ has not been raised, then our preaching is vain, your faith also is vain.
    1 Corinthians 15:14

GALATIANS

Believers' Freedom in Christ

It was for freedom that Christ set us free ... only do not turn your freedom into an opportunity for the flesh.

Galatians 5:1, 13

SESSION FORTY-EIGHT: GALATIANS
Believers' Freedom in Christ

✞ **Memory verse:** *"It was for freedom that Christ set us free ... only do not turn your freedom into an opportunity for the flesh." (Galatians 5:1, 13)*

Introduction: Paul continually struggled with the new churches and believers as they were so easily led astray as demonstrated in both 1 and 2 Corinthians. The church in Galatia was also being drawn away from the purity and simplicity of the gospel. After the church had tasted the freedom from the Mosaic Law that comes through faith in Jesus Christ, the Judaizers taught that works of the law were necessary for salvation and sanctification, that Paul was not correct, nor was he a genuine apostle. Accepting this false doctrine would put the church in grave danger and Paul was up to the task of showing them their error. With precision and clarity, he systematically built his case against this false doctrine. Justification by faith alone is defended, explained, and applied.

- **Oral Review:** Please refer to the **REVIEW Section** in the following Teaching Guide Outline.

- **Homework:** Review the homework from the book of Second Corinthians.

    Top three questions on page 84
    Questions on page 87
    Top two questions on page 88
    Question at the top of page 91
    Questions on page 93

- **Review Helps:** Written review is provided at the end of the teacher presentation. (Optional and time permitting.)

- **Teacher Presentation on the Book of Galatians**

- **Learning for Life:** You may choose to discuss all or just one or two of the questions on page 79.

- **Closing prayer:** Pray that the students would enjoy liberty in their faith and would not be in bondage to the law or works. Pray that they would have a clear understanding of grace as the Bible defines it and have joy, not bondage, in their service to Christ.

GALATIANS
Theme: Believers' Freedom in Christ

OUTLINE AID FOR TEACHERS:

I. **PAUL'S GOSPEL OF GRACE IS DEFENDED (GALATIANS 1–2)**

- **Galatians 1:1–9**
  A. Paul greeted the Galatians with the gospel of GRACE and peace and then cursed those who preached a DISTORTED gospel.

- **Galatians 1:11–17 (Good cross-reference is Acts 9:1–18)**
  B. Paul gave his biographical history to defend his APOSTLESHIP to the Galatians.

- **Galatians 1:18–2:10**
  C. Paul reminded the Galatians of the AUTHORITY of the gospel of grace and that it was APPROVED by the council in Jerusalem.

- **Galatians 2:11–21**
  D. Paul referred to correcting Cephas (Peter) on the matter of FREEDOM in Christ.

II. **PAUL'S GOSPEL OF GRACE IS DEFINED (GALATIANS 3–4)**

- **Galatians 3:1–5**
  A. The Galatians were given the Holy Spirit by FAITH not by WORKS.

- **Galatians 3:6–14**
  B. The Galatians were justified by FAITH, not by WORKS, just as Abraham was.

- **Galatians 3:15–29**
  C. The LAW was given to draw men to faith, not to SAVE them.

- **Galatians 4:1–7**
  D. The Galatians were adopted SONS of God and no longer SLAVES to the law.

- **Galatians 4:12–20**
  E. The Galatians needed to regain their freedom and blessings by FAITH, not by the LAW.

- **Galatians 4:21–31**
  F. The sons of Abraham represented the SLAVESHIP of the law versus the FREEDOM of the promise—examples: Sarah and Isaac, Hagar and Ishmael.

III. **PAUL'S GOSPEL OF GRACE IS APPLIED (GALATIANS 5–6)**

- **Galatians 5:1**
  A. Paul sought to help the Galatians RECLAIM their position and practice of LIBERTY.

GALATIANS
Theme: Believers' Freedom in Christ

- **Galatians 5:2–12**

    B. Paul explained that the principles of <u>LAW</u> and <u>LIBERTY</u> are opposite.

- **Galatians 5:22–23**

    C. Paul told the Galatians that the power of <u>LIBERTY</u> is found in the <u>HOLY SPIRIT</u>.

- **Galatians 6**

    D. Paul reminded the Galatians that they are <u>LIBERATED</u> to do good.

Galatians
[Believers' Freedom in Christ]

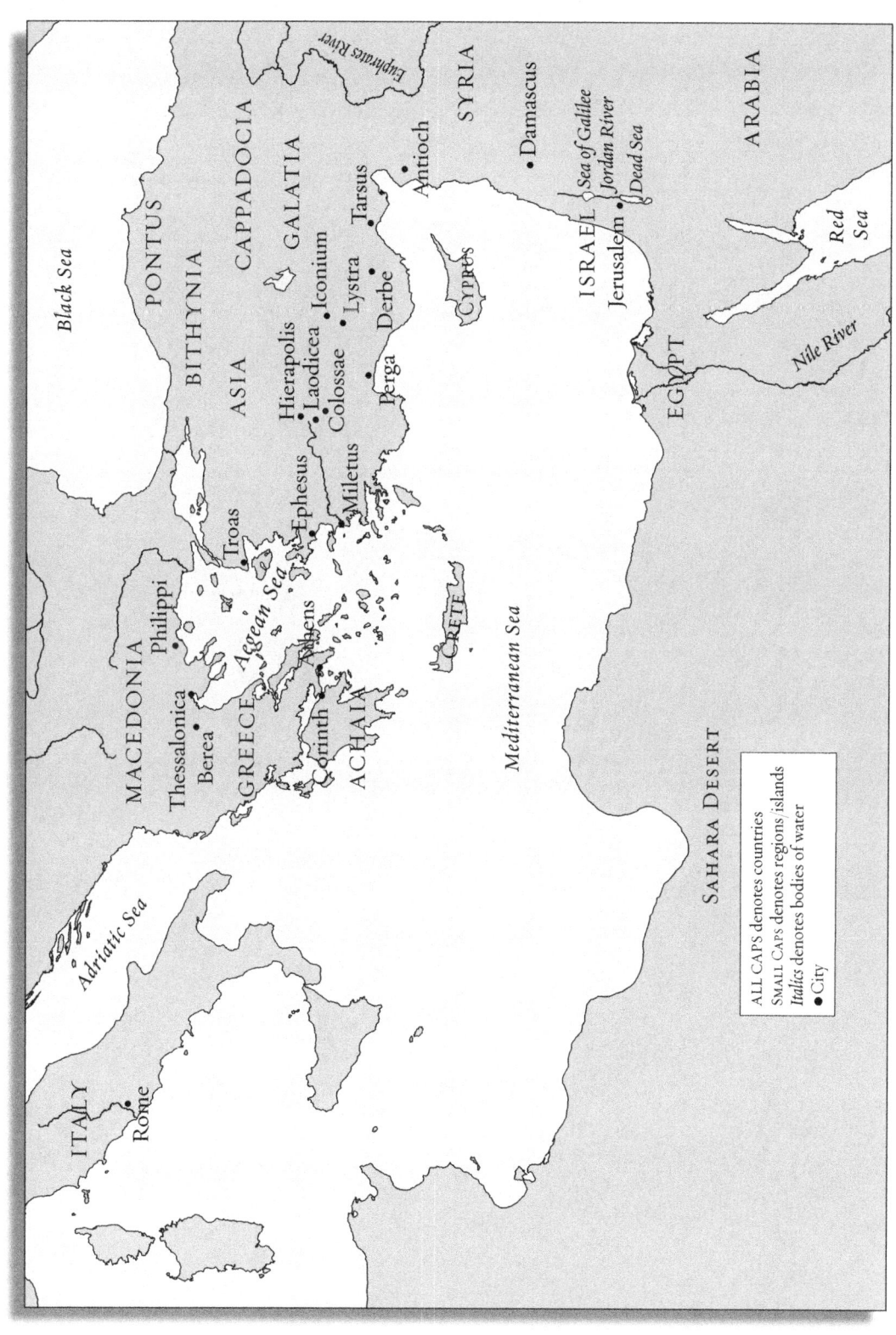

GALATIANS

GALATIANS
Theme: Believers' Freedom in Christ

THE BASICS:
- ⇨ **Who: The Author:** Paul
  Main Characters: Believers in Galatia
- ⇨ **What:** An explanation of the difference between liberty of faith in Christ Jesus and bondage to law and works
- ⇨ **When:** Written in A.D. 49 (best assumption) or A.D. 53–56
- ⇨ **Where:** Written to southern Galatia from Antioch (best assumption) or to northern Galatia from Ephesus or Macedonia
- ⇨ **Why:** To free the Galatian churches from the false teaching of law and works and to bring them back to the gospel of grace and faith, which they had learned from Paul

MEMORY VERSE: *"It was for freedom that Christ set us free … only do not turn your freedom into an opportunity for the flesh." Galatians 5:1, 13*

****

REVIEW:

- ⌑ The *Old Testament History* books shared the problem of disobedience (sin) and its consequences (slavery and death). The prophets foretold of judgment and the Messiah to come.
- ⌑ The *New Testament History* books showed that the Messiah had come and the church was born. Each gospel focused on a different aspect of Jesus:
  - ~ **Matthew:** Jesus was the long-awaited King of the Jews.
  - ~ **Mark:** Jesus was the suffering servant—a servant to all men and women.
  - ~ **Luke:** Jesus was the Perfect Man.
  - ~ **John:** Jesus was God.
  - ~ **Acts:** the church was born.
- ⌑ In *Paul's Letters to the Churches* so far, we have seen him explain who we are in Christ and the struggle to live out a righteous life.
  - ~ **Romans:** presented the truth of the gospel regarding sin, salvation, and faith.
  - ~ **1 Corinthians:** addressed problems that had arisen within the church. He explained how to live righteously with Jesus Christ.
  - ~ **2 Corinthians:** a letter that was personal and defensive as Paul responded to those who questioned his authority as an apostle over the church and in their lives.

GALATIANS
Theme: Believers' Freedom in Christ

OVERVIEW:

****

❋ **ILLUSTRATION:** Imagine seeing someone drowning in a lake. Your first thought might be: they can't swim. And then you see the real problem: a ball and chain is locked onto their ankle. Physical death is imminent if they are not set free from what is dragging them under. You jump in, pull them out, and remove the ball and chain—you essentially set them free from this deathtrap. How would you respond if they strapped the ball and chain back onto their ankle and dove into the lake again? Your first thought would probably be: why in heaven's name would they return to a deadly situation? Your second thought might be: they should know better, having been saved!

****

- In Corinth, the believers were failing to apply the gospel of truth or were applying it wrongly.
- A different and more dangerous problem existed in the Galatian church.
- Paul learned that the people he had helped free with the gospel of grace were now back in chains—bound by the teaching of the Judaizers who added the law, tradition, and rituals to the gospel message.

- The book of Galatians is referred to as the "emancipation proclamation" of the New Testament.
- And Paul is often referred to as the "Moses" of the Christian church because his whole mission was to set the people free to Christ from the bondage of sin <u>AND</u> the bondage of the law and works.
- The Galatians had returned to bondage—instead of to sin, it was back under a "works" mindset.
- It is believed that Paul wrote the Galatians from Antioch in 49 A.D.
- Tradition held that Paul gathered some of the faithful brethren together and wept and prayed all night long concerning the church in Galatia. The following morning, inspired by the Holy Spirit, he sat down with pen and papyrus and wrote this book. (Galatians 6:11)

⇨ **The purpose of the book of Galatians is to remind the people that they have freedom in Christ.**

I. PAUL'S GOSPEL OF GRACE IS DEFENDED (GALATIANS 1–2)

    A. Paul greeted the Galatians with the gospel of <u>GRACE</u> and peace and then cursed those who preached a <u>DISTORTED</u> gospel.

GALATIANS
Theme: Believers' Freedom in Christ

Galatians 1:2b–5
- Paul's greeting did not start with friendly salutations, thanksgiving, or even prayer.
- Instead, he jumped directly into the problem and was specific as to the target audience, Galatia.
- As he has done in other letters, Paul united the words "grace" and "peace."
- Paul's focus, however, was on "grace."
    - ~ He had taught them the meaning of "grace"—an undeserved gift, an unearned prize.
    - ~ They knew that they had not earned the gift of salvation, but had received it by God's grace.
    - ~ The Galatians had, in fact, received it with joy and gratitude.

Galatians 1:6–9
- But now the people were choosing to follow a teaching that denied the very truth of God's grace.
- Paul fully understood what the problem was—the teaching of the Judaizers.
    - ~ These men followed Paul from church to church.
    - ~ Every time he planted a church, they came in behind him "adding" the law and works in their teaching.

> **NOTE:** Who were the Judaizers? Jewish Christians.
> - They were Hellenistic Jews—not from the Holy Land, but from the Roman province.
> - They taught that:
>   - ~ Gentile believers needed to conform to the Law of Moses, even after the death and resurrection of Jesus Christ.
>   - ~ Circumcision was required for Gentile converts to Christianity.
> - Their teaching basically stated that if a Gentile wanted to be a "real" Christian, then he or she needed to be a "real" Jew first.

- They distorted the gospel of Christ by essentially teaching that Christ's work on the cross, His death and resurrection, was "not enough."
- The Judaizers fundamentally accused Paul of making the way of salvation too easy!
    - ~ What was easy about Jesus leaving heaven?
    - ~ What was easy about Jesus being born as a man?
    - ~ What was easy about the perfectly sinless life Jesus led?

> ★ **TEACHING TIP:**
> *Grace had a tremendous cost! And Jesus paid it—man never could "earn" salvation!*

GALATIANS
Theme: Believers' Freedom in Christ

- ~ What was easy about Jesus' trial—abandoned by friends and beaten by enemies?
- ~ What was easy about Jesus' miraculous, but promised, resurrection?
- The Judaizers, however, added to Paul's teaching with a format of "Christianity Plus":
  - ~ Faith + Circumcision = Salvation
  - ~ Faith + Obedience to the Law = Salvation

⇨ **The false teaching in the church of Galatia attacked and denied the very truth of God's amazing grace through Jesus Christ.**

B. Paul gave his biographical history to defend his <u>APOSTLESHIP</u> to the Galatians.

- The Judaizers apparently questioned Paul's position as an apostle—they questioned by whose "authority" Paul even had the right to present himself as an apostle.
  - ~ They had apparently reminded the Galatians that Paul had not been one of the original disciples, nor had he walked with Jesus during His earthly ministry as the others had.
- The Judaizers apparently had been successful in impugning Paul's character because the Galatians sent Paul a letter asking him to explain his "credentials."

> ★ **TEACHING TIP:**
> *To think that the Galatians believed the slander regarding Paul must have hurt him greatly. He had poured his life into the ministry of Jesus Christ and into these very people.*

Galatians 1:11–17 (Good cross-reference is Acts 9:1–18)

- Paul responded by giving his testimony—of who he had been before Jesus and who he was now after his encounter with Jesus.
  - ~ *Formerly*, he was a zealous Pharisee, he knew the law—all of it—and he followed it to the letter. He had been zealous for his ancestral traditions. In that fervor, he tried to destroy the Christian movement. (Galatians 1:13)
  - ~ *But* that was not God's plan for Paul's life. God had instead set Paul apart and would call Paul *through His grace* to preach Jesus Christ to the very people he had sought to persecute, specifically the Gentiles. (Galatians 1:15a)
  - ~ *Then* Paul met Jesus on his way to round up more Christians to persecute—and he received the gospel of truth from Jesus and power through the filling of the Holy Spirit. (Acts 9:1–18)
  - ~ *After* his encounter with Jesus, Paul went to Damascus and studied for three years. The Holy Spirit revealed Jesus Christ to him in every page of the Bible.

GALATIANS
Theme: Believers' Freedom in Christ

- His credentials?
  1. He knew the law better than the Judaizers claimed to know.
  2. He had been born to become Paul and not remain Saul—that had been God's plan all along—to minister to the Gentiles regarding the gospel of truth.
  3. He had not been commissioned by a man, but by the risen Lord Himself, just like the other apostles—his commissioning had just come later.
  4. Simply put: he did not need a *letter* of commissioning from men.

C. Paul reminded the Galatians of the <u>AUTHORITY</u> of the gospel of grace and that it was <u>APPROVED</u> by the council in Jerusalem.

Galatians 1:18–24
- He further explained that, after his three years of studying the Word, he went to Jerusalem for fifteen days.
- While in Jerusalem, he met with Peter and James, the brother of the Lord—both were considered "pillars" of the church—Paul shared the gospel of grace that he was preaching to the Gentiles (the "uncircumcised").
- Both men blessed Paul's message and ministry—all of Samaria, Judea, and Jerusalem celebrated Paul's ministry and how God was using him.

> ★ **TEACHING TIP:**
> *Keep the context in mind. The Judaizers taught that Gentiles needed to be circumcised first to truly become Christians. Paul stated that Jesus had commissioned him to take the gospel of grace to the "uncircumcised"—and that the ritual of circumcision was not required. God's grace was more than sufficient.*

Galatians 2:1–10
- He continued his counter-attack on the Judaizers' false teaching by reminding the people that, fourteen years later, he returned to meet with the Council at Jerusalem on the very subject of circumcision.
- Paul brought Barnabas (who the Galatians knew and loved) and Titus, the Greek Christian (who had never been circumcised).

- Paul had brought Titus with him as an illustration to the Council that circumcision was not necessary for faith in Jesus Christ.
  ~ The council examined Titus and his faith.
  ~ They concurred with Paul and determined circumcision was not necessary to become a Christian.
- Paul's point to the Galatians: a person does not need to become a Jew to become a Christian.

> ★ **TEACHING TIP:**
> *Paul, who had been the ultimate zealot of the law, became the passionate evangelist of the gospel of grace—salvation and freedom IN and through Christ alone.*

GALATIANS
Theme: Believers' Freedom in Christ

⇨ **Faith in Christ + Nothing Else = Salvation! This was the approved teaching of the Council at Jerusalem.**

D. Paul referred to correcting Cephas (Peter) on the matter of <u>FREEDOM</u> in Christ.

<u>Galatians 2:11–21</u>
- Paul used a conversation in which he corrected Peter regarding freedom in Christ to further make his point.
- In sharing this conversation, Paul was not being slanderous toward Peter; this conversation had probably been repeated to others.
- Peter was considered the head of the church, but even his thinking needed to be plumbed back to the Word of God.
  ~ Peter began spending all of his time with Jewish believers.
  ~ At the same time, he withdrew from and became aloof toward Gentile believers—he had no fellowship with them.
  ~ Paul said that Peter did this because he feared the opinions of the Jewish believers—those who had been circumcised.
  ~ Paul referred to Peter's mindset and actions as hypocritical to the true gospel, resulting in other believers, such as Barnabas who had served faithfully alongside Paul, to be led astray by Peter's actions.

> ★ **TEACHING TIP:**
> *It has been said that Judaism was the cradle for Christianity. However, it was almost the death of her as well. This was something Paul knew and wanted to prevent.*

⇨ **Paul's confrontation with Peter gave proof of Paul's authority. He needed no further credentials.**

✝ **Galatians 2:21** "I do not nullify the grace of God, for if righteousness comes through the Law, then Christ died needlessly."

⇨ **Paul's Point Reiterated: Faith in Christ + Nothing Else = Salvation! Jesus paid it all.**

II. PAUL'S GOSPEL OF GRACE IS DEFINED (GALATIANS 3–4)

- Paul wanted the Galatians to embrace the truth that God's grace alone had set them free.

A. The Galatians were given the Holy Spirit by <u>FAITH</u> not by <u>WORKS</u>.

GALATIANS
Theme: Believers' Freedom in Christ

Galatians 3:1-5
- Paul called them "fools" and asked "who had bewitched them?"
- He wanted them to consider who had turned their thinking away from the truth.
- Paul's exhortation is simple: You know this! You know the work of the Holy Spirit.
- Works had not saved them—had not changed who they were.
  - ~ They had volunteered and were still found to be unholy.
  - ~ They had donated money and were still found to be not pure.
- It was the power of the Holy Spirit that had made them different—had changed their lives.
- Paul's question: Why would they go back to the chains of the law that had not and could never bring permanent change to their lives?

****

❋ **ILLUSTRATION:** It is almost as if Paul was likening the law to a cage with bars. As with cages, the law and works were put in place for a reason—to restrain. Cages restrain beasts. The laws and works gave order and boundaries to the natural tendencies of men to sin. Neither cages nor laws/works, however, change what is restrained or confined. That is not their purpose.

If, however, the Holy Spirit came upon a tiger and taught him, trained him, guided him, and transformed him, then the cage doors could be thrown wide open! The creature would be changed—bars would no longer be necessary—so he could roam freely.

It is the same for the believer. Works did not transform them—faith in Jesus Christ did. And only through Jesus would they be free.

****

B. The Galatians were justified by <u>FAITH</u>, not by <u>WORKS</u>, just as Abraham was.

Galatians 3:6-14
- Again, it is so important to remember the context! Paul is addressing issues being caused by the Judaizers, Christian Jews, who were teaching that to become a Christian one had to become a Jew as well—adherence to the law and works was required.
- To counter this teaching, Paul used a specific Jewish example—Abraham, the father of the Jews AND the father of faith.
  - ~ There was no law when Abraham "believed" and it was counted to him as "righteousness." The law was not given to the Israelites until the time of Moses.
  - ~ Abraham was justified (just as if he had never sinned) because of his faith.

GALATIANS
Theme: Believers' Freedom in Christ

- The Judaizers had presented two teachings that opposed what Paul had taught them—what a revelation this must have been.
    - The Judaizers had taught "faith + circumcision = salvation"—Paul said, "No!"
    - The Judaizers had taught "faith + Mosaic law = salvation"—Paul said, "No!"
- Paul presented to the Galatians that, if they were true sons of Abraham, then they need to hold to the truth of "faith + nothing else = salvation."

> ★ **TEACHING TIP:**
> *It may feel like you are repeating the same truth over and over—you are! This teaching, though, requires repetition. There may be some in your study who are under the same bondage that the Galatians were—believing that there must be more than "just" faith in Jesus Christ to be truly saved.*

⇨ **People are saved by faith in Jesus Christ—believing in His death, burial, and resurrection. This is the only way of salvation.**

C. The <u>LAW</u> was given to draw men to faith, not to <u>SAVE</u> them.

Galatians 3:15–29
- God knew that man would never be able to keep the law perfectly, thus His promise to Abraham: a descendant who would save the world. (Genesis 12:2–3)
*Note: This promise was stated *prior* to the giving of the law through Moses.
- The law was given as a "tutor" to lead us to Christ.
    - It "defined" sin and its consequences.
    - It foreshadowed Jesus through its sacrifices and offerings.
    - It showed their inability to "keep" it, resulting in their condemnation, which led them to realize their need for a Savior.

> **NOTE:** Nowhere in Scripture does God commend people for "just" keeping the law and "only" doing good works. He does not say, as an example, "Yes, that Eugene, he is something else! No one keeps commandment #5 like he does." This is NOT God's way of salvation.
> - Rather He befriends, commissions, exalts men of faith. But none of them were perfect—they all erred.
> - Faith is what saved Abraham and it is what saves all believers—not perfectly working out the law.
> - ✟ **Galatians 3:26, 28-29** "For you are all sons of God through faith in Christ Jesus … There is neither Jew nor Greek, there is neither slave nor free man, there is neither male nor female; for you are all one in Christ Jesus. And if you belong to Christ, then you are Abraham's descendants, heirs according to promise."

GALATIANS
Theme: Believers' Freedom in Christ

- When Jesus Christ came, the need for a tutor was replaced by the gospel of truth.
  - ~ Under the law (the tutor), the people were placed under restraints.
  - ~ Under the gospel, they were given freedom and privileges as sons of God.
- This truth applied to both the Jews and the Gentiles who became Christians—both became "Abraham's descendants, heirs according to promise."

D. The Galatians were adopted <u>SONS</u> of God and no longer <u>SLAVES</u> to the law.

Galatians 4:1-7
- Paul used a Greek concept to explain a believer's adoption.
  - ~ The term "adoption" originated with the Greeks.
  - ~ In the Greek custom, when a boy was born to their Roman family, he was put under the authority of a trusted slave or a trustee.
  - ~ The child was expected to be obedient to this designated trustee—in essence, the child was to be a slave to the slave.
  - ~ To be obedient to the trustee was to be obedient to the father.
  - ~ If the child was obedient to the trustee, he was embraced by his father and given the full rights of "sonship" at adulthood, which included direct contact with his father and becoming his full heir.

- Paul's Point:
  1. You believers have been adopted by God the Father through your faith in Jesus Christ. You have all the rights of a son.
  2. A believer's adoption came through the work of Jesus—His perfect obedience—NOT through something a believer does or how he obeys.

E. The Galatians needed to regain their freedom and blessings by <u>FAITH</u>, not by the <u>LAW</u>.

- They were seeking freedom and blessings by the law—the absolute opposite to the truth that Paul had taught them.

Galatians 4:12-15
- Paul reminded them of their "story" with him.
  - ~ He asked them if they remembered when he came to them—when they first met.
  - ~ Their relationship was so different than it was as he wrote when they were a poor, little church:
    - * They shared a close fellowship with one another.
    - * They loved one another, a blessing in itself.
    - * They had a bond that united them together.

GALATIANS
Theme: Believers' Freedom in Christ

- * They had a mutual understanding that led to the people wanting to do everything to serve Paul.
- He recalled being terribly sick while with them—and their sacrificial love and attendance to him.

Galatians 4:16-20
✟ **Galatians 4:16** "So have I become your enemy by telling you the truth?"

- Paul basically asked, "What happened?" Or, better put, "What happened to you?"
  - ~ They had willingly returned to a restrained, restricted, unhappy, and unproductive faith!
- Essentially, Paul called them to, "Throw open the 'cage!'"
  - ~ He wanted them to remember that he was NOT their enemy.
  - ~ He desired for them to regain their freedom that came only IN and THROUGH Christ.

F. The sons of Abraham represented the <u>SLAVESHIP</u> of the law versus the <u>FREEDOM</u> of the promise—examples: Sarah and Isaac, Hagar and Ishmael.

Galatians 4:21-31

- Paul used a Jewish illustration to make his point regarding freedom versus slavery.
- He went back to the story of Abraham and Sarah in Genesis.
  - ~ God had promised them that, if they followed Him, three things would happen:
    1. They would be given a land.
    2. They would have more descendants than the stars in the heavens.
    3. The entire world would be blessed through them—the promise of the coming of the Messiah, Christ Jesus.
  - ~ To have descendants, one must get pregnant and this was a problem for Sarah. She became restless waiting for this promise to be fulfilled. (Genesis 16)
  - ~ Sarah suggested that her slave, Hagar, lay with Abraham. Hagar could become pregnant with Abraham and Sarah's child.

> **NOTE:** It is important to remember who these two women were:
> - Sarah: a free woman to whom God had made a promise of a son
> - Hagar: a slave

GALATIANS
Theme: Believers' Freedom in Christ

- ~ Hagar did have a son—Ishmael. But he was not the son of the promise, not the son of the free woman, Sarah.
- ~ Thirteen years later, God, in His perfect timing, fulfilled the promise of a son to Sarah and Abraham.
  - * Sarah was 89 and Abraham was 99 when Isaac was born—a supernatural birth, given their ages!
- Paul's point: You who believe the promise fulfilled in Jesus Christ are the true sons, the true seeds of Abraham. Your "birth" into Abraham's family is supernatural, very much like Isaac.
- Paul went one step further in his explanation:
  - ~ The sons of the promise were the sons of Jerusalem, the new Jerusalem—freedom.
  - ~ The sons of the slave, Hagar and Ishmael, were in bondage to the law—slavery.

⇨ **Paul drew a line in the sand! He told the Galatians that the Gentiles who believed in Jesus Christ were the real seeds of Abraham. The unbelieving Jews were not.**

III. PAUL'S GOSPEL OF GRACE IS APPLIED (GALATIANS 5-6)

- He wanted the Galatians to understand that their lives should be abundant, full, and free. No more chains!

A. Paul sought to help the Galatians <u>RECLAIM</u> their position and practice of <u>LIBERTY</u>.

✝ **Galatians 5:1** "It was for freedom that Christ set us free; therefore keep standing firm and do not be subject again to a yoke of slavery."

- They were not chained to the law any more nor were they bound by good works—they were free in Christ.

> ★ **TEACHING TIP:**
> *Consider Paul's point: Why would one who has received liberty through Jesus step BACK into legalism?*

B. Paul explained that the principles of <u>LAW</u> and <u>LIBERTY</u> are opposite.

<u>Galatians 5:2-12</u>

- Using the subject of circumcision once more, he reminded the people that, if they held to the law as the way to salvation, then they were under obligation to keep the whole Law—and they would not only fail in trying to keep it, but this approach to God would sever them from Christ.

GALATIANS
Theme: Believers' Freedom in Christ

- Paul reiterated that a man could not be justified by the law—it only came through God's grace.
- Paul reminded them that they had been running the Christian race well, but to adopt this false teaching of "adding" the law and works as a requirement to salvation was a destructive, lethal stumbling block for them all.
- Paul lays it out:

The Law	Liberty in Jesus Christ
◆ Man's efforts	◆ God's gift, provision
◆ Temporal	◆ Eternal
◆ Chains	◆ Glory

> ❖ **APPLICATION:** We need to apply Paul's basic point to the Galatians and to ourselves.
> ~ When a person is bound to law, can he or she experience the true joy of Jesus? Will this lead to a loss of passion? Will it ultimately lead to a loss of purpose?
> ~ What does legalism really produce? Rigidity. Pride.

C. Paul told the Galatians that the power of <u>LIBERTY</u> is found in the <u>HOLY SPIRIT</u>.

✝ **Galatians 5:22–23** "But the fruit of the Spirit is love, joy, peace, patience, kindness, goodness, faithfulness, gentleness, self-control; against such things there is no law."

- These characteristics cannot be lived out consistently through human effort.
- These traits are lived out through the power of the Holy Spirit after a man or woman comes to Jesus Christ in faith.

★ **TEACHING TIP:**
Christian character comes through the transforming power of the Holy Spirit—no law could produce this. It is produced from within, not externally.

- Paul warned the Galatians to be careful with their freedom.
    - ~ It is not a license for fleshly, disobedient behavior.
    - ~ It is not to be abused, but to be lived out.

★ **TEACHING TIP:**
The fruit of the Holy Spirit is the evidence that you are the uncaged tiger!

D. Paul reminded the Galatians that they are <u>LIBERATED</u> to do good.

Galatians 6:1–10

- Paul clearly taught that "faith + nothing = salvation."

GALATIANS
Theme: Believers' Freedom in Christ

- But, when one accepts Jesus Christ by faith and is infused with the Holy Spirit, then there will be a discernable change in that person's attitudes and actions.
- The contrast of one under the law and one under liberty:
  - Under the law, a person obeyed God because he "had or ought" to.
    * Obedience was a burden—putting one's nose to the grindstone.
  - Under liberty, through the power of the Holy Spirit and the freedom found in Christ, a person obeyed because they "wanted to"—a radically different heart perspective!
    * Obedience was no longer viewed as a chore to perform, but it was marked with love, gratitude, and a willingness to serve others.

> **NOTE:** A believer is to mirror the characteristics of Jesus Christ who:
> - showed love to the unlovely.
> - was full of joy in every circumstance.
> - exhibited peace beyond understanding.
> - was kind, good, and faithful.
> - was gentle and self-controlled.
>
> ⇨ **Liberty in Christ sets the believer free to live as Christ did—with a heart set on doing good and a desire to give God the glory.**

Galatians 6:11–18

- Paul closed his letter by contrasting the Judaizers with himself:
  - The Judaizers held tight to rituals, such as circumcision, so that they could boast in themselves—but, more importantly, they avoided being persecuted for the cross of Christ.
  - Paul willingly carried the brand marks of Jesus Christ—he was not afraid of being persecuted for the cross of Christ. Rather, that was the only thing he could boast in.

> ❖ **APPLICATION:** Be mindful that well-meaning Judaizers still exist within the body of Christ and they will try to place additional requirements upon you—falsely presenting that "faith + whatever they are *requiring*" = salvation.
>   - Beware of becoming bewitched into thinking you <u>need</u> to do good works to either *earn* or *keep* your salvation.
>
> ⇨ **Salvation is solely based on the work of Jesus Christ—not by anything we have done or not done.**

GALATIANS
Theme: Believers' Freedom in Christ

FINAL THOUGHTS AND APPLICATION

- Paul wanted the Galatians to wise up and not be foolish. He wanted them to:
    1. Remember the truth he had taught them: freedom in Christ.
    2. NOT put themselves back under the bondage of the law and works—falsely believing that anything needed to be "added" to Christ's work on the cross.

- Going back to our opening illustration of someone drowning in a lake because of a ball and chain strapped to their ankle:
    - Put yourself in as the one drowning.
    - The ball and chain represents several things—your own sin, your inability to be or do good (consistently) on your own, and your inability to completely obey God's Word.
    - Jesus is the One who jumps in and pulls you out of sinking into death.
    - Jesus is the One who cuts off the burden of the ball and chain:
        * Forgiving your sin.
        * Promising you an abundant life in Him.
        * Giving you the Holy Spirit to dwell within, so that you are empowered to live a life of obedience—transforming your heart to one that desires to serve Him and others.

- ❖ **FINAL APPLICATION:** Don't believe the lie that the gospel of works can save you. Believe the truth that the gospel of Christ can save you and set you free from the slavery of works.

- ⇨ **In Christ alone, place your trust for salvation.**

GALATIANS REVIEW HELPS

✧ **Name the New Testament book that most clearly fits the statement below.**

1. What two gospels have a genealogy of Jesus Christ?

2. What book is the longest of Paul's letters to the churches?

3. Which gospel was written to everyone?

4. What book explains salvation and justification?

5. What book shows Jesus as King of the Jews?

6. What books addresses sexual immorality in the church?

7. What book shows that Jesus is God?

8. What book uses the word "immediately" in describing the active life of Jesus?

9. In what book did Paul encounter Jesus on the road to Damascus?

10. What book describes Jesus' ascension into heaven?

11. What book has a chapter on love?

12. What book tells us there is no condemnation for those who are in Christ Jesus?

13. What book includes many women in the gospel narrative?

14. Which book tells us that "all have sinned and fall short of the glory of God?"

15. What book gives the history of the beginning of the church?

16. Who wrote nine letters to the churches?

17. Which book is about Paul's defense of his ministry and apostleship?

18. "But now faith, hope, love abide these three…"

19. "I am not ashamed of the gospel."

20. "We do not preach ourselves but Jesus Christ."

GALATIANS REVIEW HELPS
(Answers for Facilitators)

✧ **Name the New Testament book that most clearly fits the statement below.**

1. What two gospels have a genealogy of Jesus Christ? **Matthew and Luke**

2. What book is the longest of Paul's letters to the churches? **Romans**

3. Which gospel was written to everyone? **John**

4. What book explains salvation and justification? **Romans**

5. What book shows Jesus as King of the Jews? **Matthew**

6. What books addresses sexual immorality in the church? **1 Corinthians**

7. What book shows that Jesus is God? **John**

8. What book uses the word "immediately" in describing the active life of Jesus? **Mark**

9. In what book did Paul encounter Jesus on the road to Damascus? **Acts**

10. What book describes Jesus' ascension into heaven? **Acts**

11. What book has a chapter on love? **1 Corinthians**

12. What book tells us there is no condemnation for those who are in Christ Jesus? **Romans**

13. What book includes many women in the gospel narrative? **Luke**

14. Which book tells us that "all have sinned and fall short of the glory of God"? **Romans**

15. What book gives the history of the beginning of the church? **Acts**

16. Who wrote nine letters to the churches? **Paul**

17. Which book is about Paul's defense of his ministry and apostleship? **2 Corinthians**

18. "But now faith, hope, love abide these three..." **1 Corinthians**

19. "I am not ashamed of the gospel." **Romans**

20. "We do not preach ourselves but Jesus Christ." **1 Corinthians**

© 2018 Big Dream Ministries, Inc.

EPHESIANS

Believers' Holy Walk

Walk in a manner worthy of the calling with which you have been called.

Ephesians 4:1

SESSION FORTY-NINE: EPHESIANS
Believers' Holy Walk

✝ **Memory verse:** *"Walk in a manner worthy of the calling with which you have been called." (Ephesians 4:1)*

Introduction: In this great treasure, Paul writes to the church in Ephesus to help the followers of Jesus understand the great riches that was theirs in Him. Paul opens the book with words of glory spelling out with clarity and beauty all that the believer has and the great blessings the believer enjoys. These blessings, these riches, are staggering indeed! He then moves on from the blessings and the mystery of the church to show how such a blessed person should live in the world by the power of the Holy Spirit. We have all we need to live victorious over sin and joyfully as citizens of the Kingdom of God.

- **Oral Review:** Please refer to the **REVIEW Section** in the following Teaching Guide Outline.

- **Homework:** Review the homework from the book of Galatians.

    Question on page 106
    Questions at the top and bottom of page 108
    Question in the middle of page 109
    Questions at the end of page 112
    Question at the bottom of page 117
    Question at the top of page 118

- **Review Helps:** Written review is provided at the end of the teacher presentation. (Optional and time permitting.)

- **Teacher Presentation on the Book of Ephesians**

- **Learning for Life:** You may choose to discuss all or just one or two of the questions on page 127.

- **Closing prayer:** Pray that the students would gain a clear grasp of what it means to walk in a manner worthy of the calling of Jesus Christ—that their lives would reflect their love and devotion to Him.

EPHESIANS
Theme: Believers' Holy Walk

OUTLINE AID FOR TEACHERS:

I. **OUR CALLING: WHAT GOD HAS DONE—PAST (EPHESIANS 1–3)**

- **Ephesians 1:3**

  A. We are rich with all heavenly blessings when we are <u>IN</u> Christ.

- **Ephesians 1:4**

   1. The Father <u>CALLED</u> us in Him to be holy and blameless.

- **Ephesians 1:7–8a**

   2. The Son <u>REDEEMED</u> us through His blood. He forgave our sins.

- **Ephesians 1:13–14**

   3. The Holy Spirit <u>SEALED</u> us in Him, guaranteeing an inheritance.

- **Ephesians 2:1–3**

  B. Before we were in Christ, we <u>WALKED</u> according to the world, the flesh, and the Devil.

- **Ephesians 2:6–9**

  C. Now Christ has <u>SEATED</u> us with Him in heavenly places.

   1. We are not saved by our works but <u>FOR</u> good works.

- **Ephesians 2:10**

   2. Seated in Christ we are to <u>WALK</u> in His good works.

- **Ephesians 2:12–21**

  D. Christ called Jews and Gentiles into one <u>BODY</u>.

- **Ephesians 3:10**

   1. The church demonstrates to angels the <u>WISDOM</u> of God.

- **Ephesians 3:16–21**

   2. The church demonstrates to people the <u>POWER</u> of God.

II. **OUR WALK: WHAT WE ARE TO DO—PRESENT (EPHESIANS 4–6)**

- **Ephesians 4:2–6, 11–16**

  A. Walk in <u>UNITY</u>.

- **Ephesians 4:17–32**

  B. Walk in <u>HOLINESS</u>.

- **Ephesians 5:1–5**

  C. Walk in <u>LOVE</u>.

EPHESIANS
Theme: Believers' Holy Walk

- **Ephesians 5:6–14**
  D. Walk in <u>LIGHT</u>.
- **Ephesians 5:15–6:3**
  E. Walk in <u>WISDOM</u>.
- **Ephesians 6:10–18**
  F. Walk in <u>STRENGTH</u>.

Ephesians
[Believers' Holy Walk]

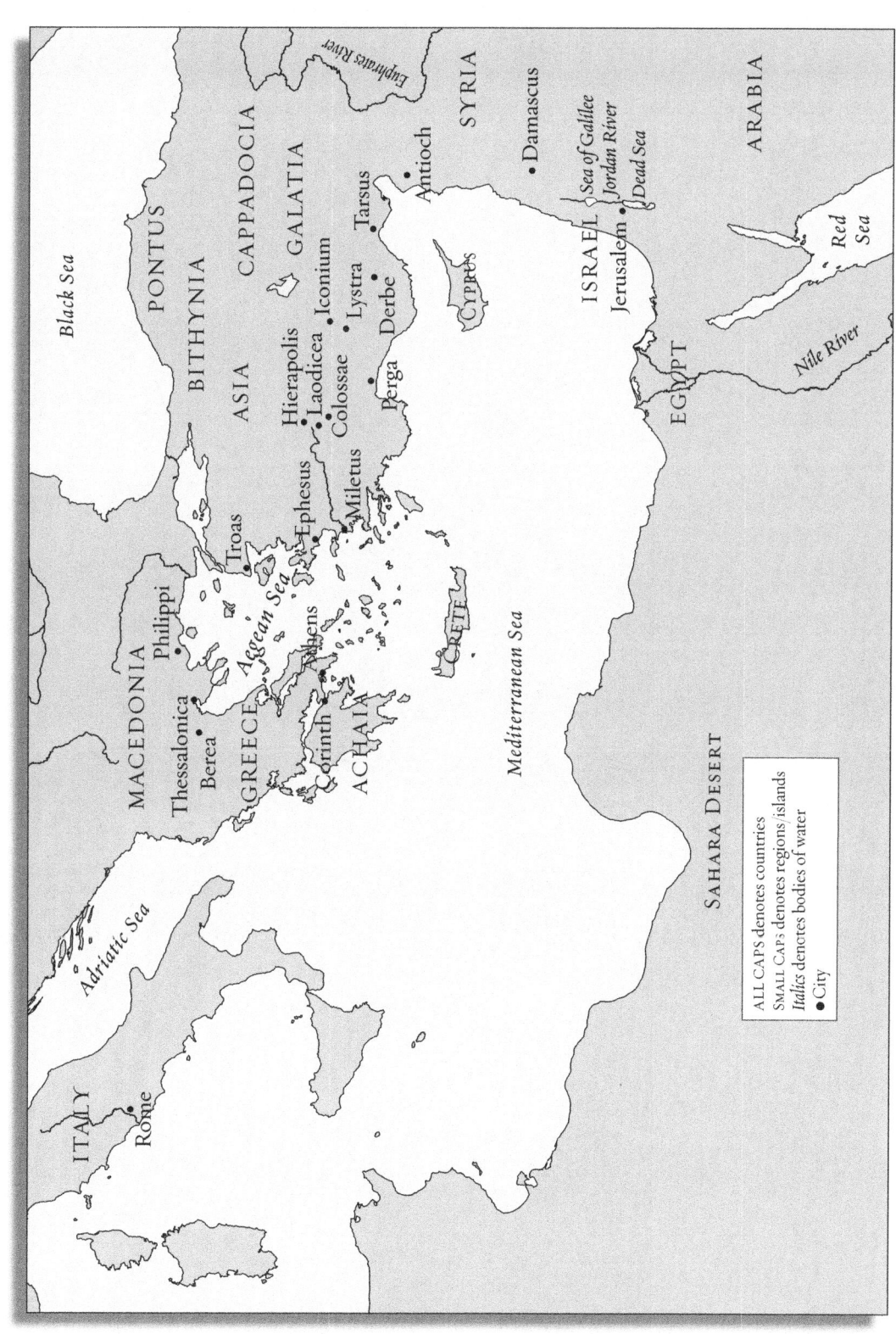

EPHESIANS

EPHESIANS
Theme: Believers' Holy Walk

THE BASICS:
⇨ **Who: The Author:** Paul
   Main Characters: Believers in Ephesus
⇨ **What:** An instruction book on Christian living
⇨ **When:** Written in A.D. 60 during Paul's first Roman imprisonment
⇨ **Where:** Written to Ephesus from Rome
⇨ **Why:** To explain the mystery of the church

MEMORY VERSE: *"Walk in a manner worthy of the calling with which you have been called." Ephesians 4:1*

****

REVIEW:
- The *Old Testament History* books shared the problem of disobedience (sin) and its consequences (slavery and death). The prophets foretold of judgment and the Messiah to come.
- The *New Testament History* books showed that the Messiah had come and the church was born.
- In *Paul's Letters to the Churches* he wrote about what faith was and how to apply it:
   ~ **Romans:** he presented the righteousness of God and how people can become righteous.
   ~ **First Corinthians:** he exhorted the believers to address sin and explained how correction should be handled.
   ~ **Second Corinthians:** he defended his own ministry and his authority as an apostle.
   ~ **Galatians:** He confronted a false teaching that was leading the people to go back under the law. He encouraged them to remember that they were free in Christ.

OVERVIEW:
****

❋ **ILLUSTRATION:** There was a story about a man in the Southwest who was living in poverty. He sold everything he had to feed his wife and children. He was down to his land being the only possession he had remaining to sell and he was about to sell it off. An oil company, however, came to town and informed him that his property was sitting on a very rich vein of oil—worth millions of dollars! The man had been rich all the time, but had lived like a pauper.

****

- Paul wrote the book of Ephesians to tell the people how rich they were *in* Christ.

EPHESIANS
Theme: Believers' Holy Walk

- This is the fifth book that he wrote.
- It was written in 60 or 61 A.D., while Paul was imprisoned in Rome.
  - This was his first imprisonment and could be likened to being under "house arrest."
  - He could not come and go from where he was staying, but people could come and visit him.
  - His visitors would take his letters and deliver them to the various churches.

- Paul wrote four letters during this first imprisonment:
  1. Ephesians
  2. Philippians
  3. Colossians
  4. Philemon

- Paul had been to Ephesus twice.

****

Background on the City of Ephesus
- It had once been a very prosperous seaport, experiencing a lot of trade via ships that came into the port.
- But the harbor became "silted in"—ships could no longer easily dock, thus export/import trade dwindled.
- The major commerce then became the sale of idols for the temple of Artemis, the Greek goddess.
  - In fact, in the book of Acts we learned that the silversmiths did not want Paul around—he was bad for their idol-making business.

****

- Ephesians contains six chapters and the book divides into two divisions, three chapters in each.
  - Division One: What We (as believers) have IN Christ. (Chapters 1–3)
  - Division Two: How We (as believers) are to Walk IN Christ (Chapters 4–6)

⇨ **The purpose of the book of Ephesians is to present the believer's holy walk—a very rich life to be lived in Jesus Christ.**

EPHESIANS
Theme: Believers' Holy Walk

I. OUR CALLING: WHAT GOD HAS DONE—PAST (EPHESIANS 1–3)

A. We are rich with all heavenly blessing when we are <u>IN</u> Christ.

> **TEACHING TIP:**
> *"Every spiritual blessing" speaks to our pardon from sin and death, redemption, our adoption into God's family, the presence of the Holy Spirit within, full joy, and peace that surpasses all understanding. This is the "rich" life.*

✞ **Ephesians 1:3** "Blessed be the God and Father of our Lord Jesus Christ, who has blessed us with every spiritual blessing in the heavenly places in Christ …"

- It is important to note the phrase "in Christ" or "in Him."
  - Paul used this phrasing thirty-nine times in this letter to the Ephesians.

> **NOTE:** Paul was most likely thinking about the Ephesians looking out at the temple of Artemis, a very grand temple.
> - It was one of the Seven Wonders of the World.
> - It was four times larger than the Parthenon.
> ⇨ **This temple had all the trappings of being "rich," but Paul wanted them to understand that the "riches in Christ" were much greater!**
> - It was also used as a bank in which the people could deposit their money.
> ⇨ **God, however, had "deposited" His riches into their lives!**

1. The Father <u>CALLED</u> us in Him to be holy and blameless.

<u>Ephesians 1:4</u>
- In explaining who believers were in Christ, he started with: "… He chose us in Him before the foundation of the world …" (Ephesians 1:4a)
- Paul went on to share the purpose of that choosing: "… that we would be holy and blameless before Him …" (Ephesians 1:4b)

****

❋ **ILLUSTRATION:** There was a woman who was given a diamond at the time of her engagement. Everyone likes diamonds … right? Not this woman. She thought the diamond she had been given was the crummiest, little diamond ring that she had ever seen. She had expected so much more; but she stayed silent about that ring until after her wedding day. Instead of verbalizing her disappointment in that diamond, she just stopped wearing it. She put it away in her jewelry box where it stayed for years. In fact, during those years, their home was robbed, but the thieves left the diamond behind! (It seemed that the robbers agreed with her … they would not even steal it!)

EPHESIANS
Theme: Believers' Holy Walk

The woman ultimately took the diamond ring to a jeweler. As he examined the diamond, he stated, "You know … this is highly unusual. This is a perfect, flawless diamond." Her attitude toward that ring immediately changed—no longer was it a crummy, little diamond … it was perfect and flawless.

Remember this story when you think of the Father's calling on your life—you were chosen to be holy and blameless before Him! His is a rich calling. Don't live a life of "is this all there is" when God wants you to live a life of "so much more!"

****

2. The Son <u>REDEEMED</u> us through His blood. He forgave our sins.

Ephesians 1:7-8a
- Paul explained that only through Jesus (being IN Him) did a man or woman have redemption because it came through Christ's blood and brought forgiveness of our sins … "according to the riches of His grace which He lavished on us …"

3. The Holy Spirit <u>SEALED</u> us in Him, guaranteeing an inheritance.

Ephesians 1:13-14
- Paul then reminded them that they had the Holy Spirit within—given to them after they had listened to the message of truth, the gospel of their salvation, and believed.
  - ~ They were now sealed in Him with the Holy Spirit.
  - ~ The Holy Spirit was given as a "pledge" of their inheritance in the kingdom of God.

> ★ **TEACHING TIP:**
> *Being "sealed" in those days referred in a sense to "setting a mark on something to denote that it was genuine, authentic, approved"—as when a deed or agreement was sealed.*

> **NOTE:** A current day example of being sealed would be a "will." A will speaks to what is being given to those who are named in it. Thus, if your name is written in the will, it is guaranteed that you will receive an inheritance.
> ⇨ **Paul wanted them to understand that the Holy Spirit was their "guarantee" of a future inheritance. In other words, he said, "You, believers, are rich."**

- Paul wanted the Ephesians to fully understand this "so much more" life—a rich life—that had been granted them through Jesus Christ. He wanted their eyes opened to God's truth about "who they were IN Him."

✞ **Ephesians 1:18-19** "I pray that the eyes of your heart may be enlightened, so that you will know what is the hope of His calling, what are the riches of the glory of His

EPHESIANS
Theme: Believers' Holy Walk

inheritance in the saints, and what is the surpassing greatness of His power toward us who believe."

- Paul wanted them to "know," which translated here means "fully be aware of, perceive, be sure of, understand" what their calling held for them:
  ~ A HOPE: that depends solely upon God's grace, not man's own "good" works.
  ~ RICHES of an INHERITANCE: that rests completely in Christ and His love for His own. The word "riches" strongly implies that there is absolutely nothing lacking in Him—rather, there is nothing more a believer could ever need than what is found in Jesus.
  ~ POWER: the very power that raised Jesus from the dead is available to a believer on a daily basis through the Holy Spirit.

> ★ **TEACHING TIP:**
> *Let these three points percolate in your soul! As it was for the Ephesians, this is true for us today. How radically would your life change if you walked in the reality of God's promises given here?*

Ephesians 1:19–23
- In wanting the Ephesians to fully understand what they had in Christ, he continued his train of thought regarding the power they had received.
  ~ It was the same power that raised Jesus from the dead.
  ~ It was the same power that seated Christ at the right hand of the Father.

⇨ **God has granted a miraculous power to those who are alive IN Christ. It is a power that provided a new life, a new hope, and an eternal inheritance.**

- Paul wanted the Ephesian believers to realize that each of them had been called individually by God, but together they had been called to be the church.
- He explained that the church acted as His body, therefore, it should conduct itself in a certain way.

B. Before we were in Christ, we <u>WALKED</u> according to the world, the flesh, and the Devil.

> ★ **TEACHING TIP:**
> *We are all "dead men walking" until God, in His mercy and love, makes us alive. It is God's work alone that brings us to life.*

Ephesians 2:1–3
- Paul reminded the people of how they had lived their lives before they were in Christ:
  ~ They had walked as "dead" men and women in their trespasses and sin—walking according to the world.
  ~ They had walked according to Satan ("the prince of the power of the air, of the spirit that is now working in the sons of disobedience.").

EPHESIANS
Theme: Believers' Holy Walk

- ~ They had walked in the lusts of their flesh, indulging their desires, living as children of wrath.
    - Paul transitioned from who they *were* with a wonderful "BUT" that focused on Who God is: One who was rich in mercy toward them and gave them life in Jesus!
- ✝ **Ephesians 2:4-5** "But God, being rich in mercy, because of His great love with which He loved us, even when we were dead in our transgressions, made us alive together with Christ (by grace you have been saved) ..."

> **NOTE:** It may be helpful to remind your students what "mercy" and "grace" mean.
> - Mercy: when God does not give you what you deserve.
> - Grace: when God gives you what you do not deserve.

⇨ **God's mercy and grace flow out of His great love for us—even when we were at our worst! Why? Because His love for us is based on Who He is, not who we are.**

C. Now Christ has <u>SEATED</u> us with Him in heavenly places.

1. We are not saved by our works but <u>FOR</u> good works.

Ephesians 2:6-9
- Paul showed the magnitude of God's mercy and grace by once more emphasizing that it was when they were at their worst (walking according to the world, the flesh, and the devil) that God raised them up and seated them in the heavenly places in Christ Jesus.

> ★ **TEACHING TIP:**
> We must not minimize the contrast that Paul made: God raised us up from the "sewer" into His celestial abode. He changed our address. That is rich!

- ✝ **Ephesians 2:8-9** "For by grace you have been saved through faith; and that not of yourselves, it is the gift of God; not as a result of works, so that no one may boast."
    - Paul reiterated that salvation was a *gift* of God.

> ❖ **APPLICATION:** If you are offered a gift, then what must you do? Receive it. It is not yours until you actually take it. It is that same way with salvation.
> - ~ Salvation is offered, as God's gift, to everyone. But, again, it is only received by those who take it.
> - ~ Salvation cannot be earned; therefore, it is not a "reward" based on the result of a man's works.
> - ~ Because salvation is a gift, there is nothing for man to boast about. In truth, the only action on man's part is *receiving* God's undeserved gift.

EPHESIANS
Theme: Believers' Holy Walk

2. Seated in Christ we are to <u>WALK</u> in His good works.

Ephesians 2:10
- Paul wanted the Ephesians to understand that people are *not* saved BY works—rather, they are saved FOR works.
  - ~ And these "works" are not self-generated but, instead, planned by God who wants to accomplish His work in and through us!

> ★ **TEACHING TIP:**
> *Have your ever questioned what your purpose in life is? Here is your answer: to do the good works that God has prepared for each of us to do.*

⇨ **Believers once walked according to the world, the flesh, and the devil—NOW they are to walk according to God's good works!**

D. Christ called Jews and Gentiles into one <u>BODY</u>.

Ephesians 2:12-21
- Each person is called by God individually, but collectively they become the body of Christ, the church.
- Paul wanted the people to fully understand who had been called by God—*both* Jews and Gentiles.
- To the Gentiles he said:

✞ **Ephesians 2:12-13** "… remember that you were at that time separate from Christ, excluded from the commonwealth of Israel, and strangers to the covenants of promise, having no hope and without God in the world. But now in Christ Jesus you who formerly were far off have been brought near by the blood of Christ."

- Up to this point, the Gentiles had been separated from Christ, excluded from the commonwealth of Israel (and all of the blessings of being part of God's chosen people).
- The Gentiles were not a part of the covenant of promise that had been made to Abraham.
- Woefully, they were a people without hope, without God in the world.
- "But now" <u>in</u> Christ, the very people who had been far off from God were brought near to Him by the blood (the sacrifice) of Jesus Christ.
- The Jews, on the other hand, were near to God through the covenant of promise, but they too needed to be reconciled to God by the blood of Christ.

✞ **Ephesians 2:14-16** "For He Himself is our peace, who made both groups into one and broke down the barrier of the dividing wall, by abolishing in His flesh the enmity, which is the Law of commandments contained in ordinances, so that in Himself He might make the

EPHESIANS
Theme: Believers' Holy Walk

two into one new man, thus establishing peace, and might reconcile them both in one body to God through the cross, by it having put to death the enmity."

⇨ **Both Jew and Gentile were reconciled to God through the cross of Christ.**

- Paul explained that, THROUGH Christ, both Jew and Gentile had access in one Spirit to the Father. (Ephesians 2:18)

⇨ **It took the blood of Christ, the cross of Christ, and the Spirit of Christ to take the Jews, who were close to God, and the Gentiles, who were far from God, and bring them into one body in Christ.**

- Paul used three different visuals in regards to describing what the church was:
    - ~ A body (Ephesians 2:16)
    - ~ A household—a family (Ephesian 2:19)
    - ~ A building—a temple (Ephesians 2:20-22)
        * They were built on the foundation of the apostles and the prophets.
        * Jesus Christ was the cornerstone—in Him the whole building fit together.
        * This was an organic building in that it continued to "grow" into a holy temple in the Lord.

> ★ **TEACHING TIP:**
> *Consider Paul's words. His words were not only amazing for that culture, but a unifying message, putting all focus on their relationship with Jesus Christ—not on their former religion or lack thereof.*

⇨ **Jewish and Gentile believers are one in Jesus Christ.**

Ephesians 3:1-9
- Paul further stated that the church was a "mystery" that was now being revealed.
    - ~ A "mystery" indicated "something that was hidden."
- In the Old Testament, the church had been hidden—nobody understood the idea of Jews and Gentiles being brought together into one family, one body.
- Paul testified that he had received a revelation from God that revealed the mystery of the church to him. (Ephesians 3:3)

1. The church demonstrates to angels the WISDOM of God.

> ★ **TEACHING TIP:**
> *Have you ever considered that angels are watching you? In this case, not "over" you, but rather to witness how wise God was in saving you!*

Ephesians 3:10
- Paul knew that one purpose of the church was to prove how wise God was in saving men.
- Consider: Angels do not know anything about salvation experientially.

EPHESIANS
Theme: Believers' Holy Walk

- ~ Those who chose to obey God continue to obey Him.
- ~ Those who disobeyed God (with Satan), continue to disobey Him.
- Jesus did not come to die for angels—He came to die for people.
- Paul wanted the Ephesian believers to understand that the angels were watching the church.

2. The church demonstrates to people the <u>POWER</u> of God.

<u>Ephesians 3:16-21</u>

✟ **Ephesians 3:16-19** "... that He would grant you, according to the riches of His glory, to be strengthened with power through His Spirit in the inner man, so that Christ may dwell in your hearts through faith; and that you, being rooted and grounded in love, may be able to comprehend with all the saints what is the breadth and length and height and depth, and to know the love of Christ which surpasses knowledge, that you may be filled up to all the fullness of God."

- Paul explained that when the Holy Spirit sealed them, He grounded them in the love of Christ.
- In being grounded, believers (the church) not only witnessed to the angels, but also to one another.

⇨ **Believers should be able to look at another believer's life and see God's power in them—unbelievers should be able to look at believers' lives and see the power of the Holy Spirit.**

✟ **Ephesians 3:20** "Now to Him who is able to do far more abundantly beyond all that we ask or think, according to the power that works within us ..."

- Paul expounded on his thought—God was able to do more than we could ever ask or think about.

****

❋ **ILLUSTRATION:** As an illustration, scuba divers can survive and do well in an alien environment because they have the right equipment.

****

- Paul's point: As believers, we live in an alien environment (we are no longer a part of this world—it is not our home). We are simply passing through, but we have been given special equipment for the journey.
  - ~ Sealed with the Holy Spirit—God's power working in us.

EPHESIANS
Theme: Believers' Holy Walk

REVIEW:
- Paul told the Ephesian believers what God had done:
    1. He had called them.
    2. He had redeemed them.
    3. He had sealed them.
    4. He had seated them in heavenly places, so that they could walk effectively in this world (with an impact on those who also believed in Jesus Christ and on those who did not).

- Paul began his next train of thought in Chapter 4 using the word "therefore." It is always important to ask the question, "What is therefore, there for?"
    - Because of all the things he had just explained to them (all that Christ had done and provided), he called them to a new walk—a walk worthy of the riches they had in Christ.

II. OUR WALK: WHAT WE ARE TO DO—PRESENT (EPHESIANS 4–6)

A. Walk in UNITY.

Ephesians 4:2–6
- He explained that to walk in humility meant to walk in humility, gentleness, patience, and showing tolerance.
    - Nit-picking at one another never has produced unity.
- Paul also stated that diligence was required by each believer to preserve unity of the Spirit in the bond of peace.
- Why? He reiterated: the church is one body, believers are to see themselves as one body with one Spirit, with one calling, having one Lord.

> ★ **TEACHING TIP:**
> *To be unified seems to be a big challenge for the church today.*

Ephesians 4:11–16
- Paul explained that God gave believers spiritual gifts in order to help them be unified.
    - Some were to be apostles, some to be prophets, some to be evangelists, some to be pastors, and some to be teachers.
- The gifts that Paul listed were given in order to equip the saints (believers) to basically grow up—to understand God's Word—so that they could attain unity in faith.

EPHESIANS
Theme: Believers' Holy Walk

> **NOTE:** Paul made a good point in vv. 13–16 that still rings true today.
> - Children can be tossed to and fro, believing in fairy tales.
> - In the same way, believers can be tossed about by believing "untruths" about God's Word. Believers can be deceived and tricked by crafty people distorting God's Word.
>
> ⇨ **God wants us to use our spiritual gifts to build unity in faith, protecting the church from those who oppose God's truth, His Word.**

****

❋ **ILLUSTRATION:** Some people have the gift of teaching. Some have the gift of service. Others have the gift of encouragement. If the encourager says to himself, "You know, my gift really isn't all that important. I don't think I will encourage anybody today." What can happen? The teacher gets tired of teaching and the server gets tired of serving—and there is no one building them up, inspiring them to continue their work for the whole body. The result? The body falters.

Each individual part of the body has to actively do his or her part. In other words, use your gift!

****

B. Walk in **HOLINESS**.

Ephesians 4:17–32

✝ **Ephesians 4:17** "So this I say, and affirm together with the Lord, that you walk no longer just as the Gentiles also walk, in the futility of their mind ..."
- Paul wanted them to remember that they had changed because of what Christ had done on the cross—His sacrifice on their behalf.
  - He did not want them to walk as they did when they were "unsaved"—spiritually dead and unable to receive the truth, thus sin marked their lives.
  - This was NOT who they were NOW.

✝ **Ephesians 4:23–24** "... and that you be renewed in the spirit of your mind, and put on the new self, which in the likeness of God has been created in righteousness and holiness of the truth."
- Paul's point: they have a radically different life now because of what Christ has done.

> ★ **TEACHING TIP:**
> *To "put on" indicates that something needs to be "put off"—in this case, they needed to put off their old life when they, as mentioned before, were essentially the walking dead. They were now new creatures in Christ!*

EPHESIANS
Theme: Believers' Holy Walk

- ~ A life that reflected the likeness of God and glorified Him.
- ~ A walk in righteousness and holiness of the truth.

- Paul listed how this new walk of unity should be lived:
  1. They should speak the truth to one another—they should not lie. (v. 25)
  2. They could be angry, yet not sin—they were not to let the sun go down on any anger they held. (v. 26)

> ★ **TEACHING TIP:**
> *Anger is never to be "nurtured" or "harbored"—a spirit of unforgiveness should never become a part of the believer's psyche.*

⇨ **To be angry gives the devil an opportunity to build up resentment in the body, thus hurting church unity.**

> ❖ **APPLICATION:** Consider the difference it would make if we simply applied this one verse in our homes! How many of us have gone to bed angry?
> - ~ In hanging on to that anger, we have all night long to "recite" it and oftentimes we "add" that anger to another anger-producing event that happened weeks ago or a year ago.
> - ~ Ultimately, we can't remember why we are mad—yet we set this self-made "grudge tape" to replay over and over again!
> - ~ Relationships are hurt (sometimes irreparably)—all because we did not obey this one verse.
> - ~ If you are upset with someone, deal with it the same day. Don't allow the devil to begin to work resentment in your life.

⇨ **Any action that causes pain to others and disrupts unity—lying, anger, unforgiveness, wrong desires, ingratitude, neglecting others, slander, etc.—will grieve the Holy Spirit within the believer. (Ephesians 4:30)**

C. Walk in <u>LOVE</u>.

Ephesians 5:1–5
- Christ's love was sacrificial and theirs should be also for one another.
  - ∗ A sweet fragrance emits from one walking in this manner—it brings joy to the heart of God.

> ★ **TEACHING TIP:**
> *Greed takes—love gives.*

EPHESIANS
Theme: Believers' Holy Walk

D. Walk in **LIGHT**.

Ephesians 5:6–14

- Paul reminded the Ephesians that they had once walked in darkness, but now they had been set free to walk in the light of the Lord—thus, they were to walk as children of the light.
- He gave adjectives in regards to the "fruit of the light": (vv. 9–10)
  1. Goodness
  2. Righteousness
  3. Truth
  4. Trying to learn what was pleasing to God

⇨ **CONSIDER:** "Fruit" grows in the light, as does spiritual fruit in the Light of Christ!

- Paul also cautioned the Ephesians that light also exposed everything—fruitful or unfruitful. (v. 13)

> ❖ **APPLICATION:** When would you prefer to judge your housekeeping efforts—on a dark, rainy day or a bright, sunny day?
> - ∼ On a rainy day, windows can appear clean but, when the sun comes out, all the smudges and smears of dirt appear.
> - ∼ The same principle applies to our lives: in the dark, we can hide a lot of what may be happening in our lives. But, once we walk in the light, God will reveal the sin.

E. Walk in **WISDOM**.

Ephesians 5:15–6:3

- Paul gave different aspects as to what made a person wise:
  1. The wise person made the most of his time. (Ephesians 5:15–16)
     * A wise man understood that he could not get that time "back."
  2. The wise person was filled with the Spirit. (Ephesians 5:18–21)
  3. The wise wife willingly submitted to her own husband, as to the Lord—and respected him (his position as the "head"). (Ephesians 5:22–33)
     * As we discussed before, Paul used the family as an illustration for the church.

> ★ **TEACHING TIP:**
> Paul explained that a Christian marriage is a "witness" for Christ to the world. A Christian marriage should reflect submission and sacrificial love—the components of a relationship with Christ.

EPHESIANS
Theme: Believers' Holy Walk

- * Here he explained that the husband was to be the head of the family.
- * In being the head of the family, the husband was called to love his wife as himself—to love her as Christ loves the church, a sacrificial love.

4. The wise child obeyed his parents. (Ephesians 6: 1–3)

F. Walk in <u>STRENGTH</u>.

<u>Ephesians 6:10–18</u>
- Paul taught that the strength a believer is to walk in is the Lord's strength, in His might—human strength will fail. (Ephesians 6:10)
- Paul further explained that this strength came from putting on the full armor of God—it was the only way in which to defend a believer against the schemes of the devil.
- Paul named the enemy: the ruler, the powers, the world forces of darkness, the spiritual forces of wickedness in heavenly places. In other words, this was a spiritual enemy that cannot be seen visibly. (Ephesians 6:12)

⇨ **Believers are involved in an unseen battle—this is spiritual warfare!**

> ❖ **APPLICATION:** Consider the assault on families today, beginning with marriage relationships. As an example, the world (through every form of media) scoffs at the concept of wives submitting to and respecting their husbands. In fact, their message is succinct, "Men are not worth being respected."

- Paul instructed the believers that, to walk in God's strength, they must put on His full armor—this would be the only way to resist every attack that may come their way.
- Paul gave a description of the armor of a soldier to illustrate the equipment God had provided His people:
  1. **Girded with truth**
     - Girded: This spoke to a "girdle or sash" that was designed to keep every part of the armor in its place and held the sword.
     - * Truth: God's Word.

★ **TEACHING TIP:**
"Great is the laxity of falsehood; truth binds the man." ~ Hugo Grotius

⇨ **When girded in truth, a believer will not be deceived!**

  2. **Breastplate of righteousness**
     - * Breastplate: protected a soldier's vital organs, including the heart, against a sword, spear, or arrow.

★ **TEACHING TIP:**
Righteousness lived out is manifested through steadfast and sincere integrity regarding one's faith in Jesus Christ.

EPHESIANS
Theme: Believers' Holy Walk

* Righteousness: bestowed upon a believer through Christ's work on the cross and lived out daily through the power of the Holy Spirit.

⇨ **When a believer walks faithfully in the light of God's righteousness, he will give Satan no opening for an attack.**

3. **Feet shod with the preparation of the gospel of peace.**
    * Feet shod: the soldier's footwear was critical to his survival in a battle. The soles were fitted with nails to give the soldier's feet the ability to stand firm, to keep him from slipping.
    * Preparation: implied readiness.
    * Gospel of peace: ready to witness for Christ, displaying a kind and compassionate spirit.

> ★ **TEACHING TIP:**
> *The questions we must ask ourselves: "Am I walking in readiness?*
> *Am I prepared to share the gospel of Christ in a spirit of kindness (with no hint of antagonism), no matter how hostile the circumstances may be?*

⇨ **When a believer wears such footwear, he can safely encounter and respond appropriately to the barbed obstacles that oppose the gospel and his pressing forward in faith.**

4. **Shield of faith**
    * Shield: was constructed to be light and strong to deflect arrows or darts. It is important to note that it actually worked to protect the other parts of the armor.
    * Faith: a full trusting in, relying upon, and adhering in Jesus Christ and the truth of all of God's promises.

> ★ **TEACHING TIP:**
> *We must never forget that, beginning in the Garden, Satan has been the corrupting source of unbelief.*

⇨ **When a believer holds up and stands firm in faith, the darts of the enemy will not find a crack in the armor!**

5. **Helmet of salvation**
    * Helmet: used to guard the head from a blow by a sword, club, or battle-axe.
    * Salvation: this referred to the "hope of salvation," the believers' ultimate salvation. This understanding of "victory in Jesus" guards the mind in conflict.

> ★ **TEACHING TIP:**
> *This hope is based on the sure Word of God. This well-founded confidence defends the mind against thoughts of doubt, despair, and defeat.*

EPHESIANS
Theme: Believers' Holy Walk

⇨ **When a believer protects his mind with the sure hope of salvation, he will continue to trust God even if the battle *seems* lost.**

6. **Sword of the Spirit, which is the word of God**
   * Sword: the ancient sword was short, usually two-edged. This was an offensive piece of equipment.
   * Of the Spirit: furnished by the Holy Spirit.
   * Word of God: God's spoken truth and promises—exactly what Jesus used in the wilderness against Satan.

> ★ **TEACHING TIP:**
> *Clichés or well-known adages cannot defend against error or falsehood—only the Word of God can!*

⇨ **When a believer is armed with the Word of God, he is able to resist and defeat the temptations and personal attacks of the evil one.**

7. **Prayer**
   * Prayers for preparation and protection—for victory.
   * Prayers of intercession for other Christian soldiers.

> ★ **TEACHING TIP:**
> *"Restraining prayer, we cease to fight;*
> *Prayer makes the Christian armor bright,*
> *And Satan trembles when he sees*
> *The meanest saint on his knees." (Barnes' Notes)*

⇨ **To have victory, a believer must pray—not an occasional prayer, but one that continually unites him with God to fight battles only the Lord can win.**

- It is important to remember that God said to put on the "full" armor—each piece was and is necessary to stand strong in spiritual warfare.

- With such impregnable equipment, Paul made his point once more that believers, the Ephesians, were rich in everything they needed.

FINAL THOUGHTS AND APPLICATION

¤ Paul basically asked, "Church, why are you living in poverty when you are so rich?"
  ~ God had given them everything they needed.
  ~ They had been called by the Father.
  ~ They had been redeemed by the Son.
  ~ They had been sealed by the Spirit.
  ~ They had been seated with Christ in heavenly places.
  ~ They had been empowered by the Holy Spirit to walk worthy in this world.

EPHESIANS
Theme: Believers' Holy Walk

- ¤ Paul explained that the believer had a responsibility in how he walked through this temporary world—but God had supplied all the equipment needed for success!
- ¤ Paul warned them that there would be battles in this life, spiritual battles—but again God had supplied all the equipment needed for victory.

- ¤ Our opening illustration told of a man living in poverty with his family, all the while residing above incredible riches. His son stated that there were three things that he did not like about being poor:
    1. His home: it was 700 square feet for four people—insufficient space.
    2. His clothing: his mother made all his clothes in size 12 when he was actually a size 4 or 6 at the time. He stated that he would enter rooms "fabric first!"
    3. His inheritance: there was none and there was no hope of one.
    - ~ This man and his family had actually been rich, yet lived as paupers.

- ¤ Jesus tells believers that they are rich with:
    - ~ A home, seated with Christ in heavenly places—far superior to the temple of Artemis.
    - ~ Clothing that equips them to walk victoriously in this world.
    - ~ An inheritance from God the Father.

- ⇨ **Paul reminded the Ephesians what believers had been given—and encouraged them that the best was yet to come!**

- ❖ **FINAL APPLICATION:** **We are called to sit with Christ, walk in His Spirit, and stand against the world, the flesh, and the Devil.**

EPHESIANS
Theme: Believers' Holy Walk

EPHESIANS REVIEW HELPS

✧ **Place the following events or people in chronological sequential order.**

Birth of the church	Abraham	Temple built
Crucifixion	Fall	Tabernacle built
Built an ark	David	Flood
Creation	Virgin birth	Fall of Israel
Jacob	Swallowed by a fish	Rebuilt temple
Paul's first missionary journey	Exile	Lions' den
The Exodus	Paul' conversion	Resurrection
Paul wrote Galatians	Paul wrote Romans	Last writing prophet

EPHESIANS REVIEW HELPS
(Answers for Facilitators)

✧ Place the following events or people in chronological, sequential order.

1. Creation
2. Fall
3. Built an ark
4. Flood
5. Abraham
6. Jacob
7. Exodus
8. Tabernacle built
9. David
10. Temple built
11. Swallowed by a fish
12. Fall of Israel
13. Exile
14. Lions' den
15. Rebuilt temple
16. Last writing prophet
17. Virgin birth
18. Crucifixion
19. Resurrection
20. Birth of the Church
21. Paul's conversion
22. Paul's first missionary journey
23. Paul wrote Galatians
24. Paul wrote Romans

PHILIPPIANS

Believers' Joy in Christ

For to me, to live is Christ and to die is gain.

Philippians 1:21

SESSION FIFTY: PHILIPPIANS
Believers' Joy in Christ

☦ **Memory verse:** *"For to me, to live is Christ and to die is gain." (Philippians 1:21)*

Introduction: Philippians is a loving thank you note from Paul to the church at Philippi, thanking them for their generosity. Though written from a prison, it is a joyful and personal letter. He exudes peace and contentment even though his circumstances were very difficult. There are no problems addressed in this letter, yet Paul does take the opportunity to encourage, inspire, and challenge those he loves so deeply. The centrality of Christ is a theme throughout this letter. Paul knew that Christ was his life, his attitude, his goal, and his strength—he encouraged the Philippians to embrace Christ likewise.

- **Oral Review:** Please refer to the **REVIEW Section** in the following Teaching Guide Outline.

- **Homework:** Review the homework from the book of Ephesians.

    Questions on pages 132–133
    Question on page 135
    Questions on pages 138–139

- **Review Helps:** Written review is provided at the end of the teacher presentation. (Optional and time permitting.)

- **Teacher Presentation on the Book of Philippians**

- **Learning for Life:** You may choose to discuss all or just one or two of the questions on page 151.

- **Closing prayer:** Pray that each of the students would come to know the true joy of the Lord, that they would be able to "see others as more important than themselves," and that they would reflect Christ's joy to those they meet.

PHILIPPIANS
Theme: Believers' Joy in Christ

OUTLINE AID FOR TEACHERS:

I. **THE HISTORY OF THE CHURCH IN PHILIPPI**

   A. The History of Philippi

   1. Philippi was a ROMAN colony.
   2. This small town was an important military outpost in MACEDONIA.
   3. The citizens had the same special privileges as the ROMAN citizens.

- **Acts 15–16**

   B. Paul and the Church in Philippi

   1. Paul founded the church on his SECOND missionary journey in A.D. 51.
   2. Some of Paul's early converts included a wealthy woman merchant, a jailor, and a SLAVE girl.

- **Acts 21–28**

   3. Paul wrote this letter to the Philippian church during his first IMPRISONMENT in Rome in A.D. 62.
   4. Philippians is Paul's most PERSONAL letter.

II. **THE LETTER TO THE PHILIPPIANS**

   A. Christ is our LIFE : "To live is Christ" (Philippians 1)

- **Philippians 1:8–11**

   1. The believer should have the same AFFECTIONS as Christ.

- **Philippians 1:12**

   2. The believer should have the same RESPONSE to circumstances as Christ.

- **Philippians 1:13–21**

   3. The believer should have the SPIRIT of Christ.

- **Philippians 1:27a**

   4. The believer should have the CONDUCT of Christ.

   B. Christ is our ATTITUDE: "Have this attitude in yourselves which was also in Christ Jesus…" (Philippians 2)

- **Philippians 2–4**

   1. The believer should have the HUMILITY of Christ.
   2. We should regard others as more important than OURSELVES.

PHILIPPIANS
Theme: Believers' Joy in Christ

- **Philippians 2:5–8**
    3. Christ's obedience is our <u>MODEL</u>.
- **Philippians 2:14–15**
    4. Do all things without <u>GRUMBLING</u>.
- **Philippians 2:16**
    5. Hold fast to the <u>WORD</u> of life.

C. Christ is our <u>GOAL</u>: "I have suffered the loss of all things, and count them but rubbish so that I may gain Christ." (Philippians 3)

- **Philippians 3:7–11**
    1. The believer's goal is to <u>KNOW</u> Christ intimately.

D. Christ is our <u>STRENGTH</u>: "I can do all things through Him who strengthens me." (Philippians 4)

- **Philippians 4:4**
    1. Christ is the believer's <u>JOY</u>.
- **Philippians 4:7**
    2. Christ is the believer's <u>PEACE</u>.
- **Philippians 4:10–12**
    3. Christ is the believer's <u>SATISFACTION</u>.
- **Philippians 4:13**
    4. Christ is the believer's <u>STRENGTH</u>.

Philippians
[Believers' Joy in Christ]

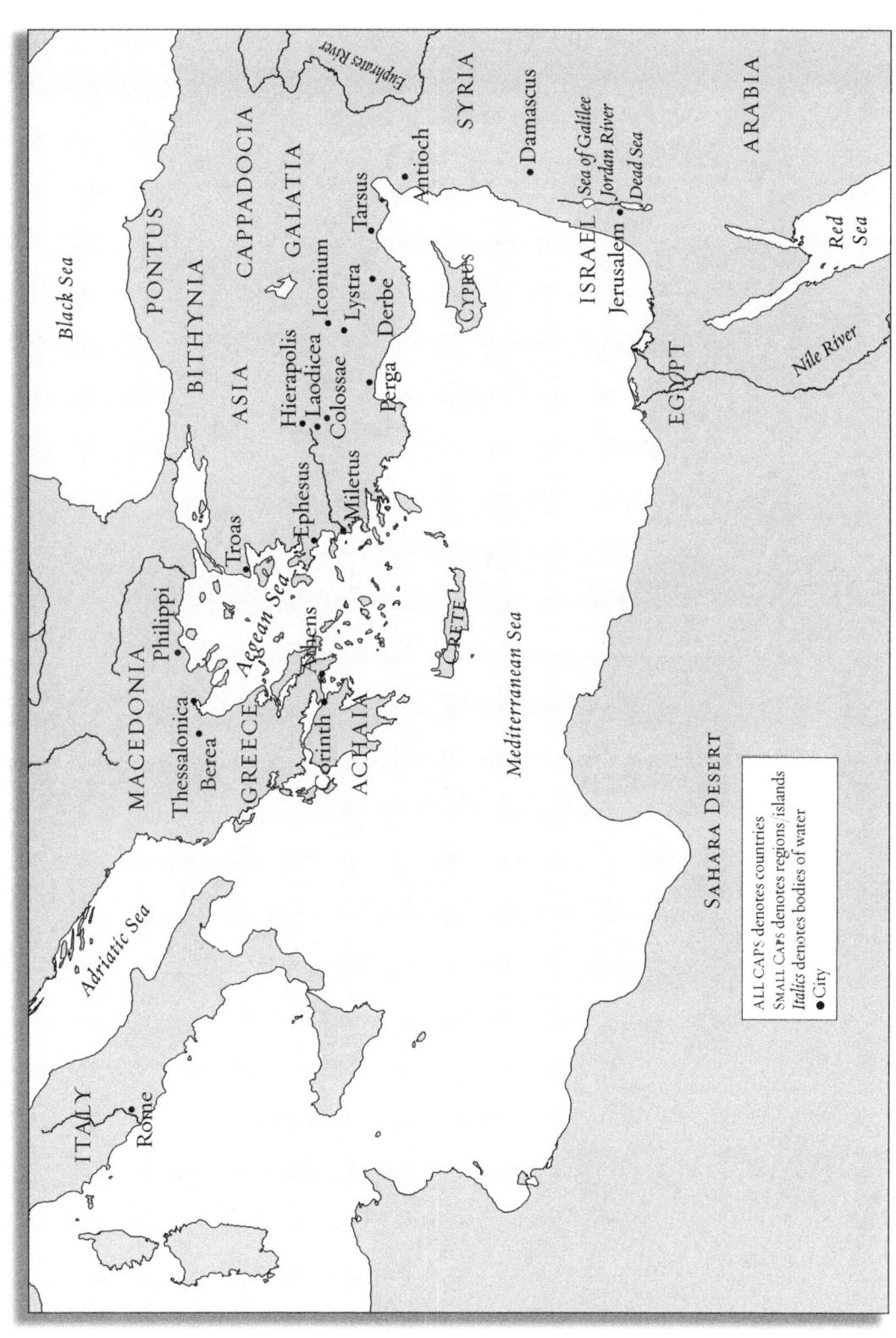

PHILIPPIANS

PHILIPPIANS
Theme: Believers' Joy in Christ

THE BASICS:
⇨ **Who: The Author:** Paul
   Main Characters: Believers in Philippi
⇨ **What:** A thank-you letter to the Philippian church
⇨ **When:** Written in A.D. 62
⇨ **Where:** Written to Philippi from a Roman prison
⇨ **Why:** To give thanks to the Philippians and to encourage them

MEMORY VERSE: *"For me, to live is Christ and to die is gain."* Philippians 1:21

****

REVIEW:
- The *Old Testament History* books:
  - Shared the problem of disobedience (sin) and its consequences (judgment and death).
  - The prophets foretold of judgment and the Messiah to come.
- The *New Testament History* books:
  - Showed that the Messiah had come.
  - The church was born.
- In *Paul's Letters to the Churches*:
  - **Romans:** A deep and instructive book on the righteousness of God and how man can become righteous—through belief in Christ alone.
  - **First Corinthians:** A direct and confrontational book addressing sin in the church and how it was to be handled.
  - **Second Corinthians:** A personal and defensive book regarding Paul's ministry and authority as an apostle.
  - **Galatians:** A book confronting false teaching and the believers' inclination to forget that they were free in Christ.
  - **Ephesians:** An inspiring doctrinal book with practical application to daily life.

OVERVIEW:

****

✻ **ILLUSTRATION:** Have you ever met someone who knows the Word of God better than anyone else that you know? Have you ever had another believer invest their time and their life in you? Have you watched them in their relationships with others, whether their spouse, children, other family members, or friends, and witnessed God's Word applied and lived out?

PHILIPPIANS
Theme: Believers' Joy in Christ

If you have, then you probably have experienced their ability to know the right scripture to share at your point of need—a verse that you can hold onto, a verse that helps you to look up to your Lord and Savior. The amazing attribute of these type of people—those who are truly sold out to the Lord—is their deep seated joy: a joy based on their understanding of Jesus Christ and His love for them.

****

- Paul had such a relationship with the people in Philippi.
- He was with them for a short period of time but, while he was there, he just loved them—and the people loved him back.
- This is a book that is full of affection—it is also filled with joy!
    - You will find the word "joy" and "rejoice" used over and over again.
    - Even though Paul is writing from a difficult situation (imprisoned), there is a real sense of joy within him.
- Paul's words give a picture of Christ that is found in no other book in the Bible.

I. THE HISTORY OF THE CHURCH IN PHILIPPI

A. The History of Philippi.

1. Philippi was a <u>ROMAN</u> colony.

- It was not a very big city, but it was very prestigious because it was a Roman colony.
- Rome imported many people from Italy to this little town.
- It was a diverse city made up of Greeks and Italians.
- Unlike the Corinthians, who were known for their immorality, the Philippians were not immoral. Instead, they were known for being a straightforward and affectionate people.
- They did have one negative: the Philippians were very conscious of one's "social status."
    - There was a sense that a higher status could be achieved by gaining "honors."
- Philippi also had a medical center and school. Some scholars believe that Luke, the great physician, may have actually attended this medical school and had perhaps lived there. (Note: this is an interesting thought, but cannot be proven.)

2. This small city was an important military outpost in <u>MACEDONIA</u>.

3. The citizens had the same special privileges as the <u>ROMAN</u> citizens.

PHILIPPIANS
Theme: Believers' Joy in Christ

> **NOTE:** This was an incredibly effective political tool used by Rome with its conquered nations. Such privileges included:
> - The right to vote and make legal contracts.
> - Not being submitted to torture.
> - The right to have a trial before a court to defend oneself.
> - If sentenced to death, no Roman citizen could be sentenced to die on a cross.
>
> ⇨ **Both Paul and Peter were found guilty of the same crime but, because Paul was a Roman citizen, he was beheaded—while Peter, not being Roman citizen, was crucified.**

B. Paul and the Church in Philippi

- This was the first church that Paul established in Europe.

1. Paul founded the church on his <u>SECOND</u> missionary journey in AD 51 (see Acts 16:11–40).

☦ **Acts 16:11–13** "So putting out to sea from Troas, we ran a straight course to Samothrace, and on the day following to Neapolis; and from there to Philippi, which is a leading city of the district of Macedonia, a Roman colony; and we were staying in this city for some days. And on the Sabbath day we went outside the gate to a riverside, where we were supposing that there would be a place of prayer; and we sat down and began speaking to the women who had assembled."

- As a reminder, Luke wrote the book of Acts. In his use of "we," it appears that it is at Troas that Luke joined this missionary party led by Paul.
- There are several things to note in this Acts passage about Paul's time in Philippi:
  ~ It was the Sabbath and Paul was looking for a synagogue.
  ~ There was no synagogue in Philippi—ten Jewish men are needed to start one, so apparently there were not ten Jewish men in Philippi. (*This indicates that the Jewish population in general was very small in this city.*)
  ~ Paul went down to the banks of a river (in reality, it was quite a small stream) and found a group of Jewish women praying and worshiping God.
  ~ Though the site of worship seems odd to us, there was a reason for its location:
    * It is believed that this was the area that the Jews were given to worship.
    * It was not against the law to be a Jew nor was it against the law to worship one God—BUT it was against the law to invite others to come join you to worship your God.

PHILIPPIANS
Theme: Believers' Joy in Christ

⇨ **The culture that Paul entered into basically limited the Jews from sharing their faith.**

> **TEACHING TIP:**
> *Can you imagine the scene that unfolded? Paul had come to town to share the good news of the Gospel. He would <u>never</u> keep his faith in Christ to himself!*

    2. Some of Paul's early converts included a wealthy woman merchant, a jailor, and a <u>SLAVE</u> girl.

Acts 16:14–15
- Paul met a businesswoman, Lydia, at the river's bank.
    - She sold very expensive purple cloth.
    - This description of her indicated that she was probably quite wealthy and successful.
- Lydia listened to the words of Paul regarding Jesus Christ, she believed what she heard, and gave her life to Christ.
- It appeared that Lydia's newfound belief was enthusiastic and contagious, as her entire household came to the Lord as well.
- Paul actually stayed in Lydia's home for a short period of time.

⇨ **Lydia was the first European convert by Paul.**

Acts 16:16–23
- Paul encountered a slave girl that had followed him. She was exclaiming that Paul was telling the people to believe in Jesus and be saved—one would think that this was a good thing.
- But apparently the manner of her words—whether sarcastic, unkind, or off-putting—communicated disrespect or disdain for Jesus.
- Paul allowed this situation to go on for a short period of time until he had had enough:

✝ **Acts 16:18** "But Paul was greatly annoyed, and turned and said to the spirit, "I command you in the name of Jesus Christ to come out of her!" And it came out at that very moment."

> **TEACHING TIP:**
> *This slave girl generated profits for her masters as a fortune-teller. In their mind, Paul had impacted their bottom-line, which was far more important to them than the fate of a slave girl. And he needed to pay!*

- The masters of this slave girl were enraged by Paul's actions because he had just destroyed their lucrative business.
    - These men had used the demonic being within their slave to make them money.
    - When the slave girl lost the demon, she also lost her power to fortune-tell—and they had lost their money-maker.

PHILIPPIANS
Theme: Believers' Joy in Christ

- Instead of being happy that this woman had been set free of a demon, they became angry.
- ✝ **Acts 16:20–23** "… and when they had brought them to the chief magistrates, they said, 'These men are throwing our city into confusion, being Jews, and are proclaiming customs which it is not lawful for us to accept or to observe, being Romans.' The crowd rose up together against them, and the chief magistrates tore their robes off them and proceeded to order them to be beaten with rods. When they had struck them with many blows, they threw them into prison, commanding the jailer to guard them securely; …"
  - Paul and Silas were brought before the authorities and were savagely beaten.
  - And then they were thrown into prison—the jailer being strongly instructed to guard these men.

Acts 6:24–34
- ✝ **Acts 16:24** "… and he, having received such a command, threw them into the inner prison and fastened their feet in the stocks."
  - It must be noted that their physical condition must have been incredibly painful, but Scripture relates that about midnight (after being beaten), Paul and Silas were praying and singing.

> ★ **TEACHING TIP:**
> *When a person was put into stocks, the only way to lie down was on one's back. In Paul's and Silas' case, they had been severely beaten, so their backs were probably raw from where the skin had been torn.*

> ❖ **APPLICATION:** Take a second to let this scene sink in.
> ~ These two men had not only been treated horribly, but unjustly.
> ~ They had been thrown into prison and put in a position that caused further pain from the beatings they had endured.
> ~ AND they are singing … praising God … singing hymns!
> ⇨ **Be honest—would this be your response in such an unfair circumstance? Or would you be complaining, asking God, "Why me?!"**

- There were other prisoners in that jail and they were listening to Paul and Silas. All of a sudden, there was an earthquake. The ground shook, the prison doors opened, and the chains fell off of every prisoner—setting them all free.
  - BUT no one left. Why? They all saw this event as a great work of God.

PHILIPPIANS
Theme: Believers' Joy in Christ

- The jailer (who was under strict orders regarding Paul) was awakened by the earthquake and he came running into the cell area. He saw that the doors were all opened and assumed the prisoners had fled.
- The jailer pulled out his sword and was prepared to kill himself.

✞ **Acts 16:28** "But Paul cried out with a loud voice, saying, 'Do not harm yourself, for we are all here!'"

> ★ **TEACHING TIP:**
> *The jailer knew that his responsibility was to make sure the prisoners stayed securely in their cells. He knew that failure would lead to his death for not successfully doing his duty.*

- The jailer lit the lanterns and there were all of his prisoners—securely sitting in their cells, with their chains on the floor and the doors wide open! Not one prisoner had fled, but they all were praising God.
- It is hard to imagine what must have run through this jailer's mind, but he had one question for Paul and Silas:

✞ **Acts 16:30b** "Sirs, what must I do to be saved?"

- The jailer, like the other prisoners, saw this event as one that God had miraculously orchestrated.
- Paul and Silas responded: "Believe in the Lord Jesus, and you will be saved, you and your household." (Acts 16:31)

REVIEW:
- Here, the church in Philippi was born with Lydia, a slave girl, and a jailer.
- It would not be a stretch to think that some of the women at the river and some of the prisoners in the jail also became part of this church.
- It is good to remember that this church was an unusual group of people brought together, especially as Paul addressed them in his letter.

3. Paul wrote this letter to the Philippian church during his first IMPRISONMENT in Rome in AD 62. (See Acts 21–28)

- A brief understanding of Paul and his ministry may be helpful:
  - Paul had been on three missionary journeys and had returned to Jerusalem.
  - He was arrested. He demanded to be tried in Rome, which was his right as a Roman citizen.
  - After being taken to Rome, he spent two years in jail. It was during this time that he wrote this letter and several others.
  - Paul would eventually be released from jail, only to be re-arrested after a few years. He was brought back to Rome, where he would ultimately be executed.

PHILIPPIANS
Theme: Believers' Joy in Christ

4. Philippians is Paul's most __PERSONAL__ letter.

- It is essentially a thank-you note for how they had ministered to him.
  - On two different occasions, they had sent him financial gifts that he desperately needed.
  - When they learned of this imprisonment, they sent him more money and clothes.
- Paul, however, expressed more than "thank you" to this church—he poured out his love for them and his joy in Christ.

II. THE LETTER TO THE PHILIPPIANS

- The book contains four chapters and is divided into four thoughts:
  - Christ is our life
  - Christ is our attitude
  - Christ is our goal
  - Christ is our strength

A. Christ is our __LIFE__: "To live is Christ" (Philippians 1)

1. The believer should have the same __AFFECTIONS__ as Christ.

✝ **Philippians 1:8** "For God is my witness, how I long for you all with the affection of Christ Jesus."

- Paul wanted these believers to understand that he was allowing the love of Christ to flow through him to these people.

Philippians 1:9–11
- His affection poured forth through his prayers for them:
  - That their love would abound—for God, for one another, for the lost.
    * This was not just "mushy" blind affection, but an intelligent love based on an understanding of God and His truth.
    * This was a discerning love, having spiritual perceptiveness of what was true and of real value.
  - That their walk with the Lord would be wise, recognizing good from evil.
  - That their faith would be sincere—authentic.
  - That their faith would be productive—serving others.

2. The believer should have the same __RESPONSE__ to circumstances as Christ.

PHILIPPIANS
Theme: Believers' Joy in Christ

✝ **Philippians 1:12** "Now I want you to know, brethren, that my circumstances have turned out for the greater progress of the gospel, …"

- Paul recognized his circumstances—in a prison—as God's opportunity to present the gospel to those in need.

> ★ **TEACHING TIP:**
> *Paul looked at all of his circumstances, good or bad, as being given to him from Jesus Christ and his job was to bring glory to Christ in that circumstance.*

****

❋ **ILLUSTRATION:** There was a man on the ten most wanted list of the FBI. He was captured and put into solitary confinement in prison. While he was there, he was given a small New Testament. He read the book of John. He was overcome with the love of Jesus Christ and, in that cell, he fell on his knees, received Christ, and committed to be His servant. It would be many years before he was freed. He took that time to study God's Word, know Jesus better, and tell others of Him.

Later, when he was married, the guests included prisoners, ex-prisoners, and prison guards. The wedding was attended by the many people that had been led to Christ through this man's great work.

Yes, this man had been in prison, but he realized that he had work he could do for Christ there! People's lives were changed forever because a man took his circumstances and used them with the power of God working through him to bring about great good. He still has a prison ministry.

****

3. The believer should have the <u>SPIRIT</u> of Christ.

Philippians 1:13–21
- Paul shared that there was a good chance that he would never leave jail because he could very well be executed.
- He posed his personal reality in verse 21: "For to me, to live is Christ and to die is gain."
  - ~ It is as if he questions within himself which was best.
    - ★ If he lived, he had great work to accomplish for Christ.
    - ★ If he died, he would be in the presence of Christ.
- Paul exemplified a "heavenly vision" toward his life and circumstances.

> ★ **TEACHING TIP:**
> *If you live Christ's life <u>through</u> you, then you are going to be very different (alien) to those who live in the ways of this world.*

PHILIPPIANS
Theme: Believers' Joy in Christ

****

❋ **ILLUSTRATION:** There was a woman, Vesta, who had cancer. Her friends prayed for her and witnessed a miraculous recovery. And then, many years later, the cancer returned. The doctor told her that there were no other options; nothing else could be medically done for her. A friend called her and said, "I just heard the news and I wanted to tell you I am so sorry." Vesta asked, "Why?" The friend responded, "Well, I heard that you were told you were going to die." Vesta responded, "Yes, I am, and I am so excited! I have been reading God's Word. I want to know more about my Savior and I want to know more about heaven. I am telling you that He has prepared a wonderful place for us and I can't wait to get there!" The friend answered, "Okay, I am not sorry for you, but I am sorry for me. I am going to miss you so much." Vesta's heavenly perspective: "For crying out loud, you are going to be with me before I even finish my tour of heaven!"

> ★ **TEACHING TIP:**
> *Time goes by so fast, in a blink. We need a heavenly perspective—one that understands that this world is not our "home," but we are headed there with eyes focused on the Savior.*

****

4. The believer should have the **CONDUCT** of Christ.

✞ **Philippians 1:27a** "Only conduct yourselves in a manner worthy of the gospel of Christ, …"

- Paul wanted these believers to remember that they were citizens of the kingdom of heaven—this earth is not our home.

⇨ **As we pass through this temporary home, the believer is to bring honor to Christ.**

B. Christ is our **ATTITUDE**: "Have this attitude in yourselves which was also in Christ Jesus …" (Philippians 2)

Philippians 2:2–4

1. The believer should have the **HUMILITY** of Christ.

2. We should regard others as more important than **OURSELVES**.

> ★ **TEACHING TIP:**
> *Humility is not thinking of yourself as "first" or "last"—it is just not thinking of yourself at all.*

PHILIPPIANS
Theme: Believers' Joy in Christ

- Paul called the Philippians to be:
    ~ Like-minded versus having strife with one another—united and unified with the gospel work of Christ.
    ~ Maintaining the same love for one another—opinions could differ, but their love for each other should remain a constant.
    ~ United in spirit, intent on one purpose—their harmony would draw others to them, while strife and divisions would drive people away.
    ~ Guided by a mindset of humility, not from selfish or conceited ambition. Thinking of others first—their needs, their welfare.

3. Christ's obedience is our **MODEL**.

- Paul then gave these believers the perfect example of the mindset he was calling them to—he shared the attitude of Jesus Christ. (These may be some of the most beautiful verses in the Bible.)

> ★ **TEACHING TIP:**
> *"It is only because he became like us that we can become like him."*
> *— Dietrich Bonhoeffer, The Cost of Discipleship*

☦ **Philippians 2:5–8** "Have this attitude in yourselves which was also in Christ Jesus, who, although He existed in the form of God, did not regard equality with God a thing to be grasped, but emptied Himself, taking the form of a bond-servant, and being made in the likeness of men. Being found in appearance as a man, He humbled Himself by becoming obedient to the point of death, even death on a cross."

- Given the culture, this example was radical because it used the words "bondservant" and "cross."
    ~ The bondservant would be low on any status ladder.
    ~ The most horrible way to die was the cross.
- But Paul stated clearly that Jesus Christ, the Son of God, became a bondservant and He humbled Himself to the point of death on a cross—and He, Jesus Christ, is the example to follow. Period.
- Paul called these believers to pour themselves out for others, for the good of others.
    ~ Paul basically said, "Do not think that it is all about you. It is not."

> ★ **TEACHING TIP:**
> *As you read these verses, remember that the Philippian culture was "status" driven with an emphasis on receiving honors.*

⇨ **Jesus Christ's attitude is to be our attitude—one of humility and obedience.**

PHILIPPIANS
Theme: Believers' Joy in Christ

4. Do all things without <u>GRUMBLING</u>.

<u>Philippians 2:14–15</u>

- Paul returned to the call for unity, which cannot exist when the people are dealing with one another in a testy, argumentative, complaining manner.
- Paul wanted them to understand that grumbling, whether verbally or non-verbally, communicated clearly that Christ's attitude of putting others first was missing.

> ★ **TEACHING TIP:**
> *Think about it: a spirit of humility and a spirit of divisiveness cannot peaceably co-exist!*

****

❋ <u>**ILLUSTRATION:**</u> A woman, Pat, experienced a time in her life when events seemed to present a "tightrope" journey. Her daughter, Cameron, had begun her sophomore year in high school with a sense of excitement and her mother whose health was failing moved in with their family, bringing a sense of uncertainty. Two seasons of life colliding.

By the time Cameron was a senior, her grandmother had a health crisis requiring a tracheostomy, resulting in paralysis—she now needed 24-hour care, 7 days a week. Someone needed to be by the bedside to ensure that the trach never clogged. Pat was resigned to learning the many medical procedures needed to care for her mother; but she was not happy about becoming a "nurse" (just not in her DNA!).

Cameron volunteered to help her mom and said, "Mom, you know I am really excited about this! We are going to learn something different!" Pat thought, "I hope you are going to enjoy this because I am not." Every afternoon, when Cameron arrived home from school, she would put her books down and go into her grandmother's room, "Mom, your turn is done. It is my turn." And Cameron would take over, suction the tracheotomy, and bathe her grandmother.

Cameron's graduation drew near with parties being given for the seniors. Participation was often impacted by a crisis with the grandmother's health. Pat began to feel increasingly heavy-hearted for her daughter because of all that she had "missed" in her senior year.

The day after Cameron's graduation, her grandmother died and went home to be with the Lord. Once more it seemed that a time of joy for Cameron was overshadowed by a time of sorrow for the grandmother. Pat experienced mixed emotions—as a daughter herself, she was sad to have lost her mother, but as a mother she felt guilty that she had deprived her daughter of what should have been a memorable, fun senior year.

PHILIPPIANS
Theme: Believers' Joy in Christ

Cameron headed off to college. One of her first class assignments was to write about the most important event in her life. Cameron wrote about the joy she had received in serving her grandmother in her time of need. She ended the paper with these words, "That time shaped my life and showed me that I wanted to be a nurse. I loved serving my grandmother."

Pat realized how wrong her eyesight had been. Her daughter had not been deprived; rather the Lord had given Cameron a great gift—the blessing that comes from having a servant's attitude, Christ's attitude.

****

5. Hold fast to the <u>WORD</u> of life.

- Instead of grumbling and disputing, Paul exhorted the Philippians to be "holding fast the word of life." (Philippians 2:16)
    - ~ "Hold fast" translates to "hold forth."
    - ~ The "word of life" is the gospel, which is a message that promises life or is "life giving."
- Paul wanted the Philippians to understand that they should be consistently holding out Jesus Christ to a world that needed Him!

> ❖ **APPLICATION:** Grumbling about our circumstances or holding forth the light of God's gospel in them is a daily choice—either hold tight to "self," which will result in a self-centered irritability *or* hold tight to God's Word, which will result in the joy and blessings of a "life giving" witness.

C. Christ is our <u>GOAL</u>: "I have suffered the loss of all things, and count them but rubbish so that I may gain Christ." (Philippians 3)

<u>Philippians 3:7–11</u>

- Paul had been considered a man of stature, one who was very accomplished.
    - ~ As a Pharisee, he would not only have been considered a Jew's Jew but would have been recognized as a highly educated man.
    - ~ He was well-known for being zealous in his Jewish faith.
- Paul, before his encounter with Jesus Christ, had great confidence in himself.
- But he was more than willing—he was enthusiastic—to give all of his accomplishments up for knowing Christ. There was no comparison to Christ.

> ★ **TEACHING TIP:**
> *Think about Paul's words here: to the Philippians he is saying that all of the status and honors he had gained were meaningless in comparison to knowing Jesus Christ!*

PHILIPPIANS
Theme: Believers' Joy in Christ

> **NOTE:** Often as we read Paul's letters, we forget about how much he gave up to follow Christ.
> - He went from a high position in his society to become the lowest—giving up all the privileges that came with being a man at the top.
> - The Jews did not like his messages regarding Jesus, so he was treated as an outcast.
> - Almost every time he entered a town, he was physically beaten, mocked in some way, or thrown in jail.

⇨ **Paul could have had confidence in himself—his position and power—but he gave it all up willingly and put his confidence in Christ!**

1. The believer's goal is to **KNOW** Christ intimately.

- The word "know" that Paul used means to be "fully acquainted with His nature, character, work, and with the salvation that He was worked out."
- Paul explained that there were two aspects of knowing Christ—
    - **The power of His resurrection**: a sustaining hope is found in this powerful truth—because He lives, I will live eternally.
    - **The fellowship of His suffering**: recognizing that when a believer truly identifies with Christ, he will suffer as Christ did—and will see such suffering as an honor.

> ★ **TEACHING TIP:**
> *To know they were redeemed was critical, but Paul exhorted them to know their "Redeemer" up close and personal.*

> ★ **TEACHING TIP:**
> *"Persecution is simply the clash between two irreconcilable value systems." ~ John Stott, Anglican cleric*

> ❖ **APPLICATION:** Knowing Christ intimately—is that your goal?
> - Do you faithfully set aside time to meet with God through prayer, studying, and meditating on His Word?
> - What is your motive? To know Christ better or to mark off a task on your "to do" list?
>
> ⇨ **The purpose of these questions is not to be unkind or harsh—but to have you truly think about your desire to "know" Christ and make changes if this is not your goal.**
> - This is not about "putting time in" a Bible study or prayer group—these are simply ways to the goal of knowing Christ.
>
> ⇨ **Christ is to be our goal—our hope and our identity, even in suffering.**

PHILIPPIANS
Theme: Believers' Joy in Christ

D. Christ is our <u>STRENGTH</u>: "I can do all things through Him who strengthens me." (Philippians 4)

- Paul sat in prison and penned these words—he did not see himself as "weakened" by his circumstances but strengthened by the One who had permitted them.
- Paul gave a prescription for achieving this mindset of total reliance upon the Lord.

1. Christ is the believer's <u>JOY</u>.

<u>Philippians 4:4</u>
- Paul instructed them—"Rejoice in the Lord always."
    - These words were spoken by a man sitting in prison, encouraging people who were free to go as they pleased.
    - His rejoicing was not based on his circumstances, but on the character and promises of His Lord and Savior.

> ★ **TEACHING TIP:**
> *Paul used the word "rejoice" or "joy" over sixteen times. Paul was a man overflowing with joy!*

2. Christ is the believer's <u>PEACE</u>.

<u>Philippians 4:6</u>
- Paul exhorted them: "Be anxious for nothing, pray about everything."
    - Paul was not suggesting that a believer was not to care about worldly matters (such as providing for one's family), but rather there was a confidence in God that freed a believer's mind from anxiety.
    - Paul instructed the people pray about everything.
    - He encouraged them by stating God would respond with His peace—one that would guard their hearts and minds, the very places where anxiety seeks to take root!

> ★ **TEACHING TIP:**
> *"Anxiety does not empty tomorrow of its sorrows, but only empties today of its strength." ~ Charles H. Spurgeon, Pastor*

⇨ **Prayer is the antidote to worry—they cannot co-exist.**

PHILIPPIANS
Theme: Believers' Joy in Christ

> ❖ **APPLICATION:** On a scale of 1–10, how would you rate your anxiety level (with 10 being "off the charts")?
> - ~ If worry, fear, anxiety, and doubt stir like a cyclone in your thoughts and emotions, it is time to get on your knees!
> - ~ There is absolutely nothing that you are presently facing or will face that God will not strengthen you to endure—you must, however, put it in His hands.
> - ~ Paul did not say that God would strengthen us for *some* things—he stated confidently that Christ would strengthen us in ALL things because nothing is too great for our Savior and Lord to handle.
>
> ✝ **Psalms 16:8** "I have set the Lord continually before me;
> Because He is at my right hand, I will not be shaken."

3. Christ is the believer's **SATISFACTION**.

Philippians 4:10–12
- Writing from prison, Paul said he had learned to be content in humble times or times of prosperity.

4. Christ is the believer's **STRENGTH**.

Philippians 4:13
- Paul relied on Christ to strengthen him whenever, wherever, and however.
- Paul's strength to endure and experience joy and peace in his dire circumstances came through the power of His Lord.
- Paul clearly did not view himself as a "victim" of his circumstances—he always and only saw "victory" in Jesus Christ in all matters of life.

> ★ **TEACHING TIP:**
> *"O satisfy us in the morning with Your lovingkindness, that we may sing for joy and be glad all our days."*
> *(Psalms 90:14)*

FINAL THOUGHTS AND APPLICATION

****

❋ **ILLUSTRATION:** A young pastor found a website that amazed him with its promises. It claimed that it could tell a person the exact date and time he or she would die. The site requested specific information, such as age, health, happiness level, etc., to assist them in determining a person's lifespan. The pastor was intrigued and responded to the questions. The website informed him that he would die on April 14, 2064 at 4:00 p.m.

The pastor knew that the length of his days had already been determined by God Himself (Psalms 139:16)—something no computer software could ever do. He decided, however,

PHILIPPIANS
Theme: Believers' Joy in Christ

to mark this date on his calendar. Why? As a reminder and motivator to not waste his time—not one minute, one hour, one day. He wanted Christ to be his goal in all the time the Lord gave him.

****

- Though short in length, Philippians is a powerful book focusing on what matters most—Jesus Christ.
    - **He is our life**: "To live is Christ…"(Philippians 1:21)
        - Jesus should be first in every aspect of our life.

    - **He is our attitude**: "Have this attitude in yourselves which was also in Christ Jesus…" (Philippians 2:5–8)
        - Our thoughts, decisions, and actions should model our Lord and Savior.

    - **He is our goal**: "I have suffered the loss of all things, and count them but rubbish so that I may gain Christ…" (Philippians 3:8)
        - Nothing is more important or precious than knowing Christ —no achievement, possession, or position.

    - **He is our strength**: "I can do all things through Him who strengthens me…" (Philippians 4:13)
        - We can be confident that the Lord will use any and all situations in life to grow us up and glorify Himself—He will fortify us to endure.

- ❖ **FINAL APPLICATION: Let Christ be your greatest joy regardless of your circumstances.**

PHILIPPIANS REVIEW HELPS AND ANSWERS

✧ **Have the students write the names of the books we have studied so far in the New Testament (Five New Testament History books and five of Paul's Letters to the Churches).**

- Put the books in order.
- By each name, write the theme of the book.
- Do not work as a team—this is an "individual" challenge!

✧ **Answers are below.**

....

1. **Matthew:** *Jesus is King of the Jews*

2. **Mark:** *Jesus is the Suffering Servant*

3. **Luke:** *Jesus is the Perfect Man*

4. **John:** *Jesus is the Son of God*

5. **Acts:** *The Birth of the Church*

6. **Romans:** *God's Righteousness Described*

7. **First Corinthians:** *Church's Problems Corrected*

8. **Second Corinthians:** *Paul's Ministry Defended*

9. **Galatians:** *Believers' Freedom in Christ*

10. **Ephesians:** *Believers' Holy Walk*

PHILIPPIANS

COLOSSIANS

Believers' Completion in Christ

For in Him all the fullness of Deity dwells in bodily form.

Colossians 2:9

SESSION FIFTY-ONE: COLOSSIANS
Believers' Completion in Christ

☦ **Memory verse:** *"For in Him all the fullness of Deity dwells in bodily form."* (Colossians 2:9)

Introduction: In the book of Colossians, Paul, writing from prison, brilliantly defends the supremacy of Christ as the image of the invisible God, the firstborn of all creation, and the creator of all things. Some Judaizers were confusing the Colossians, adding some of their legalistic laws. Others encouraged the worship of angels and the practice of asceticism, which stemmed from the belief that the body was evil. Paul exalts Christ and His teachings over all these false teachings and goes on to encourage the Colossians that they had an exalted calling.

- **Oral Review:** Please refer to the **REVIEW Section** in the following Teaching Guide Outline.

- **Homework:** Review the homework from the book of Philippians.

    Question at the bottom of page 153
    Questions on page 154
    Question at the top of page 159
    Top two questions on page 163
    Additional Question: What robs you of joy and makes you discontent?

- **Review Helps:** Written review is provided at the end of the teacher presentation. (Optional and time permitting.)

- **Teacher Presentation on the Book of Colossians**

- **Learning for Life:** You may choose to discuss all or just one or two of the questions on page 176.

- **Closing prayer:** Pray that the students would grow in their knowledge of and love for Jesus Christ as the Perfect Man and as God Who is Lord of all.

COLOSSIANS
Theme: Believers' Completion in Christ

OUTLINE AID FOR TEACHERS:

I. **CHRIST'S SUPREMACY WAS PROVEN THROUGH HIS PERSON AND WORK (COLOSSIANS 1:1–23)**

- **Colossians 1:3–8**
    A. Paul greeted the Colossian believers first with words of PRAISE.
- **Colossians 1:9–12**
    B. Paul revealed the PRAYER he and coworkers in Rome had prayed for them.
    C. Paul revealed Christ's CHARACTER.
- **Colossians 1:15–22**
    1. He is the visible IMAGE of the invisible God.
    2. He is the FIRSTBORN of all creation.
    3. All things were CREATED by Christ and for Christ.
    4. He is BEFORE all things and because of Him all things HOLD together.
    5. He is the HEAD of the church (body).
    6. He is the beginning, the firstborn of the DEAD.
    7. He is to have first place in EVERYTHING.
    8. The full ESSENCE of God dwells in Him.
    9. He RECONCILES all things to Himself through His death.
    10. His DEATH made them holy, blameless, and presentable to God.

II. **CHRIST'S SUPREMACY WAS WITNESSED THROUGH HIS CHURCH (COLOSSIANS 1:24–2:7)**

- **Colossians 1:24–29**
    A. Paul's purpose was to reveal the MYSTERY hidden for ages.
    B. Paul wanted the Colossians to understand that faith in Christ makes all believers FAMILY.
- **Colossians 2:2c-5**
    C. True wisdom and knowledge would prevent their being led astray by false teaching and persuasive ARGUMENTS.

COLOSSIANS
Theme: Believers' Completion in Christ

- **Colossians 2:6–7**
  D. Paul wanted the Colossians, having begun in Christ and now growing in Him, to <u>WALK</u> accordingly.

III. **CHRIST'S SUPREMACY WAS REVEALED THROUGH RELIGIOUS TEACHINGS (COLOSSIANS 2:8–23)**

  A. Paul warned of being enslaved to worldly <u>PHILOSOPHIES</u> and empty deceptions.

  B. Christ's teaching is superior to:

- **Colossians 2:8–23**
  1. <u>LEGALISM</u>, which is being enslaved to the law.
  2. Mystic insights and the worship of <u>ANGELS</u>.
  3. <u>ASCETICISM</u>, which is self-neglect, self-denial, and self-abuse for religious purposes.

IV. **CHRIST'S SUPREMACY WAS REVEALED THROUGH PRACTICAL EXPERIENCE (COLOSSIANS 3–4)**

- **Colossians 3:1–4**
  A. Believers were to set their minds on things <u>ABOVE</u>, not things on earth.

- **Colossians 3:5–17**
  B. Believers were <u>DEAD</u> to certain accepted worldly actions.

- **Colossians 3:18–4:1**
  C. Behavior within the <u>FAMILY</u> and between masters and slaves is God's plan.

- **Colossians 4:2–4**
  D. Believers were encouraged to devote themselves to <u>PRAYER</u>.

- **Colossians 4:5–6**
  E. Instructions for being a Christian <u>WITNESS</u> were given.

- **Colossians 4:18**
  F. Paul ended with a request to be <u>REMEMBERED</u>.

Colossians
[Believers' Completion in Christ]

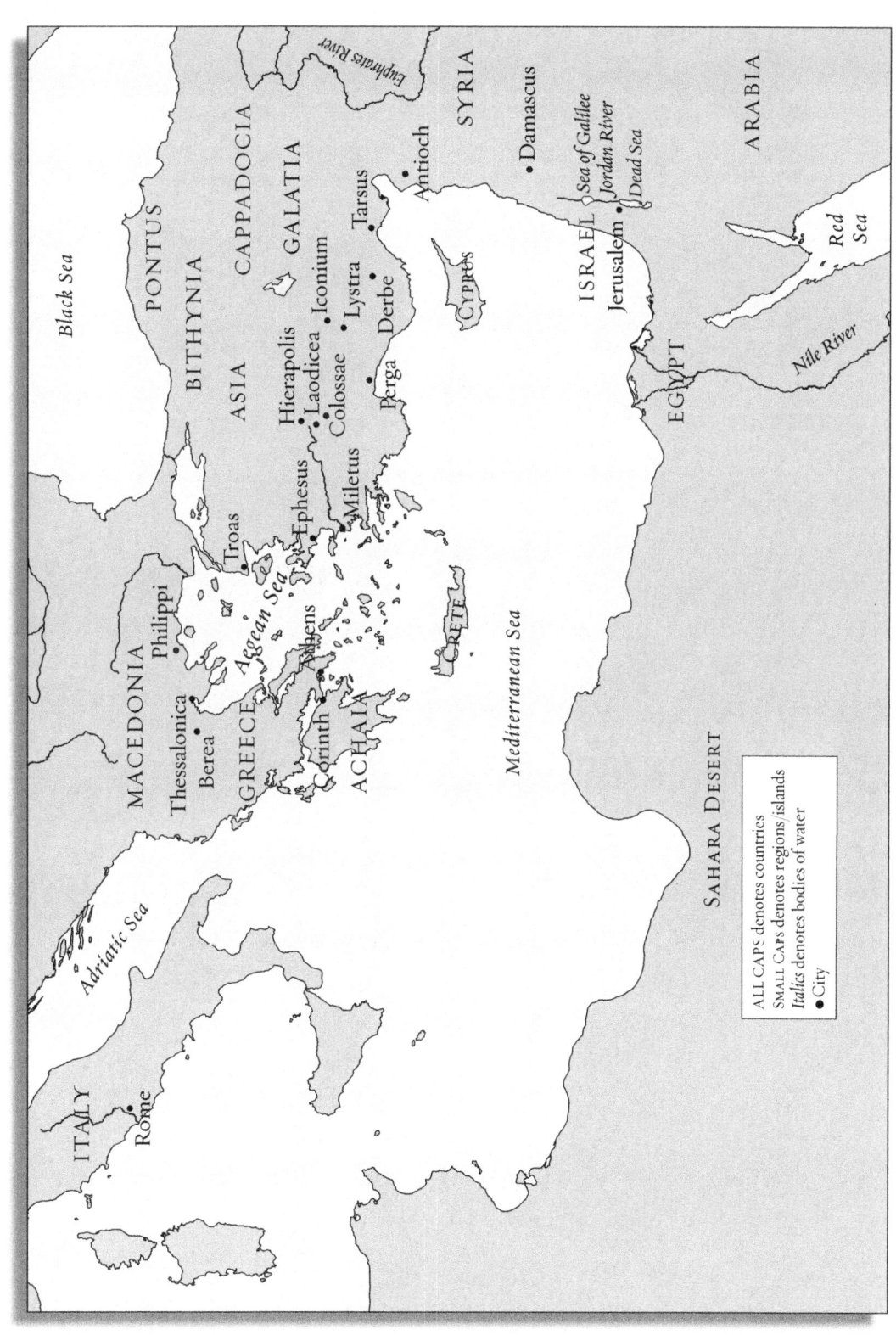

COLOSSIANS

COLOSSIANS
Theme: Believers' Completion in Christ

THE BASICS:
⇨ **Who: The Author:** Paul
      Main Characters: Believers in Colossae
⇨ **What:** A letter to correct false teaching in Colossae
⇨ **When:** Written in A.D. 60–61
⇨ **Where:** Written to Colossae from a Roman prison
⇨ **Why:** To respond to concerns shared by Epaphras, the pastor of the church in Colossae, who visited Paul in Rome and informed him that heresy was being taught in the church

MEMORY VERSE: *"For in Him all the fullness of Deity dwells in bodily form." Colossians 2:9*

****

REVIEW:
- The *Old Testament History* books:
  - Shared the problem of disobedience (sin) and its consequences (judgment and death).
  - The prophets foretold of judgment and the Messiah to come.
- The *New Testament History* books:
  - Showed that the Messiah had come.
  - The church was born.
- In *Paul's Letters to the Churches*:
  - **Romans:** Focused on the righteousness of God and how man could become righteous.
  - **First Corinthians:** Dealt with sin in the church and how it was to be addressed.
  - **Second Corinthians:** Defended his ministry and authority as an apostle.
  - **Galatians:** Confronted false teaching and warned the believers' to remember that they were free in Christ.
  - **Ephesians:** Taught doctrine, giving practical application.
  - **Philippians:** Thanked the people for their continued support and encouragement. Also stressed the centrality of Christ around whom all of life and death revolves.

OVERVIEW:
- Colossians was written about 61 A.D. from Rome— around the same time that Paul wrote the book of Ephesians.
- The city was located about 100 miles east of Ephesus. (Refer to map in the workbook.)
- It was also a Roman colony and an active commercial center due to its location on a busy trade route.
- The Colossians produced a beautiful dark red wool cloth (*colossinum*) for which they became famous.

COLOSSIANS
Theme: Believers' Completion in Christ

- However, as its neighboring cities, Laodicea and Hierapolis, increased in importance, Colossae declined.
- Paul never physically visited Colossae; he never directly met the people to whom he penned this letter. He had just heard about them from those who had been active in this early church.

****

✺ **ILLUSTRATION:** Have you ever ruined something that was perfectly good until you decided to "add" to it? As an example, you taste a dish that has been cooking on the stove—it tastes pretty good, but you decide it needs a "little" salt and, before you know it, it is inedible! Another example: you have sat down to a wonderful meal, eaten, and are completely satisfied—and then you decide to have "one more" helping and you become sick to your stomach! Often we can find ourselves in trouble just because we decided to add something that we did not need.

****

- Paul faced such a situation within the church at Colossae—there was danger that some heresy could infiltrate the church.
    - ~ Heresy involves deviating from the truth, God's Word.
    - ~ In the case of the Colossian church, there were several different groups involved, but the end result was a teaching that combined Jewish tradition, Greek philosophy and speculation, and oriental mysticism.
    - ~ The church needed to be warned of what was being "added."

> ★ **TEACHING TIP:**
> *Sounds very similar to what is going on today in many churches.*

- Paul received this news from one of his converts, Epaphras, who visited him in prison.
    - ~ Epaphras had sat under Paul's teaching in Ephesus.
    - ~ He went to Colossae and apparently started a church there.
- Paul took the opportunity to write the Colossians and state firmly that Christ was supreme over all—His Word was above and over any teaching that they were attempting to add.
- He also wanted the believers in this church to understand the practical application of submitting to the supremacy of Christ.

> **NOTE:** Not long after this letter was written, Laodicea, Hierapolis, and Colossae were destroyed by an earthquake. Colossae did recover, but many died. Given that historical context, this letter becomes all the more poignant as a reminder that we do not know what tomorrow may bring, but we do know Who holds all of our tomorrows.

COLOSSIANS
Theme: Believers' Completion in Christ

⇨ **The purpose of Colossians was to communicate the supremacy of Jesus Christ—that believers are "complete" in Him.**

I. CHRIST'S SUPREMACY WAS PROVEN THROUGH HIS PERSON AND WORK (COLOSSIANS 1:1–23)

A. Paul greeted the Colossian believers first with words of <u>PRAISE</u>.

- The greeting comes from Paul and Timothy.

Colossians 1:3–8
- Paul lays out the reasons for his praise of this church:
  ~ Their faith
  ~ Their love of one another
  ~ They are fruit-bearing—bringing others into the kingdom

> ★ **TEACHING TIP:**
> *Paul demonstrates an excellent communication style—he emphasized what these people were doing right before he addressed and corrected where they were going wrong.*

B. Paul revealed the <u>PRAYER</u> he and coworkers in Rome had prayed for them.

Colossians 1:9–12
- Paul's praise for these believers was followed by his unceasing prayers for them.

✝ **Colossians 1:9–12** "For this reason also, since the day we heard of it, we have not ceased to pray for you and to ask that you may be filled with the knowledge of His will in all spiritual wisdom and understanding, so that you will walk in a manner worthy of the Lord, to please Him in all respects, bearing fruit in every good work and increasing in the knowledge of God; strengthened with all power, according to His glorious might, for the attaining of all steadfastness and patience; joyously giving thanks to the Father, who has qualified us to share in the inheritance of the saints in Light."

- He prayed specifically for them:
  1. That they be filled with the knowledge of God's will in all spiritual wisdom and understanding.
     * Paul wanted them to know and understand God's will to the point of applying it.
     * This would be possible through the supernatural help of the Holy Spirit.
  2. That they would walk in a manner worthy of the Lord.
     * With a desire to please Him in all respects.
     * To bear fruit in every good work.
     * To increase in the knowledge of Him.

COLOSSIANS
Theme: Believers' Completion in Christ

3. That they would be strengthened with all power.
   * According to God's glorious power—not "humanly" generated.
   * Attaining steadfastness and patience with joyful thanksgiving to the Father—having an ability to stand firmly under trials with a "shining, not whining" mindset.

> ❖ **APPLICATION:** This passage in Colossians is one of the most precious prayers in all of Scripture.
> ~ Often our own prayers are just generic: *"Lord, please bless (fill in the blank)"* or *"Lord, please be with (fill in the blank)."* God has blessed them and is with them! We need to mature in how we pray for others.
> ~ Encourage your students to pray through this verse and put in their names, then the names of those they care about—this is how to pray "personally" through God's Word.

C. Paul revealed Christ's **CHARACTER**.

Colossians 1:15

1. He is the visible **IMAGE** of the invisible God.

- We often hear people say, "Why doesn't God show Himself? Why can't we see Him?"
- The word "image" here means "exact likeness and perfect Representative."
- Paul wanted the Colossians to fully understand that God did show Himself in Jesus—the visible of the invisible!

☦ **John 14:9b** "... He who has seen Me has seen the Father ..."

2. He is the **FIRSTBORN** of all creation.

- The word "firstborn" speaks to status—it is *not* a reference to place or time.

- Paul spoke to Jesus' superiority over all of creation.

★ **TEACHING TIP:**
The term "firstborn" is similar to our referring to the President's wife as the "First" Lady. She is not the first "First" Lady. This title speaks to her status or position.

Colossians 1:16

3. All things were **CREATED** by Christ and for Christ.

- Christ is both the source and the agent of creation.
- We found Christ in the book of Genesis as creation took place.

COLOSSIANS
Theme: Believers' Completion in Christ

Colossians 1:17

4. He is BEFORE all things and because of Him all things HOLD together.

- His power causes the earth's axis to rotate.
- His power causes the stars to come out at night.
- His power holds the sun, moon, and solar system in place.

> ★ **TEACHING TIP:**
> This should give us a new appreciation for something we all take for granted—gravity!

✝ **Matthew 28:18** "And Jesus came up and spoke to them, saying, 'All authority has been given to Me in heaven and on earth.'"

Colossians 1:18

5. He is the HEAD of the church (body).

- When Paul wrote the Ephesians, he emphasized that there was only <u>one</u> body of Christ—believers.
- Here in Colossians, Paul wanted to underscore that Christ was the head of the church, the body of believers.
- Jesus, alone, has the power and authority over the church—He is the final word in the church.

6. He is the beginning, the firstborn of the DEAD.

> **NOTE:** This may cause some confusion in your class because Lazarus may come immediately to mind.
> - Jesus was not the first one to rise from the dead—He raised not only Lazarus, but others, from the dead.
> - It is important to understand that the people who were raised from the dead in Scripture died again.

- Jesus was the first who rose from the dead to immortality—He rose to die no more.

7. He is to have first place in EVERYTHING.

- Paul was telling the Colossians that Jesus was "supreme."
- To be supreme means:
  ~ To hold the highest rank or authority.
  ~ To be sovereign.
  ~ To be the greatest, the utmost, the ultimate.

COLOSSIANS
Theme: Believers' Completion in Christ

⇨ **When a person goes to Jesus, he goes to the top—there is no higher authority!**

- Paul's point to the Colossians was that Jesus was to hold "first place" in all aspects of their lives

Colossians 1:19

8. The full ESSENCE of God dwells in Him.

- Paul stressed that Jesus was fully man and fully God—Jesus was and is God.
- This was the very reason Jesus was to take precedence over everything.
- Paul made this point twice. Look at Colossians 1:19 and Colossians 2:9:

✝ **Colossians 1:19** "For it was the Father's good pleasure for all the fullness to dwell in Him, …"

✝ **Colossians 2:9** "For in Him all the fullness of Deity dwells in bodily form, …"

- Though we may not be able to fully understand this, it does not change the truth—Jesus and God are one.

Colossians 1:20–21

9. He RECONCILES all things to Himself through His death.

- Paul reminded the Colossians that it was Christ's death that enabled them to get right with God—He was the remedy for their estrangement.
- Paul recapped who they once were before Christ:
  ~ Alienated from God, enemies of God.
  ~ Hostile in mind, deliberate enmity against God.
  ~ Engaged in evil deeds; sin was acted out publicly.
- As we learned in the book of Genesis, this estrangement began in the Garden of Eden when Adam and Eve sinned—impacting all mankind.
  ~ The only way to God was through His requirement of a blood sacrifice.
  ~ So the Jewish people constantly offered up sacrificial lambs to "cover" their sin.
- Paul wanted these believers to remember the huge gulf that separated them from God.
- The word "reconcile" means to "change, exchange." In this context, because of Christ's sacrifice on their behalf, there was a great exchange—from enmity with God to a restored, reunited relationship.

> ★ **TEACHING TIP:**
> *It is important to take a moment and remember that Paul is speaking to us as well in this passage.*

****

✷ **ILLUSTRATION:** There was young woman who wrote poetry and was very successful in having her work published. A young man read her work and was so drawn to it that he

COLOSSIANS
Theme: Believers' Completion in Christ

wanted to meet the author. He found a way to meet her. They discovered that they held a lot in common and fell in love. The young woman was Elizabeth Barrett and the young man was Robert Browning.

Elizabeth's father was not happy with this relationship. She went to him to share her intention to marry Robert. Her father said, "If you do, you will be disinherited. I will disown you." Elizabeth married Robert and her father was true to his word.

For ten years, Elizabeth grieved over her broken relationship with her father. She wrote him every week and begged for reconciliation—her desire was to make things right between them. One day, she received a package from her father. It contained all of her letters—unopened. He had never read one of them but instead sent them back. They were never reconciled.

****

> ❖ **APPLICATION:** We have been sent a love letter. The love letter is Jesus Christ.
> - ~ Jesus is the only way that we can be reconciled to God—the only way to approach God.
> - ~ It has been said that with two boards and three nails Jesus built a bridge.
> - ~ The cross of Christ bridged the gulf—made the way to God.

Colossians 1:22

10. His <u>DEATH</u> made them holy, blameless, and presentable to God.

- How did this happen?
  - ~ God required blood to cover sin.
  - ~ Christ's blood covers our sin.
- When God looks down at us, He does not see us and our sin, He sees the blood of Jesus and our sins are forgiven.
- Paul wanted the believers to understand this—it was just as if they had never sinned. They had been "justified" by Christ's work on the cross.
- Paul presented the incredible hope that believers have in Jesus Christ.

- In this teaching, Paul set forth with clarity that Jesus Christ is God—He is in charge and over all creation.

> ★ **TEACHING TIP:**
> *To be "justified" is to be set free from the penalty of sin, separation from God, and death.*

COLOSSIANS
Theme: Believers' Completion in Christ

II. CHRIST'S SUPREMACY WAS WITNESSED THROUGH HIS CHURCH (COLOSSIANS 1:24–2:7)

A. Paul's purpose was to reveal the <u>MYSTERY</u> hidden for ages.

<u>Colossians 1:24–29</u>
- What is the mystery hidden for ages and for generations? It is the church.
  - The church that includes everyone—not exclusively the Jewish people.
  - The church that includes Jew and Gentile, slave and free.

> **NOTE:** This may not be a radical thought as we study this passage of Scripture today, but it was drastically different from what the Jews had anticipated regarding the Messiah.
> - The Jews believed that the Messiah was coming—they were looking for him. Jesus was not the Messiah, however, they had expected.
>   - They thought the Messiah would be solely for them.
>   - They thought He would come as a mighty warrior removing the Roman oppression.
>   - The Jews most certainly did not think the Messiah would associate with sinners or constantly rebuke their own religious leadership as being hypocrites.
> - The Jews rejected the Messiah and put Him on a cross. After that, the mystery of the church was revealed: everyone was now welcome.

B. Paul wanted the Colossians to understand that faith in Christ makes all believers <u>FAMILY</u>.

- They were a family bound together in love.
- They did not know Paul personally—he had never been to their church, but Paul wanted them to grasp that they were family In Christ.

> ★ **TEACHING TIP:**
> Unity in Christ far outweighs any diversity of ethnicity, language, culture, etc. As believers, we are one in Christ —a family.

****

❋ <u>**ILLUSTRATION:**</u> Have you ever moved from your hometown to a new city or country? Often, it is as if a spotlight shines down upon how different you are in your "new" surroundings, beginning with your accent—whether Southern, Northern, British, French, Spanish, etc. But, as a believer, the moment you become connected in a Bible study or church, you "belong" as a brother or sister in Christ because you are, indeed, a member of

COLOSSIANS
Theme: Believers' Completion in Christ

God's family! Yes, it may take some time to understand each other's inflections or pronunciations, but it doesn't matter. That is what Paul was trying to show the Colossians.

****

C. True wisdom and knowledge would prevent their being led astray by false teaching and persuasive <u>ARGUMENTS</u>.

<u>Colossians 2:2c–5</u>
- The Colossians had practical truth (wisdom) and doctrinal truth (understanding) through the Word of God—there was no need for anything else … period.
- But they were being enticed into persuasive arguments in which those who they debated offered "plausible, enticing" words that "sounded" wise.

> ★ **TEACHING TIP:**
> *There were people in their midst trying to deceive them, leading them <u>away</u> from the truth. This is happening today, isn't it?*

⇨ **Paul wanted these believers to be on the alert and prepared—the gospel was their foundation. Any and all teaching must "plumb" to it or must be ignored.**

D. Paul wanted the Colossians, having begun in Christ and now growing in Him, to <u>WALK</u> accordingly.

<u>Colossians 2:6–7</u>
- Paul basically said, "You have the roots to grow. You have the foundation necessary to grow. It's the gospel. It is time to grow up and act like it—walk your talk!"

> **NOTE:** In his commentary on this passage, Warren Wiersbe states it this way: *"As you were saved by faith, so walk by faith. As you were saved by the Word, so walk according to the Word. As you were saved through the work of the Spirit, so walk in the Spirit. The Christian life continues as it began, by faith in God."* (Wiersbe's Expository Outlines (NT))

III. CHRIST'S SUPREMACY WAS REVEALED THROUGH RELIGIOUS TEACHINGS (COLOSSIANS 2:8–23)

- Paul continued his warning of the false teaching that had become prevalent because he understood that it was not only deceptive, but destructive, to those who would listen to it.

COLOSSIANS
Theme: Believers' Completion in Christ

- ~ The Colossians were being told, in effect, that they needed "something more" than what the gospel presented.

> ★ **TEACHING TIP:**
> *False teachers often use biblical words but do not use God's definition for those words! We need to heed Paul's warning today.*

- Paul wanted these believers to fully understand who they were in Christ—*they were complete in Him, in need of nothing else.*

✝ **Colossians 2:10a** "… and in Him you have been made complete, …"
  - ~ Believers in Christ need NOTHING MORE for salvation—it is found in Christ alone.
  - ~ A believer's justification (set free from the penalty of sin), a believer's sanctification (set free from the power of sin), and a believer's glorification (one day to be set free from the presence of sin) come only through Christ and His work on the cross.

A. Paul warned of being enslaved to worldly <u>PHILOSOPHIES</u> and empty deceptions.

- The church had been infiltrated with teachers who mixed oriental mysticism with Greek philosophy and Jewish tradition into the gospel message. Paul was warning them that this was all false teaching.
- In effect, the Colossian church was being corrupted by heresy—the world's "view" of truth—and this was all very dangerous for this church.
- Paul wanted these believers to know the truth for themselves so that they could immediately detect anything false—and recognize that Satan was behind all false teaching.

B. Christ's teaching is superior to:

1. <u>LEGALISM</u>, which is being enslaved to the law.

<u>Colossians 2:8–17</u>
- What were some trying to add to the gospel?
  - ~ Strict adherence to the Jewish law, including circumcision.
  - ~ Recognition of various Jewish sacrifices, feasts, and Sabbath days.
- The message was clear: "You can have Jesus, BUT you have to do all these things, too."
- The Old Testament is full of sacrifices, rites, and traditions, but they were all mere shadows of what was to come—God's perfect plan was Jesus.

✝ **Colossians 2:11–14** "… and in Him you were also circumcised with a circumcision made without hands, in the removal of the body of the flesh by the circumcision of Christ; having

COLOSSIANS
Theme: Believers' Completion in Christ

been buried with Him in baptism, in which you were also raised up with Him through faith in the working of God, who raised Him from the dead. When you were dead in your transgressions and the uncircumcision of your flesh, He made you alive together with Him, having forgiven us all our transgressions, having canceled out the certificate of debt consisting of decrees against us, which was hostile to us; and He has taken it out of the way, having nailed it to the cross."

2. Mystic insights and the worship of ANGELS.

<u>Colossians 2:18–19</u>
- These false teachers were claiming to have had incredible visions, but Paul knew these were "tall tales" in an attempt to gain attention. Paul told the people that they were being "defrauded" by these claims.
- Paul told them to stop worshipping angels—Christ alone was to be worshipped.

> **NOTE:** Angels are a big business industry today:
> - There are entire stores and departments in stores dedicated to angels (some are dedicated to teaching about angels and worshiping them).
> - There are books on angels that have been on the bestseller list.
> - There have been television series' about angels—even fallen angels have been developed as almost sympathetic creatures.
>
> ⇨ **To worship angels is, however, heresy!**

3. ASCETICISM, which is self-neglect, self-denial, and self-abuse for religious purposes.

<u>Colossians 2:23</u>
- The false teachers had introduced a "worship lifestyle" that included neglecting the body when Jesus had clearly taught believers to care for their bodies.
- The concept of this false teaching was to produce humility by, in a sense, punishing oneself.
  - ~ Being conceived by men, the real result was just an "appearance of humility."
  - ~ True, authentic humility is "lived out" in and through Jesus Christ.

> ★ **TEACHING TIP:**
> *Before he came to know Christ, Martin Luther continually punished himself in an attempt to make himself worthy. Instead, he stayed in a state of depression—apart from Christ, man cannot be worthy!*

COLOSSIANS
Theme: Believers' Completion in Christ

⇨ **The basis of Christianity: Christ's work on the cross + nothing.**
  ~ Satan, as the father of all lies, will try his best to deceive us by thinking that man must "do" something more than simply believe in the basic truth of the gospel.

IV. CHRIST'S SUPREMACY WAS REVEALED THROUGH PRACTICAL EXPERIENCE (COLOSSIANS 3-4)

A. Believers were to set their minds on things <u>ABOVE</u>, not things on earth.

<u>Colossians 3:1-4</u>
- Paul wanted the Colossians to reset their focus: upward NOT downward or sideways.
  ~ When we look above to Jesus, we look at things we can know are permanent.
  ~ When we look around us, we look at a temporary situation.

⇨ **It is critical that believers remember: Who they belong to, Who they represent, where their true home is.**

B. Believers were <u>DEAD</u> to certain accepted worldly actions.

<u>Colossians 3:5-9</u>
- The meaning behind being "dead" is "to not indulge sin," but to make a "corpse of those desires."
  ~ A good visual is how we handle weeds in our gardens or yards—we actively destroy them so they will not spread.
- People have a bent towards sinning, but the desire to sin changes when a person becomes a Christian.
  ~ A believer's heart is more attuned to what Christ wants for him or her.
- Paul gives some specifics regarding what a believer once did and is to stop doing:

> ★ **TEACHING TIP:**
> *The Greek, Roman, and oriental religions did not say much or anything about personal holiness.*

  ~ Immorality   ~ Greed   ~ Malice
  ~ Impurity   ~ Idolatry   ~ Slander
  ~ Passion   ~ Anger   ~ Abusive Speech
  ~ Evil Desire   ~ Wrath   ~ Lying to Others

- Paul is basically saying: "Don't live your old life—you have a new life to live!"
  ~ We have learned that when a person comes to Christ, he or she becomes a new creature.

COLOSSIANS
Theme: Believers' Completion in Christ

Colossians 3:10–17
- How is it possible to refrain from these deeply imbedded actions, such as envy?
  - Lay aside the "old self"—take off the old, selfish, untruthful life (its thoughts and actions), which is inconsistent to the call of Jesus Christ.
  - Put on the "new self," which is renewed to the true knowledge of Jesus Christ.

> **NOTE:** A good visual for this is how we physically dress ourselves.
> - When we purchase a brand new outfit, we do not put it on and wear it over an old one.
> - We take the old outfit off, and then put on the new one.

⇨ **Christ is now your life—your daily lifestyle choices and actions should now reflect Him.**

- Paul summed up the new life a believer was to live: *"Whatever you do in word or deed, do all in the name of the Lord Jesus, giving thanks through Him to God the Father." (Colossians 3:17)*

C. Behavior within the <u>FAMILY</u> and between masters and slaves is God's plan.

- Following his instruction regarding *whatever they said or did* should be done in a way that glorified the Lord, Paul turned to how they were to conduct themselves in their families and the workplace. How they interacted in these relationships should also glorify God.

Colossians 3:18–21
- As we study these verses, we recognize immediately that they run counter-cultural to what is promoted in the world today. Such words as "submission" and "obey" are viewed as weak—but not in God's economy in which believers should live.

> ★ **TEACHING TIP:**
> *There will be some in your class who will bristle at these instructions.*

✝ **Colossians 3:18** "Wives, be subject to your husbands, as is fitting in the Lord."
  - God has placed the husband as the authority in the family—husbands did not create this role for themselves.
  - A wife's submission to her husband is expressed through respecting the position that God has placed him in and following his leadership.
  - Note: Paul put this in its proper perspective—*"as is fitting in the Lord"*—this is really about being obedient to Jesus Christ, our Lord.

COLOSSIANS
Theme: Believers' Completion in Christ

- ✝ **Colossians 3:19** "Husbands, love your wives and do not be embittered against them."
  - This is not a "Hollywood" screen scene of love! This is "agape" love.
  - The word "love" here calls for a sacrificial love, putting someone and their needs above oneself, giving them priority in your life.
  - The phrase "do not be embittered against them" is, in fact, the opposite of the love God calls the husband to show. Bitterness, unkindness, and mistreatment of any sort should not be exhibited by the husband.
  - Paul is basically calling the husband to consistently display a loving tenderness toward his wife.

> ★ **TEACHING TIP:**
> *Husbands, are you kinder, more polite and loving to others outside your home than you are to your own wife? If so, she is not the problem—your obedience to God is.*

- ✝ **Colossians 3:20-21** "Children, be obedient to your parents in all things, for this is well-pleasing to the Lord. Fathers, do not exasperate your children, so that they will not lose heart."
  - Once again, we see that Paul explained the "why" of this instruction—*"it is well-pleasing to the Lord."*
  - When Christian children rebel against their parents, they are, in essence, rebelling against Jesus.
  - On the other hand, fathers must be diligent to not be a continual "fault-finding" parent.
    - ~ Fathers are not to discourage their children to the point that they break their spirit—leading a child to believe that he or she will never be able to please them.
    - ~ This is not instructing fathers to give "fake" flattery, but to praise a child's achievements and/or efforts.

****

- ❋ **ILLUSTRATION:** There was a young woman who simply adored her father and wanted to please him in all that she did. He was a good man and he loved his daughter. However, he had the tendency to compliment her in this way, "What a good job … *but* you could have or should have …" As an adult, this woman still waits for a "but" to follow any compliment given to her—she expects that whatever she does will somehow not be quite good enough.

****

- ⇨ **This is all about our relationship to Jesus—whether as a wife, husband, child, or father.**

Colossians 3:22–4:1
  - For us today, this passage would apply to employer-employee relationships.

COLOSSIANS
Theme: Believers' Completion in Christ

- Slaves (employees) were taught to obey their masters with sincerity.
  - ~ This was a call to work with an authentic single-focus: to please God in one's labor—not merely being a man-pleaser.
- Masters (employers) were instructed to treat their slaves (employees) justly and equally.
  - ~ This was a call to give those who worked for them what they ought to have, what was their fair due.
- Paul summed up how believers were to conduct themselves in the workplace: *"Whatever you do, do your work heartily, as for the Lord rather than for men, knowing that from the Lord you will receive the reward of the inheritance. It is the Lord Christ whom you serve." (Colossians 3:23-24)*

> ★ **TEACHING TIP:**
> *It has been said that Christians are the only Bible some people may ever read. What are they learning about Jesus from your life?*

> ❖ **APPLICATION:** Can you imagine how radical it would be if we would apply Colossians 3:17, 23, and 24 to our daily lives?
> - ~ Laundry, yardwork, cooking, and parenting could take on a whole new "light" *and* "lightness."
> - ~ Attitudes toward parents, employers, and employees could all be transformed.
>
> ⇨ **Consider the questions that such living would compel others to ask, giving us an opportunity to share Jesus as the basis of our "different approach" toward our spouse, child, parent, employer, or employee.**

D. Believers were encouraged to devote themselves to **PRAYER**.

Colossians 4:2-4

- Paul called the believers to pray not only for themselves, but for others who were serving the Lord—for opportunities and clarity of words.
- And Paul instructed them to pray with an attitude of thanksgiving.

> ★ **TEACHING TIP:**
> *Prayer makes a difference! The diligent prayers of others (many of you reading this) undergirded the writing and completion of The Amazing Collection and the Teaching Guides. Thank you for praying for the Big Dream team!*

COLOSSIANS
Theme: Believers' Completion in Christ

E. Instructions for being a Christian WITNESS were given.

✝ **Colossians 4:5–6** "Conduct yourselves with wisdom toward outsiders, making the most of the opportunity. Let your speech always be with grace, as though seasoned with salt, so that you will know how you should respond to each person."

- Paul called these believers at Colossae to be good witnesses to strangers.
- He wanted them to understand that people who did not know the Lord were looking at them. What did those unbelievers see and hear?

⇨ **Paul's point: every interaction a believer has with others may be an opportunity to share the reality of Jesus Christ. A Christian's talk and walk matter!**

F. Paul ended with a request to be REMEMBERED.

Colossians 4:18
- Paul asked them to remember him in prison—he wanted and needed their prayers.

> ❖ **APPLICATION:** We need to be interceding for people that are in hard places—people that are in bondage are on battlefields. Perhaps, not literally, but there are many things in the world that can enslave someone and there are most certainly battlefields of life that we all face. We need to be lifting each other up in prayer, just as Paul requested.

FINAL THOUGHTS AND APPLICATION

- We are not much different from the people in Colossae as we look at the culture in which we live.
- Heresy is everywhere—even within the church, there are still some adding to the gospel.

⇨ **Danger is everywhere for the believer in Jesus Christ—but the danger today is not so much the adding *to* the gospel, as it is the subtracting *from* the gospel.**
  - In Colossae, the formula was: Jesus *plus* other requirements.
  - Today, the formula is: Christianity *minus* Jesus Christ.
- There is no Christianity without Christ—Jesus Christ is not one among many—He is superior to all.

⇨ **Paul warns us: Do not "add to" or "subtract from" Jesus Christ. Why? He is perfect.**

❖ **FINAL APPLICATION: We are to know who Christ is by knowing His Word. This will prevent us from being persuaded by false doctrine or arguments to the contrary and will enable us to walk in a way that is worthy of Him.**

COLOSSIANS REVIEW HELPS AND ANSWERS

✧ Put the names of the books that have been covered so far on cards. You may wish to begin with Genesis or, if the group is small and there is a time restriction, begin with the New Testament books. Have them work as a group and put the cards in the order they appear in the Bible. If using only the New Testament, have each person choose a card and tell what that book is about and what it teaches about God. The group can help as needed.

....

Genesis	Isaiah	Romans
Exodus	Jeremiah	1 Corinthians
Leviticus	Lamentations	2 Corinthians
Numbers	Ezekiel	Galatians
Deuteronomy	Daniel	Ephesians
Joshua	Hosea	Philippians
Judges	Joel	Colossians
Ruth	Amos	
1 Samuel	Obadiah	
2 Samuel	Jonah	
1 Kings	Micah	
2 Kings	Nahum	
1 Chronicles	Habakkuk	
2 Chronicles	Zephaniah	
Ezra	Haggai	
Nehemiah	Zechariah	
Esther	Malachi	
Job	Matthew	
Psalms	Mark	
Proverbs	Luke	
Ecclesiastes	John	
Song of Solomon	Acts	

COLOSSIANS

FIRST THESSALONIANS

Return of the Lord

*May the Lord ... establish your hearts
without blame in holiness before our God and Father
at the coming of our Lord Jesus with all His saints.*

1 Thessalonians 3:12–13

SESSION FIFTY-TWO: FIRST THESSALONIANS
Return of the Lord

✝ **Memory verse:** *"May the Lord ... establish your hearts without blame in holiness before our God and Father at the coming of our Lord Jesus with all His saints."*
(1 Thessalonians 3:12–13)

Introduction: Two thousand years ago, Christ came to earth the first time as a helpless baby born into humble means. He spent His time on earth teaching, preaching, and healing, and then He died a substitutionary death so that men might be saved through His sacrifice. Before He left, He said He would come back. The Thessalonians were waiting for His return but there was much confusion about how and when that event would take place. The second coming will be like a thief in the night, so Paul encouraged his readers to be alert and live a life of faithful holiness while they wait for His return.

- **Oral Review:** Please refer to the **REVIEW Section** in the following Teaching Guide Outline.

- **Homework:** Review the homework from the book of Colossians:

    All questions on page 181
    Question in the middle of page 184
    Last question on page 187
    What one, great truth have you taken away from the book of Colossians?

- **Review Helps:** Written review is provided at the end of the teacher presentation. (Optional and time permitting.)

- **Teacher Presentation on the Book of First Thessalonians**

- **Learning for Life:** You may choose to discuss all or just one or two of the questions on page 199.

- **Closing prayer:** Pray for the students that God would "establish their hearts without blame in holiness before our God and Father at the coming of our Lord Jesus with all His saints."

FIRST THESSALONIANS
Theme: Return of the Lord

OUTLINE AID FOR TEACHERS:

I. **PAUL'S PERSONAL REFLECTIONS TO THE THESSALONIANS (1 THESSALONIANS 1–3)**

- **1 Thessalonians 1**
  A. Paul offered congratulations for their <u>FAITHFULNESS</u>.
- **1 Thessalonians 2:2–20 (Acts 17 as a cross-reference)**
  B. Paul reminisced about <u>FOUNDING</u> the church.
- **1 Thessalonians 3:1–11 (Acts 17 as a cross-reference)**
  C. Paul commended Timothy for <u>STRENGTHENING</u> the church.

II. **PAUL'S PRACTICAL EXHORTATIONS TO THE THESSALONIANS (1 THESSALONIANS 4)**

- **1 Thessalonians 4:1–7**
  A. Paul encouraged them to <u>WALK</u> in a manner worthy of God.
- **1 Thessalonians 4:8–12, 5:16–18**
  B. Paul gave them directions for their spiritual <u>GROWTH</u>.
- **1 Thessalonians 4:13–18**
  C. Paul gave a revelation concerning the <u>DEAD</u> in Christ.

III. **PAUL'S DESCRIPTION OF THE RETURN OF THE LORD TO THE THESSALONIANS (1 THESSALONIANS 5)**

- **1 Thessalonians 5:1**
  A. Paul admonished them to wait and <u>WATCH</u> for the glorious presence of the Lord.
- **1 Thessalonians 5:4–23**
  B. Paul prayed that they would be blameless and <u>HOLY</u> when the Lord returns with His holy ones.
- **1 Thessalonians 5:2–3**
  C. Paul warned them that the Lord's return will be <u>SUDDEN</u>, audible, and visible.

I Thessalonians
[Return of the Lord]

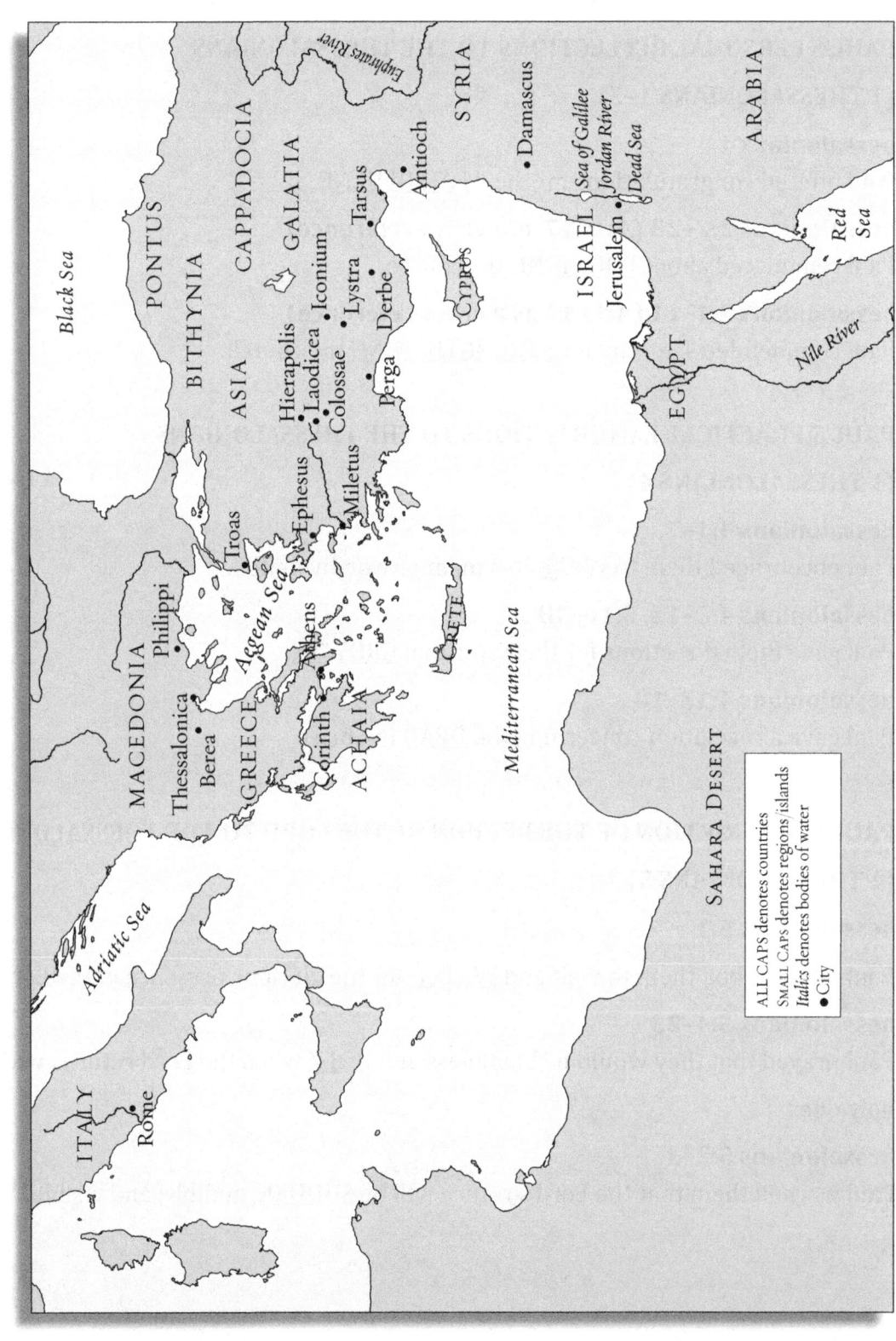

FIRST THESSALONIANS
Theme: Return of the Lord

THE BASICS:
- **Who: The Author:** Paul
  Main Characters: Believers in Thessalonica
- **What:** A letter of encouragement for the new converts during their trials and a charge to stay faithful concerning godly living and daily work
- **When:** Written in A.D. 51
- **Where:** Written to Thessalonica from Corinth
- **Why:** To exhort believers to grow in their faith and love while they continue in their labor for the Lord

MEMORY VERSE: *"May the Lord ... establish your hearts without blame in holiness before our God and Father at the coming of our Lord Jesus with all His saints." 1 Thessalonians 3:12-13*

****

REVIEW:
- The *Old Testament History* books:
  - Shared the problem of disobedience (sin) and its consequences (judgment and death).
  - The prophets foretold of judgment and the Messiah to come.
- The *New Testament History* books:
  - Spoke to Jesus' time on earth—His first coming.
  - Related how the church came into being.
- In *Paul's Letters to the Churches*:
  - **Romans:** The righteousness of God and how man could become righteous.
  - **First Corinthians:** Sin in the church must be addressed.
  - **Second Corinthians:** Defense of Paul's ministry and apostleship.
  - **Galatians:** Believers' freedom in Christ.
  - **Ephesians:** Church doctrine with practical application.
  - **Philippians:** Jesus Christ is central to every aspect of life and death.
  - **Colossians:** Jesus Christ is supreme over everything—under Whom all are in submission.

OVERVIEW:

****

- **ILLUSTRATION:** Have you ever been inspired by an article on "modern day heroes?" Usually those being highlighted are just ordinary people that had done an extraordinary

FIRST THESSALONIANS
Theme: Return of the Lord

act—perhaps their "feats" were fueled by adrenaline or fear or instinct, but whatever the motivation, the outcome was something incredible.

As an example, there was a young boy who was vacationing with his family in Hawaii. He was having a wonderful time in the surf on his boogie board. He noticed, however, that many people were swimming to shore. He saw a young woman, just beyond the break of the water, being attacked by a shark. While everyone else was fleeing the danger, he paddled toward it—he saved the young woman by beating off the shark with his boogie board! He ultimately brought her safely back to shore. He was a hero, indeed.

****

- The apostle Paul was a hero—fueled by the power of the Holy Spirit, his love for God, and his love for others.
  - ~ A hero for whom there were no trophies or rewards. Instead of receiving honor, he was persecuted, beaten, shipwrecked, bitten by a snake, and, finally, martyred.
- Paul was a hero to the Thessalonians.
- He founded the Thessalonian church on his second missionary journey.
- This letter poignantly expressed his love for these believers.

- It's important to understand the backdrop of Paul's letter to the Thessalonians.

The City of Thessalonica
- It was the capital of Macedonia.
- When the Romans invaded and conquered the area, they made Thessalonica the capital for two reasons:
  1. It was at the head of the Thermaic Gulf, which made it a busy trading port—merchants from the known world could easily get in and out of this port.
  2. It was on the Roman highway or the Aegean Highway, which was the main road of travel.
- Thessalonica was booming in trade. It was also very rich and worldly.
- The city was very polytheistic.
  - ~ It was the home of the Pantheon, the place where people from the whole known world would come to worship their various gods.
  - ~ It was also the site of Mount Olympus—the home of Greek gods and Greek mythology.

⇨ **The purpose of First Thessalonians was to exhort the people to look for the coming of the Lord!**

I. PAUL'S PERSONAL REFLECTIONS TO THE THESSALONIANS (1 THESSALONIANS 1–3)

A. Paul offered congratulations for their <u>FAITHFULNESS</u>.

FIRST THESSALONIANS
Theme: Return of the Lord

1 Thessalonians 1
- Paul was congratulating them on who they had become—faithful believers.
  - In 1 Thessalonians 1:3 Paul characterized their lives—
    - Their work for God was produced by faith.
    - Their labor was prompted by love.
    - Their endurance was inspired by hope in the Lord Jesus Christ.

> ★ **TEACHING TIP:**
> *Could your life be described in such a manner? Faith ... Love ... Hope. These qualities were evident in their daily lives. What a witness to a pagan society!*

- Their lives had changed drastically:
- ✞ **1 Thessalonians 1:9b** "... and how you turned to God from idols to serve a living and true God, ..."
  - These were a people who had previously worshipped everything.
  - When Paul arrived in the city, he had gone to the synagogue and found the people worshiping many gods as "God-fearing pagans" and "God-fearing Jews."
  - They had moved *from* monotheism *to* full-out polytheism—BUT, in hearing the gospel, they had returned to the one true God!
  - They had become servants of the Lord in faithfulness and complete submission to Christ.

- And, because of that radical transformation, they were impacting those around them.
  - They went from being isolated individuals to becoming a loving community that served one another.
  - They went from moral compromise (in worshipping many gods) to compromising nothing for the name of Christ.
  - The dramatic change in these believers had brought hope to those around them, and, as a result, many in Macedonia and Greece believed in Christ.

⇨ **These believers in Thessalonica were "little heroes" to this community because of their godly impact—pointing others to Jesus Christ.**

> ❖ **APPLICATION:** The Thessalonian believers were being the "Bible" to a place that did not have the Bible. They were the "Word" in action to a place that did not know the Word.
>   - Have you known anyone like that? Someone that has lived out what they believed?
>   - Have you ever been that "someone?"

FIRST THESSALONIANS
Theme: Return of the Lord

B. Paul reminisced about <u>FOUNDING</u> the church.

1 Thessalonians 2:2-8
- Paul first remembered the converts, then he looked back at the evangelists who had come into this community: Paul, Silas, and Timothy.
  - They had boldly shared the gospel amid much opposition—in other words, great effort had been necessary. (v. 2)
  - Their preaching of the gospel had not been in error or deceitful—nor had it in any way led them to impure living, but rather had exhorted them to holiness. (v. 3)
  - They had not sought to please men, but only to please God Who would examine their hearts and motives. They had been straightforward with the people. (v. 4)
  - They did not try to "flatter" them into belief, but rather spoke the simple truth. (v. 5)
  - They did not come with greed or self-glory in mind. (v. 5)
  - They did come in love with gentle, tender care for them in sharing the gospel—the Thessalonians were dear to these evangelists. (vv. 7-8)

1 Thessalonians 2:9-20
- It seemed that Paul deemed it necessary to give a personal defense against speculations regarding why he had not returned to visit them—his love for them had been questioned.

- Luke's words in Acts can help us better understand Paul's words to the Thessalonians because he explained the dynamics of the church's founding.

Acts 17:1-10
  - Paul, Silas, and Timothy came to the synagogue.
  - For three Sabbaths, they reasoned with the people from Scripture, explained, and gave evidence of the gospel.
  - There was a large Jewish population in Thessalonica and they were very threatened by Paul's teaching—they wanted these Christian missionaries ousted!
    * They first formed a mob and set the city in an uproar.
    * Then they attacked the home of Jason in which Paul, Silas, and Timothy were staying. They demanded that he give them the three men, but they were not there.
    * They took Jason and others before the Roman authorities and accused him and his missing "guests" of treason—they were worshiping another "king" and it was not Caesar, but Jesus.
    * In reality, Jason could have lost everything—not just his standing in the community or his home or his family, but his very life.

FIRST THESSALONIANS
Theme: Return of the Lord

- * The three evangelists left Thessalonica and went to Berea in order to protect Jason and those in the city who had become followers of Christ.
- Paul reminded them how the three evangelists (during their founding of this church in the Acts passage) had worked so as not to be a burden to any of them—they had conducted themselves in a manner worthy of the God Who had called these Thessalonian believers to His kingdom. As stated earlier:
  - ~ They had not tried to please men at the expense of pleasing God.
  - ~ They had not tried to "woo" them through flattery.
  - ~ They had not been covetous of what they had—this was a church of rich people.
    - * They never wanted any of the people's "stuff" nor had they demanded payment for their missionary work.
- Paul further recapped how he had labored day and night, as a tentmaker, so as never to ask anything of anyone—and when he wasn't working, he was ministering.

⇨ **Paul wanted them to recall who these three evangelists were—how they had conducted themselves when they were with them—how they had encouraged them as "fellow" workers.**

> **NOTE:** The manner in which Paul, Silas, and Timothy conducted their ministry was in total contrast to the preachers, pastors, priests, and proselytes of that day who demanded to be served and not to serve.
> - ♦ Paul, our "hero," was living out Jesus for the Thessalonians.
>   - ~ He came to serve, not be served.
>   - ~ He came to give God glory, not to get glory.
>   - ~ He came to encourage these people, not demand encouragement from them.

- Paul explained that he had hoped to return to them after a brief period of time but, though absent from them, he held the Thessalonians close to his heart.
  - ~ He stated that Satan had hindered his return—obstructions had been thrown in his way to prevent his return to Thessalonica.

C. Paul commended Timothy for <u>STRENGTHENING</u> the church.

- In Acts 17, the missionary journey of Paul, Silas, and Timothy was further shared.
  - ~ When the three men left Thessalonica at night, they went to Berea.
  - ~ In Berea, they began their ministry in the synagogue—sharing that the God they worshiped had a Son and his name was Jesus.

FIRST THESSALONIANS
Theme: Return of the Lord

- ~ As they shared about Jesus to the Bereans, disgruntled people from Thessalonica came into the city and riled up the citizens in Berea against the three evangelists.
    * They told the Bereans that these men were traitors who needed to be thrown out of their town.
    * They ultimately chased them out of Berea.
- From Berea they went into Athens.

✞ **1 Thessalonians 3:1-2** "Therefore when we could endure it no longer, we thought it best to be left behind at Athens alone, and we sent Timothy, our brother and God's fellow worker in the gospel of Christ, to strengthen and encourage you as to your faith, …"

- While in Athens, the three evangelists regrouped and determined that they had left the Thessalonian believers with many questions unanswered—they had not been told everything they needed to know.
- It was decided that Timothy would return to Thessalonica and take care of the young church.

> **NOTE:** Most commentators believe that Paul sent Silas back to Philippi at the same time, while he traveled further south to Corinth (from where he penned this letter).

1 Thessalonians 3:3-5

- Timothy had been sent to encourage them from becoming unsettled in their faith when facing the trials their newfound belief would bring—he came to help them remain steadfast and stand firm in Jesus amidst all the opposition.
- Paul was concerned that the "tempter" might have tempted them away from their faith in Jesus—for Satan was, indeed, a great author of persecution for the early church.

> ★ **TEACHING TIP:**
> *Sending Timothy back was an act of love because he was Paul's son in the faith and a personal source of encouragement to the apostle.*

- Timothy reported to Paul that the Thessalonian believers had questions, but they were being faithful and standing firm in what they knew.
    - ~ They were, in fact, an incredible witness for the Lord.
    - ~ Their faith was an encouragement to others, especially Paul.
    - ~ This church was learning God's Word and applying it.

⇨ **Paul learned that these young believers were living out what they said they believed—what they were learning for life!**

FIRST THESSALONIANS
Theme: Return of the Lord

II. PAUL'S PRACTICAL EXHORTATIONS TO THE THESSALONIANS (1 THESSALONIANS 4)

- Paul transitioned his message from "where they had come from—their beginnings," to "where they were now" and how they were to live.

A. Paul encouraged them to <u>**WALK**</u> in a manner worthy of God.

☦ **1 Thessalonians 4:1–2** "Finally then, brethren, we request and exhort you in the Lord Jesus, that as you received from us instruction as to how you ought to walk and please God (just as you actually do walk), that you excel still more. For you know what commandments we gave you by the authority of the Lord Jesus."

> ★ **TEACHING TIP:**
> *What a word for us today! We live in a time of spiritual mediocrity—oh, that we might respond enthusiastically to Paul's exhortation in v. 1—what a difference our lives could make in our communities.*

- Paul called them to behave "practically" in their faith—to walk in the instructions they had received regarding how to live out their belief in Christ.
- Paul exhorted them to live in a way that pleased God.
- He acknowledged that they were doing well in this area, but he implored them to go even further in their endeavors—to "excel" in their journey of faith.

⇨ **As we walk "normally," we are called to also walk "spiritually."**

1 Thessalonians 4:3–7
- Paul followed his call for them to "excel" in their walk with a focus on sexual sin.
  - Why? These believers were surrounded by an immoral society and many of these believers had come from Greek and Roman backgrounds.
    * They had not grown up with access to the Mosaic Law.
    * They had not been trained in the way of Jewish customs—they had never been taught to behave morally.
    * Immoral sin was prevalent—it was what everyone did.
- Paul wanted these believers to know that they had a much higher standard!
  - He acknowledged their natural longings.
  - He instructed them, however, to put those longings under God's control.
    * Whether impulses or thoughts or actions.

FIRST THESSALONIANS
Theme: Return of the Lord

> **NOTE:** Paul's words would have also struck a chord with the married believers—they were to stay pure in their covenant relationship, being faithful (including sexually) to their spouse.
> - Paul's instructions were a radical call to all Thessalonian believers—to no longer participate in the sins of the community.

****

✷ **ILLUSTRATION:** Many of us have heard the saying, "Make your walk match your talk." Some believe that a Native American pastor actually came up with this phrase after watching his congregation interact with the rest of the tribe in their community. His church members would come to worship on Sundays and agree "verbally" with all that had been taught from the Word of God, but would leave and do whatever they wanted to do on Mondays through Saturdays.

One day the church members came in and the pastor simply said, "There is much crooked walk from those who make straight talk."

****

- Paul wanted the young converts in Thessalonica to understand that their talk about Jesus needed to be supported by their walk in Jesus because people in Greece and Macedonia were watching them.

⇨ **If Christians do not live out what they believe, then the world will not accept what Christians say they believe.**

- Paul wanted the Thessalonians to keep up their faithful walk—they were making a difference in the world.

B. Paul gave them directions for their spiritual <u>GROWTH</u>.

1 Thessalonians 4:8
- Paul explained that God had provided the power that they needed to obey the instructions they were given—it would be through their reliance on the Holy Spirit.
- Knowing that God had given believers the Holy Spirit as their "Helper," Paul made a strong statement about obedience—when a believer rejects the instructions from the Word, they are rejecting God Himself, not a human being.

> ★ **TEACHING TIP:**
> *Paul knew that he was not a "super-hero"—he was able to do what he did only through the power of the Holy Spirit and the Thessalonians had that same power available to them.*

FIRST THESSALONIANS
Theme: Return of the Lord

1 Thessalonians 4:9–12
- Paul stated that this church understood how they were to love one another.
- But he basically followed that compliment with a simple message: "mind your own beeswax!"
  - ~ Don't worry about what others are doing, do what you have been called to do.
- He exhorted them to treat each other with integrity.
- He told them to go about their daily lives in a manner that would bring respect from outsiders—and not be beholden to anyone.

> **NOTE:** Long before Brother Lawrence said, "Practice the presence of God," Paul was delivering the same message.
> - Be mindful of the unseen world.
> - As you breathe, pray.
> - As you move through life, be aware that God is using you and you are empowered by His Holy Spirit.

****

❋ **ILLUSTRATION:** This can be a struggle for many, especially young converts —to be mindful all the time of representing Christ.

A Christian woman stated that she wrote "Jesus" on a piece of paper and put it by her bed. Every morning when she awoke, it was the first thing she saw—it reminded her to walk her faith that day *before* her feet hit the ground running.

Bill Hybels shared the manner in which he got into a good habit of practicing the presence of God and walking continually in the Spirit. He used a timer! He would set it to go off every fifteen minutes. When the timer beeped, he would stop whatever he was doing and say, "All right, Lord, I have just been working on my own here for fifteen minutes. What is it You want me to do? How is it You want me to behave?"

****

⇨ **Paul called believers to live out their faith—do life differently than the world in which you live! Because the whole world is dying to see people do what they say they believe.**

- In 1 Thessalonians 5, Paul said:
✞ **1 Thessalonians 5:16–18** "Rejoice always; pray without ceasing; in everything give thanks; for this is God's will for you in Christ Jesus."
  - These words were spoken to believers who were becoming outcasts in their community.

FIRST THESSALONIANS
Theme: Return of the Lord

- They were admired for their integrity and generosity, but alienated because of their faith.

> ❖ **APPLICATION:** It is difficult to be in a hard place and be continually thankful, isn't it?
> - ~ When you are persecuted or lonely or have been rejected or are experiencing troubles and trials, remain thankful to God! Continue to give Him thanks, no matter your circumstances.
> - ~ Why? Such a response is so very different from the world that it causes people to wonder how you can be thankful when hurting. It will give you a platform to share

****

❋ **ILLUSTRATION:** There was a story about a New England pastor who is known as the "Praising Pastor." He admitted, however, that there was a time in his life when, after serving a congregation for over thirty years, he thought, "I am tired of this. I have got to quit before I lose my faith because I feel like these members are the most ungrateful flock that I have ever been around!" And he did quit and became a recluse for three years.

One day, a former parishioner arrived at his door with a fruit basket. The pastor thanked him and the man went on his way. The pastor's wife saw the gift and asked him, "Aren't you going to write him a thank you note?" He responded, "Why should I? They should be loading me down with fruit baskets."

The wife's words, however, hit the mark! The pastor went into his study and thought, "Perhaps, I should write this man a note. I should be thankful that he thought of me after three years of absence—and brought me this gift."

The pastor related that the most incredible thing happened—as he prayed about what he should write to the man, God's Spirit came over him and, with a grateful heart, he wrote every parishioner in that church, thanking them for the way they had touched his life in some manner. And that is how he became known as the "Praising Pastor."

****

- Paul encouraged the Thessalonians to be thankful—no matter their circumstances.
    - ~ Why? It isn't "normal!" Everyone can complain, feel depressed, and burdened in hard times.
    - ~ But the person who can give thanks in the midst of trials is "walking their talk."

FIRST THESSALONIANS
Theme: Return of the Lord

C. Paul gave a revelation concerning the <u>DEAD</u> in Christ.

<u>1 Thessalonians 4:13–18</u>
- When Timothy returned with his letter from this church, one of the questions must have been: "What happens to our loved ones who were believers, but have died?"
  - ~ Their concern revolved around whether their dead fellow believers would be left behind when Christ returned?

> ★ **TEACHING TIP:**
> *It is interesting to note that the word "cemetery" means "a sleeping place."*

✟ **1 Thessalonians 4:13** "But we do not want you to be uninformed, brethren, about those who are asleep, so that you will not grieve as do the rest who have no hope."

- Paul gave a beautiful visual regarding those believers who had died: they were "asleep." It was their bodies that slept—their souls had gone to be with Christ.
- A believer has hope! The hardest thing about the death of a loved one is the separation—but one day believers will all be together with the Lord … forever!

> ★ **TEACHING TIP:**
> *What hope! If they could, those we mourn would tell us themselves, "Don't mourn me now. Don't worry. I will be coming back with the Lord!"*

✟ **1 Thessalonians 4:16–18** "For the Lord Himself will descend from heaven with a shout, with the voice of the archangel and with the trumpet of God, and the dead in Christ will rise first. Then we who are alive and remain will be caught up together with them in the clouds to meet the Lord in the air, and so we shall always be with the Lord. Therefore comfort one another with these words."

- When Christ returns, believers who have died will be raised first.
- They will be with Him in the air and He then will receive those who are still alive.

⇨ **An important and comforting truth to embrace—take your eyes off the grave of a loved one and look to the heavens!**
  - ~ *It is VERY important to remember, however, that Paul is writing to believers! This passage of hope cannot be experienced by one who does not believe in Jesus Christ.*

III. PAUL'S DESCRIPTION OF THE RETURN OF THE LORD TO THE THESSALONIANS (1 THESSALONIANS 5)

- Paul had the Thessalonians:
  - ~ Look to their past and remember their lives before Christ.

FIRST THESSALONIANS
Theme: Return of the Lord

- ~ Look to their present and walk in a manner worthy of Christ.
- Paul closed this letter with having the people:
  - ~ Look to their future and toward the coming of Christ

> **NOTE:** The theological term for the end times and future events is "eschatology."
> - In 2 Thessalonians we will go into a deeper study of the events to come.

A. Paul admonished them to wait and <u>WATCH</u> for the glorious presence of the Lord.

✝ **1 Thessalonians 5:1** "Now as to the times and the epochs, brethren, you have no need of anything to be written to you."
- ~ In *The Message* it says: "I don't think, friends, that I need to deal with the question of when all this is going to happen."

- Paul stated basically that those who are called to "watch" for Christ's coming do not need to know the hour when it will occur.

B. Paul prayed that they would be blameless and <u>HOLY</u> when the Lord returns with His holy ones.

<u>1 Thessalonians 5:4–11</u>
- When Christ returned they were not to be found participating in the ways of the world.
  - ~ In 1 Thessalonians 5:4–11, he reminded them with clarity as to who they were:
    - * They were no longer in darkness—living in immorality.
    - * They were children of light, Christ's light—they were to walk in faith, hope, and love while waiting and watching for Jesus' coming.

✝ **1 Thessalonians 5:23** "Now may the God of peace Himself sanctify you entirely; and may your spirit and soul and body be preserved complete, without blame at the coming of our Lord Jesus Christ."

⇨ **Paul brought them back full circle to his call for them to "walk in a manner worthy" of the Lord.**

C. Paul warned them that the Lord's return will be <u>SUDDEN</u>, audible, and visible.

<u>1 Thessalonians 5:2–3</u>
- The Lord will return unexpectedly, like a "thief in the night."

> ★ **TEACHING TIP:**
> *Consider: A thief does not announce his coming—in fact, a thief will take all precautions to prevent a household from knowing it.*

FIRST THESSALONIANS
Theme: Return of the Lord

- He will return suddenly—this spoke to the certainty of His return.
- Unbelievers will not expect it nor will they escape it. Why? They never believed God's Word!
  - These are people who have lived under a false security—very much like the people in Noah's day before the flood.
  - Unbelievers will be unprepared, but believers will be alert to what is coming.
- Paul reminded them of the very character of Christ—words of incredible hope.

✝ **1 Thessalonians 5:24** "Faithful is He who calls you, and He also will bring it to pass."

FINAL THOUGHTS AND APPLICATION

- Paul began by praising the Thessalonian believers for their faithfulness—reminding them how far they had come in the Lord.
- He exhorted them to live in a manner worthy of the Lord, as they walked in a world of darkness that desperately needed Christ.
  - They could be "heroes" of the faith through the power of the Holy Spirit.
- He encouraged them by clarifying that this life and death was not the end of a believer's story.
  - In this, they were given hope of reuniting with others in the faith that had died—more importantly, the hope of being united with Christ.
- He instructed them to be watchful, on the alert, for Christ's coming—to live as if He was coming today.

❖ **FINAL APPLICATION:** **The world is desperately looking for Christians who live what they say they believe.**

FIRST THESSALONIANS
Theme: Return of the Lord

FIRST THESSALONIANS REVIEW HELPS AND ANSWERS

✧ **Have each student write down what difference "Christ in you, the hope of glory" has made in their lives. (Colossians 1:27)**

✧ **Choose three or four people to read what they have written.**

FIRST THESSALONIANS

SECOND THESSALONIANS

Day of the Lord

Let no one in any way deceive you …

2 Thessalonians 2:3a

SESSION FIFTY-THREE: SECOND THESSALONIANS
Day of the Lord

☦ **Memory verse:** *"Let no one in any way deceive you..." (2 Thessalonians 2:3a)*

Introduction: The church was looking for the coming of Jesus but there had been some misunderstanding among the church at Thessalonica about the day of the Lord. Paul needed to address this error and clarify what they needed to know about the second coming of Christ. Some believed that the judgment had already begun. The result was that some had stopped working and were waiting in anticipation. Paul addressed this error and others in this small but important letter.

- **Oral Review:** Please refer to the **REVIEW Section** in the following Teaching Guide Outline.

- **Homework:** Review the homework from the book of 1 Thessalonians:

    Question on page 203
    Question at the top of page 204
    Question at the top of page 208
    Two questions on page 211
    Question on page 214

- **Review Helps:** Written review is provided at the end of the teacher presentation. (Optional and time permitting.)

- **Teacher Presentation on the Book of Second Thessalonians**

- **Learning for Life:** You may choose to discuss all or just one or two of the questions on page 223.

- **Closing prayer:** Pray that the students will live expectantly for the Lord's return and that they will reflect the love of Christ and His character while they wait for Him.

SECOND THESSALONIANS
Theme: Day of the Lord

OUTLINE AID FOR TEACHERS:

I. PERSECUTION BEFORE THE DAY OF THE LORD (2 THESSALONIANS 1)

- **2 Thessalonians 1:3–5**
  A. Paul commended the Thessalonians for enduring persecution and <u>AFFLICTION</u>.

- **2 Thessalonians 1:6–12**
  B. Paul comforted the Thessalonians by saying Jesus is coming again
    1. For the believer, He is coming to <u>RELIEVE</u> affliction.
    2. For the unbeliever, He is coming to deal out eternal <u>DESTRUCTION</u> and separation from His presence.

II. MISUNDERSTANDING ABOUT THE DAY OF THE LORD (2 THESSALONIANS 2)

  A. Three events or signs must take place before the Day of the Lord comes.
    1. <u>APOSTASY</u> must come first.
    2. The <u>MAN</u> of lawlessness will be revealed.
    3. He who <u>RESTRAINS</u> will be taken out of the way.

- **2 Thessalonians 2:3a**
  B. Apostasy means a <u>FALLING AWAY</u> or departing from the faith.

- **2 Thessalonians 2:3b–12; Daniel 7:21–25; Revelation 13**
  C. The man of lawlessness will <u>SIT</u> in the temple as if he were God.
    1. He will have the power to perform <u>MIRACLES</u>.
    2. He is probably the one called the <u>ANTICHRIST</u>.
    3. He will wage war with the <u>SAINTS</u> for three and a half years.

- **2 Thessalonians 2:7–8**
  D. He who restrains is probably the <u>HOLY SPIRIT</u>.
    1. God promised that the Holy Spirit will never be taken away. (see John 14:16–17)
    2. The restrainer of sin will be taken <u>OUT</u> of the way.

III. BEHAVIOR IN LIGHT OF THE DAY OF THE LORD (2 THESSALONIANS 3)

- **2 Thessalonians 2:15**
  A. Paul asked the Thessalonians to <u>STAND</u> firm on the Word of God.

- **2 Thessalonians 3:1–7**
  B. He asked them to <u>PRAY</u> for him and that the Word would spread.

- **2 Thessalonians 3:8–13**
  C. Paul commanded them to <u>WORK</u> until Jesus comes.

2 Thessalonians
[Day of the Lord]

SECOND THESSALONIANS
Theme: Day of the Lord

THE BASICS:
- ⇨ **Who: The Author:** Paul
  - **Main Characters:** Believers in Thessalonica
- ⇨ **What:** A letter of encouragement to persevere and obey because Christ is coming
- ⇨ **When:** Written in A.D. 51, shortly after 1 Thessalonians was written
- ⇨ **Where:** Written to Thessalonica from Corinth
- ⇨ **Why:** To correct the false teaching that the Day of the Lord had already come

MEMORY VERSE: *"Let no one in any way deceive you ..."* 2Thessalonians 2:3a

****

REVIEW:

- ⌑ The *Old Testament History* books:
  - ~ Addressed disobedience (sin), its consequences (judgment and death), and the promise of the Messiah to come.
- ⌑ The *New Testament History* books:
  - ~ Spoke to Jesus' time on earth—His first coming—and the birth of the church.
- ⌑ In *Paul's Letters to the Churches*:
  - ~ **Romans:** The righteousness of God and how man could become righteous.
  - ~ **First Corinthians:** Sin in the church must be addressed.
  - ~ **Second Corinthians:** Paul's defense of his ministry and apostleship.
  - ~ **Galatians:** Believers' freedom in Christ.
  - ~ **Ephesians:** Church doctrine with practical application.
  - ~ **Philippians:** The centrality and significance of Jesus *in everything*.
  - ~ **Colossians:** The supremacy of Christ *over everything*.
  - ~ **First Thessalonians:** An explanation of Christ's return (in the future)—it would be completely different from His first (in the past).

OVERVIEW:

****

❊ **ILLUSTRATION:** There was a young woman who passed by a rock that had a phrase painted on it: "Are you prepared?" She thoroughly discounted the question as being posed by religious fanatics attempting to scare people. But when she turned 26 years old, she accepted Jesus as her Savior and began to attend a Bible study on 1 Thessalonians.

One day after the class, she related to her husband (with much excitement) all that she had learned: "Did you know that the Bible says Jesus ascended into heaven while the disciples

SECOND THESSALONIANS
Theme: Day of the Lord

were watching? And did you know that the angels said that Jesus would return the same way he left?! Did you know that Jesus said He was going to prepare a place for believers, so that we can be with Him? And, the best part—it could happen today!"

That same evening they went to sleep. During the night she awoke to the sounds of a sick child and decided to stay in the baby's room. The next morning, her husband awoke and reached over to find that his wife was gone! He thought, "Oh, no! It's happened and I am still here!"

He did not feel prepared. The question for each of us: am I prepared?

****

- Paul wrote nine letters to the churches—this is the final one.
- As you may recall, they are placed in order of their size *not* in order of the date—it was actually the third letter written.

> **NOTE:** There is a "musical" approach in which to remember the purposes of these letters—Paul wrote a quartet, a trio, and a duet.
> - The Quartet: includes Romans, 1 and 2 Corinthians, and Galatians—focused on Christ and the cross.
> - The Trio: includes Ephesians, Philippians, and Colossians—focused on Christ and His church (both Jews and Gentiles were called into the church).
> - The Duet: 1 and 2 Thessalonians—focused on Christ and His Coming.
>
> ⇨ **This, in fact, is a perfect order! We have to *know about* Christ and the cross—so that we can *become part* of Christ and His church—so that we can *look forward* to Christ and His coming.**

- The second coming of Christ is mentioned about 318 times in the New Testament.
- Without a doubt, there are differences and divisions among Christians as to the details of Christ's second coming—but one thing is sure ... He is coming!
- The study of His second coming is called eschatology which means "the study of last things or future events."

****

❋ **ILLUSTRATION:** A young couple traveled to an out-of-town wedding. Their young son had accompanied them. A baby sitter was brought in to watch over all of the children while their parents attended the ceremony. Instead of just leaving their son behind, the couple explained to him, "We are going to leave you now, but we are coming back, so that where we are you will also be. While we are gone, you have a job to do. We want you to play with these other children who may be frightened because their parents are gone, too. Your job will be to take care of them. And when we come back, we will take you to a

SECOND THESSALONIANS
Theme: Day of the Lord

"mansion" (a hotel) and we will have a good time!" Their son's trepidation about their departure turned to excitement about their return because he knew the plan.

****

- Paul had told the people of Thessalonica the plan.
  - ~ He had preached to them himself for three Sabbaths before he was driven out of town by an angry Jewish mob because he was teaching about another king—King Jesus.
- Paul knew that these believers were suffering persecution.

REVIEW:

- In 1 Thessalonians 4:14, Paul encouraged them about those who had died before Christ's return.
- **1 Thessalonians 4:14** "For if we believe that Jesus died and rose again, even so God will bring with Him those who have fallen asleep in Jesus."
  - ~ Jesus would bring with Him those believers who had died.

- **1 Thessalonians 4:16** "For the Lord Himself will descend from heaven with a shout, with the voice of the archangel and with the trumpet of God, and the dead in Christ will rise first."
  - ~ When a believer dies, his spirit goes to be with the Lord—he is "absent from the body, present with the Lord." (2 Corinthians 5:6–8)
  - ~ But the believer's physical body is buried in the ground.
  - ~ When a believer returns with Jesus, he will receive his new body.

- **1 Thessalonians 4:17** "Then we who are alive and remain will be caught up together with them in the clouds to meet the Lord in the air, and so we shall always be with the Lord."
  - ~ Believers who are still alive at Christ's coming will be snatched up together with those who had died—in the clouds to meet the Lord in the air.
  - ~ And believers will always be with the Lord.

> ★ **TEACHING TIP:**
> *What comforting words! Believers will be reunited—those still alive with those who have died—all will live forever with the Lord!*

- In 1 Thessalonians 5:2–3, Paul spoke about the day of the Lord:
- **1 Thessalonians 5:2–3** "For you yourselves know full well that the day of the Lord will come just like a thief in the night. While they are saying, "Peace and safety!" then destruction will come upon them suddenly like labor pains upon a woman with child, and they will not escape."

SECOND THESSALONIANS
Theme: Day of the Lord

> **NOTE:** The Jews knew that the day of the Lord was a day of God's judgment. Through our study of the Old Testament, we read many times about the day of the Lord.
> - Isaiah 2 said it was a day when man's pride would be humbled and the Lord Himself would be exalted.
> - Isaiah 13:9 described it as a day when the Lord will come, cruel with fury and burning anger. He will exterminate sinners from the earth.

- It is very important to see that Paul spoke about two different aspects of the Lord's coming in 1 Thessalonians 4 and 5.
  - First: He would come to gather up believers—with trumpets blaring!
  - Second: He would come like a thief in the night while people on earth were proclaiming peace and safety—while destruction came upon them suddenly and there would be no escape.

- Paul reminded the people in his first letter to them that they were not in the dark about these things—Christ's coming would not be a surprise for them.

- While they waited for Christ's return, Paul gave them instructions:
  - Watch and be sober: the Lord's coming is an event that will most certainly occur.
  - Put on the breastplate of faith and love.
  - Put on the helmet of the hope of salvation.

- Paul exhorted them to remember that they, as believers, were not destined for God's wrath:

✝ **1 Thessalonians 5:9–10** "For God has not destined us for wrath, but for obtaining salvation through our Lord Jesus Christ, who died for us, so that whether we are awake or asleep, we will live together with Him."

⇨ **This was the message that Paul had given them in 1 Thessalonians—one that clarified the Lord's coming, giving great comfort and hope—but something had happened.**
  - A false letter had arrived stating that the Thessalonians were now in the day of the Lord.
  - This letter falsely claimed that their current suffering and persecution was the "proof" that the day of the Lord had come, the day of God's judgment.

- Paul wrote this second letter to address and correct the error of this false teaching.

⇨ **The purpose of 2 Thessalonians was to exhort the people to not be deceived by false teachers regarding the Day of the Lord.**

SECOND THESSALONIANS
Theme: Day of the Lord

I. PERSECUTION BEFORE THE DAY OF THE LORD (2 THESSALONIANS 1)

A. Paul commended the Thessalonians for enduring persecution and AFFLICTION.

2 Thessalonians 1:3–5
- Paul began his letter by giving thanks for these believers—for their growing faith and love for one another.
- He stated that he "bragged" about them to other churches regarding their perseverance and faith in the midst of great persecutions and afflictions.
- He commended them for enduring in their difficult circumstances—because they were suffering for the kingdom of God.

B. Paul comforted the Thessalonians by saying Jesus is coming again.

1. For the believer, He is coming to RELIEVE affliction.

✝ **2 Thessalonians 1:6–8** "For after all it is only just for God to repay with affliction those who afflict you, and to give relief to you who are afflicted and to us as well when the Lord Jesus will be revealed from heaven with His mighty angels in flaming fire, …"

- Paul encouraged them by reminding them that the Jesus would return.
- And when He returned, their affliction would end!

2. For the unbeliever, He is coming to deal out eternal DESTRUCTION and separation from His presence.

✝ **2 Thessalonians 1:8–10** "… dealing out retribution to those who do not know God and to those who do not obey the gospel of our Lord Jesus. These will pay the penalty of eternal destruction, away from the presence of the Lord and from the glory of His power, when He comes to be glorified in His saints on that day, and to be marveled at among all who have believed — for our testimony to you was believed."

- Paul explained that there would be a future judgement—punishment would come to those who now persecuted these believers.
- When Paul spoke about "retribution" for those who did not know God, the word "retribution" may be translated as "vengeance" in some Bible translations.
  ~ Paul stated that God would execute His righteous judgment upon the wicked.
- Paul presented a clear contrast between the responses of the believer and the unbeliever at Christ's return:
  ~ The unbeliever would pay the penalty of eternal destruction away from the presence of the Lord.

SECOND THESSALONIANS
Theme: Day of the Lord

- * The word "destruction" used in this verse does not denote annihilation, but rather an ongoing punishment.
- ~ The believer would glorify the Lord in that day—they will marvel at Him.

> **NOTE:** Do you see the contrast that Paul made that supports his words in 1 Thessalonians regarding Christ's coming?
> - Believers will be caught up in the clouds to Him and they will always be present with Him.
> - Unbelievers—those who don't know God and don't obey the gospel—will experience an eternal torment.
>
> ⇨ **Temporary suffering is hard, indeed. But it does not compare to the one who will suffer being eternally separated from God.**

- He ended these thoughts with a prayer for the believers:

☦ **2 Thessalonians 1:11–12** "To this end also we pray for you always, that our God will count you worthy of your calling, and fulfill every desire for goodness and the work of faith with power, so that the name of our Lord Jesus will be glorified in you, and you in Him, according to the grace of our God and the Lord Jesus Christ."
  - ~ That they would live worthy of their high calling in Christ.
  - ~ That they would allow God to work out His perfect will in faith and power.
  - ~ That God would be glorified in and through their lives.

- After offering up a prayer for these believers, Paul's primary purpose for writing them is addressed.

II. MISUNDERSTANDING ABOUT THE DAY OF THE LORD (2 THESSALONIANS 2)

☦ **2 Thessalonians 2:1–2** "Now we request you, brethren, with regard to the coming of our Lord Jesus Christ and our gathering together to Him, that you not be quickly shaken from your composure or be disturbed either by a spirit or a message or a letter as if from us, to the effect that the day of the Lord has come."

- Paul began with two distinctions with the purpose of instilling confidence:
  1. The coming of the Lord Jesus Christ.
  2. The gathering of believers to Him.

SECOND THESSALONIANS
Theme: Day of the Lord

- A false message had been presented that appeared to have come from Paul and it had not. Its impact was shaking their faith (which he had just commended).

> **NOTE:** It is clear that something was causing a disturbance among these believers and their confidence in the Lord's coming. Paul addressed three possibilities. Commentators suggest the following regarding them:
> 1. A spirit: a person in their midst who had professed to have the spirit of prophesy, but presented false claims. (1 John 4:1–3)
> 2. A message: someone who alleged to be sharing the words of Paul but, again, perverting truth. (2 Thessalonians 2:5, 15)
> 3. A letter: Paul had written them once, but perhaps another had come purporting to be from him. It was not, instead it was a forgery. (2 Thessalonians 3:17)

- Whoever or whatever, the message being spread was not the truth.
- Paul warned them: Do not be deceived.
- He then shared that certain events had to occur before the Lord returned.

A. Three events or signs must take place before the Day of the Lord comes.

    1. <u>**APOSTASY**</u> must come first.

    2. The <u>**MAN**</u> of lawlessness will be revealed.

    3. He who <u>**RESTRAINS**</u> will be taken out of the way.

B. Apostasy means a <u>FALLING AWAY</u> or departing from the faith.

✝ **2 Thessalonians 2:3a** "Let no one in any way deceive you, for it will not come unless the apostasy comes first …"

- "Apostasy" is when a person moves away from the teachings of Jesus, the apostles, and the forefathers (Abraham, Isaac, and Jacob).

> ❖ **APPLICATION:** We are living in an age of apostasy.
> ~ We are religious, aren't we? There is no problem in the world today with having a "religion" because most will claim to be "spiritual."
> ~ What many do not have is a relationship with the God of the Bible.
>
> ⇨ **Sadly, today there are many who take the position that the use of Jesus' name should be avoided so as not to "offend" anyone.**

SECOND THESSALONIANS
Theme: Day of the Lord

C. The man of lawlessness will <u>SIT</u> in the temple as if he were God.

✞ **2 Thessalonians 2:3b–4** "… and the man of lawlessness is revealed, the son of destruction, who opposes and exalts himself above every so-called god or object of worship, so that he takes his seat in the temple of God, displaying himself as being God."

- It is important to note that Paul did NOT refer to a religion or a church or a government. He pointed to a "man."
- Paul described this man as:
  - The man of lawlessness.
  - The son of destruction.
  - One who will oppose and exalt himself above every so-called god or object of worship.
  - One who will take his seat in the temple of God.
  - One who will display himself as being God.

> ★ **TEACHING TIP:**
> *To be able to take a seat in the temple, the temple would have had to be rebuilt by this time.*

~ **This man will either think he is God or will, at least, portray himself as God.**

- Paul reminded them that this was not new information. He had taught them about the second coming of Christ during those three Sabbaths when he was with them. (2 Thessalonians 2:5)
  - This was NOT "new" news!
  - He had given them all the details.

1. He will have the power to perform <u>MIRACLES.</u>

2. He is probably the one called the <u>ANTICHRIST.</u>

<u>2 Thessalonians 2:9–12</u>
- "Antichrist" means both "against Christ," as well as "instead of Christ."
- Paul continued his characterization of what was to come prior to Jesus' return:
  - The man of lawlessness will come in accord with the activity of Satan.
    - He will work "under and through" the energy and operation of Satan.
  - He will come with all power and signs and false wonders.
    - Power: That which Satan can exhibit—which will be a great exertion of power in this case.
    - Signs: This word often denotes real miracles, but it may be applied to "pretended" miracles as well.

> ★ **TEACHING TIP:**
> *Just as the magicians in Egypt imitated Moses' miracles, this man of lawlessness will imitate Christ's powers*

SECOND THESSALONIANS
Theme: Day of the Lord

* False wonders: "Lying wonders." A further comment on false miracles—but they would be such to cause wonder and excitement.

> ❖ **APPLICATION:** This is a warning to us today! Do not believe everything that "seems" miraculous—it could come from a false spirit.
>
> ✝ **1 John 4:2–3** "By this you know the Spirit of God: every spirit that confesses that Jesus Christ has come in the flesh is from God; and every spirit that does not confess Jesus is not from God; this is the spirit of the antichrist, of which you have heard that it is coming, and now it is already in the world."
>
> ⇨ **Plumb everything you see or hear to the Word of God.**

- ~ Paul presented two ideas of the depravity that would come:
  - * Deceit that used fraudulent methods.
  - * A purposeful promotion of wickedness.
- ~ And there would be those who refused to receive the love of the truth, so as to be saved, and would engage in this depravity and perish.

> ★ **TEACHING TIP:**
> *Paul made it clear that godless activities would increase. Do we not see that happening in our culture today?*

> **NOTE:** What we see in this passage is that men would prefer to believe the lie rather than the truth. Those who choose to follow the man of lawlessness will worship and serve the "creature" instead of their Creator. (Romans 1:25)

⇨ **NOTE: This will be the rise of a world dictator—not a world system, but one who will head up a world system.**

3. He will wage war with the <u>SAINTS</u> for three and a half years. (See Daniel 7:21–25; Revelation 13)

- The man of lawlessness is not a new figure in the Word.
  - ~ Daniel referred to him as the "abomination of desolation."
  - ~ The apostle John called him the "antiChrist."
- Daniel described these future events. He explained:
  - ~ There would be seventy weeks of prophecy (future events).
  - ~ A week equals seven years, thus 490 years.
  - ~ Sixty-nine weeks of Daniel's prophecy have been fulfilled, so there remains seven years of prophecy yet to occur.

SECOND THESSALONIANS
Theme: Day of the Lord

⇨ **It is as if we are presently living in the "pause of time" between the sixty-ninth and seventieth year of prophetic history.**

- Daniel described this last seven year prophetic period:
  - The man of lawlessness will make a covenant with many—this covenant is to last for a seven year time period.
  - He will break the covenant in the middle—after three and a half years.
  - The man of lawlessness will exalt himself and oppose God.
    - He will say awful things against the God of gods.
    - He will wage war with the saints and overcome them.

> **NOTE:** The book of Revelation states that this man of lawlessness will only be given authority for three and a half years.
> - It also states that "all" will worship him on earth "who do not have their names written in the Book of Life."

⇨ **When this man of lawlessness does come, he will have a big following of people who are deluded—*but* he will only have three and a half years to conduct his vile agenda.**

- The book of 2 Thessalonians explains what will happen to him:

✝ **2 Thessalonians 2:8** "Then that lawless one will be revealed whom the Lord will slay with the breath of His mouth and bring to an end by the appearance of His coming …"

⇨ **Paul gave us the "end of the story" for the man of lawlessness—it has already been determined. He will be brought to an end by Jesus' coming!**

- This mystery of lawlessness is at work—we see that in all the difficulties in our world today.
- But the "mystery" will be dispelled and the lawless one will be revealed once another event takes place.

D. He who restrains is probably the <u>HOLY SPIRIT</u>.

1. **God promised that the Holy Spirit will never be taken away (see John 14:16–17).**

2. **The restrainer of sin will be taken <u>OUT</u> of the way.**

- Paul set out the order of events: the lawless one would not come until the restrainer was taken out of the way.

SECOND THESSALONIANS
Theme: Day of the Lord

- ✝ **2 Thessalonians 2:7** "For the mystery of lawlessness is already at work; only he who now restrains will do so until he is taken out of the way."

  - The first question that comes to mind: Who is the "restrainer?"
    - Scripture is clear that God has a "restrainer" working in the world that is holding back Satan's evil program.
    - And he will continue to hinder Satan's activities until he is "taken out of the midst."

  > **NOTE:** There is disagreement as to who the "restrainer" is:
  > - Some ascribed it to be the government—the Roman government.
  >   - The Roman government, however, no longer holds worldwide sway.
  >   - Plus, human governments do not restrain sin, often they endorse sin.
  > - Some think it is the church.
  > - Others think it is Michael, the archangel.
  > - There are many who believe this is the Holy Spirit who is clearly restraining the full onslaught of sin today.

  > **NOTE:** Warning! This is where the study can become difficult. If the "restrainer" is indeed the Holy Spirit, then many would say that God would not take Him out of the world without taking believers out of the world with Him. They base this on:
  > - Ephesians 1:13 (*Believers are sealed with the Holy Spirit.*)
  > - John 14:16 (*Jesus promised believers that the Helper would be with them forever.*)
  > - Hebrews 13:5c (*God promises never to leave/forsake those who are His.*)
  > - Romans 5:5, 1 Corinthians 6:19 (*The Holy Spirit is given from God and resides within a believer.*)
  >
  > ⇨ **Many believe that the Holy Spirit works in and through the church today—therefore, His being "taken out of the way" would coincide with the rapture of the church.**

- ⌑ Second Thessalonians could bring deeper understanding to the revelation in 1 Thessalonians 4.
  - Paul explained that believers would one day be "caught up" to be with Jesus Christ.
  - Knowing that the Holy Spirit resides in believers, it seems that when believers are "taken up" to be with Jesus Christ, the Holy Spirit will be with them.
  - Thus when believers are "taken up," the Holy Spirit, the restrainer of sin, is gone.

SECOND THESSALONIANS
Theme: Day of the Lord

✝ **2 Thessalonians 2:8** "Then that lawless one will be revealed whom the Lord will slay with the breath of His mouth and bring to an end by the appearance of His coming; ..."

> **NOTE:** Most agree that there will be a seven year period called the "tribulation."
> - However, there is disagreement concerning "when" believers will be "taken up."
>   - Pre-Tribulation: Believers (the church) will be taken before the tribulation begins.
>   - Mid-Tribulation: Believers (the church) will be taken in the middle of the seven year period.
>   - Post-Tribulation: Believers will go through the tribulation and will not be taken until the end.

- In Matthew 24:9–30, Jesus spoke to Daniel's prophecy:
  - A day would come when believers would experience tribulation, death, hatred, and betrayal.
  - Many false prophets (and false "christs") would arise to mislead many and lawlessness would increase, showing great signs.
  - A day would come when the man of lawlessness would be seen standing in the holy place.
  - When this occurred, He exhorted them to "flee to the mountains."
  - He explained that there would be a great tribulation, such as has not occurred since the beginning of the world—until now—nor ever would.
  - Jesus said that unless those days were cut short, no life would be saved.
  - Immediately following the tribulation, the sun will get dark, the moon will not give its light, the stars will fall down, and Jesus will come in all His glory.

> ★ **TEACHING TIP:**
> *There is a big difference between experiencing daily tribulations due to one's faith in Christ and the "great tribulation" to come.*

> **NOTE: For the teacher's purposes only.** Three verses that support the pre/mid tribulation views are:
> ✝ **1 Thessalonians 5:9** "For God has not destined us for wrath, but for obtaining salvation through our Lord Jesus Christ, ..."
> ✝ **1 Thessalonians 5:10** "... who died for us, so that whether we are awake or asleep, we will live together with Him."
> ✝ **Revelation 3:10** "Because you have kept the word of My perseverance, I also will keep you from the hour of testing, that hour which is about to come upon the whole world, to test those who dwell on the earth."

SECOND THESSALONIANS
Theme: Day of the Lord

> ⇨ **Warning: Do not let your teaching get "stuck" here. Agree to it all being a "mystery" to us now. And agree that we do know two aspects of the second coming of Christ:**
> 1. It will involve the deliverance of some.
> 2. It will involve the destruction of others.

- The problem that Paul faced involved false teachers deceiving the believers by stating that the reason they were suffering was because they were IN the great tribulation.
- Paul addressed the misunderstanding of the day of the Lord—he wanted them to know that they were not in it.

****

❋ **ILLUSTRATION:** A believer shared that, before she read this passage, she thought, "If I share Christ with my family and friends … and they do not accept Him … and Christ comes and catches me up into the clouds to be with Him … well, at least those left behind will think that I knew what I was talking about." She went on to muse, "They will probably say, 'I will pay attention now!'"

But this passage makes it clear that those who have rejected the truth (in order to be saved) will be deluded—even with witnessing the Rapture as a miraculous event. Now is the time to pray, to fast, and to share Jesus with others.

****

- He once again closed this teaching with a prayer for them. (2 Thessalonians 2:16-17)
- Paul, at this point, had offered up two prayers—both dealt with their works.
- Why? Because false teaching will always lead to wrong behavior.

III. BEHAVIOR IN LIGHT OF THE DAY OF THE LORD (2 THESSALONIANS 3)

A. Paul asked the Thessalonians to **STAND** firm on the Word of God.

- Paul gave this instruction in chapter 2:

✝ **2 Thessalonian 2:15** "So then, brethren, stand firm and hold to the traditions which you were taught, whether by word of mouth or by letter from us."

B. He asked them to **PRAY** for him and that the Word would spread.

2 Thessalonians 3:1
- Paul knew there was power in prayer—even though Satan was at work, believers could pray to God and see Him answer!

> ★ **TEACHING TIP:**
> Paul's heart was to see God's Word glorified in a world (a culture) that wanted to ignore it.

SECOND THESSALONIANS
Theme: Day of the Lord

- Paul requested they pray for his ministry—he was sharing the truth of God with the goal to counteract the impact of Satan's lies.

2 Thessalonians 3:4–7
- Paul noted his confidence in the Thessalonian believers to continue in their obedience to the Lord.
- He then instructed them to keep away from every brother who led an unruly life, who did not live according to the traditions of the Word.
- He exhorted them to follow their example (Paul, Silvanus, and Timothy).

> ★ **TEACHING TIP:**
> *Can you imagine the impact on the world IF each Christian personally committed to obeying God's Word?*

C. Paul commanded them to **WORK** until Jesus comes.

2 Thessalonians 3:8–13
- Paul led by example:
✝ **2 Thessalonians 3:8–9** "… nor did we eat anyone's bread without paying for it, but with labor and hardship we kept working night and day so that we would not be a burden to any of you; not because we do not have the right to this, but in order to offer ourselves as a model for you, so that you would follow our example."
  - Paul had been consistent with this teaching. He worked with his own hands to support himself and his co-laborers.
  - Paul felt strongly that if a man refused to work, then he should not eat. (2 Thessalonians 3:10)

> ★ **TEACHING TIP:**
> *Through history, there have been some who have suggested, "We ought to give up our jobs and wait for Jesus to come."*

⇨ **It would seem to be an oxymoron—but believers are to be busy in the waiting on the Lord's return!**

- Paul reasoned that men with too much time on their hands became "busybodies"—resulting in a bad testimony to the unbelievers around them. (2 Thessalonians 3:11)
- Paul clearly instructed what believers should do until Jesus returned:

✝ **2 Thessalonians 3:13** "But as for you, brethren, do not grow weary of doing good."

2 Thessalonians 3:14–18
- Paul ended his letter with the exhortation that the Word of God was to be heard and to be lived out.
  - Apparently there were church members who were refusing to obey what Paul had taught them.

SECOND THESSALONIANS
Theme: Day of the Lord

- ~ Believers have accountability to one another in that we should encourage others into obedience to God—in the context here, a member should not encourage laziness.
  - Paul prayed one last time:
- ✞ **2 Thessalonians 3:16** "Now may the Lord of peace Himself continually grant you peace in every circumstance. The Lord be with you all!"
  - ~ They needed peace!
    - * They were experiencing personal tribulations for their faith.
    - * Some had died.
    - * Others were choosing not to live in disobedience to God's Word.
    - * All on top of the false teaching that was in their midst.

⇨ **Real, genuine peace can only come from the Lord of peace!**

FINAL THOUGHTS AND APPLICATION

- ⌑ Why study prophecy?
  1. It is comforting:
     - ~ To know what the future holds and that God holds the future.
     - ~ To know that God will spiritually deliver believers and destroy His enemies.
  2. It is a call to accept Jesus Christ:
     - ~ In understanding prophecy, we had better realize the need to be prepared for His coming.
     - ~ Are you prepared? If Jesus came today, would you be delivered or destroyed?
  3. It is a challenge to live for Christ daily.

****

- ❋ **ILLUSTRATION:** There are two typical responses if you tell your children, "Clean up your room. I will be back in a few minutes to check on you." If they have cleaned their room, they will come running out of their room with a desire for you to see what they have done. If they have not cleaned up their room, they do not look forward to your return and are anxious about seeing you.

  The question for each one of us is: Have we answered the call of Jesus Christ and, thus, look expectantly for His return?

****

- ❖ **FINAL APPLICATION:** Jesus is coming. Are you prepared? Stand firm, work, and persevere until He comes.

SECOND THESSALONIANS
Theme: Day of the Lord

SECOND THESSALONIANS REVIEW HELPS

✦ **Answer the questions below.**

1. How were the letters named?

2. What book describes God's righteousness?

3. Where was Paul when he wrote the book of Romans?

4. What was the theme of First Corinthians?

5. Which gospel tells of Jesus the Suffering Servant?

6. Which gospel tells of Jesus as the Perfect Man?

7. Which gospel tells of Jesus as the King of Kings?

8. Which gospel tells of Jesus as the Son of God?

9. In the first part of the book of Acts, what happened to Jesus?

10. What happened to Paul on the road to Damascus?

11. Describe one problem the church in Corinth was having.

12. What does Paul say happens when we die?

13. What is the greatest thing: faith, hope, or love?

14. Tell one attribute of love.

15. Finish the statement:
    "For I am not ashamed of the gospel … for in it the righteousness of God is ____."

16. What book deals with our "walk in a manner worthy of our calling?"

17. Complete: "For in Him all the fullness of _____ dwells in _____ form."

18. What book tells about Jesus' return?

19. In what book does Paul give a defense of his ministry, apostleship, and authority?

20. Complete: "For to _____ to live is _____ and to die is _____."

SECOND THESSALONIANS REVIEW HELPS
(Answers for Facilitators)

✧ **Answer the questions below.**

1. How were the letters named? **Name of the city the church was located**

2. What book describes God's righteousness? **Romans**

3. Where was Paul when he wrote the book of Romans? **In Corinth**

4. What was the theme of First Corinthians? **Church's problems corrected**

5. Which gospel tells of Jesus the Suffering Servant? **Mark**

6. Which gospel tells of Jesus as the Perfect Man? **Luke**

7. Which gospel tells of Jesus as the King of Kings? **Matthew**

8. Which gospel tells of Jesus as the Son of God? **John**

9. In the first part of the book of Acts, what happened to Jesus? **He ascended into heaven**

10. What happened to Paul on the road to Damascus? **Jesus spoke to him from heaven, blinded him, and he was converted.**

11. Describe one problem the church in Corinth was having. **Various answers: Immorality; taking sides; not understanding the work of the cross; Holy Spirit.**

12. What does Paul say happens when we die? **Will have bodies that are imperishable**

13. What is the greatest thing: faith, hope, or love? **Love**

14. Tell one attribute of love. **See First Corinthians 13:4–8 for complete list.**

15. Finish the statement—
    "For I am not ashamed of the gospel ... for in it the righteousness of God is **salvation**."

16. What book deals with our "walk in a manner worthy of our calling"? **Ephesians**

17. Complete: "For in Him all the fullness of **deity** dwells in **human** form."

18. What book tells about Jesus' return? **First Thessalonians**

19. In what book does Paul give a defense of his ministry, apostleship, and authority? **Second Corinthians**

20. Complete: "For to **me** to live is **Christ** and to die is **gain**."

© 2018 Big Dream Ministries, Inc.

PAUL'S LETTERS TO THE CHURCHES AT A GLANCE
****
CHARTS

SET 9

Paul's Letters to the Churches at a Glance

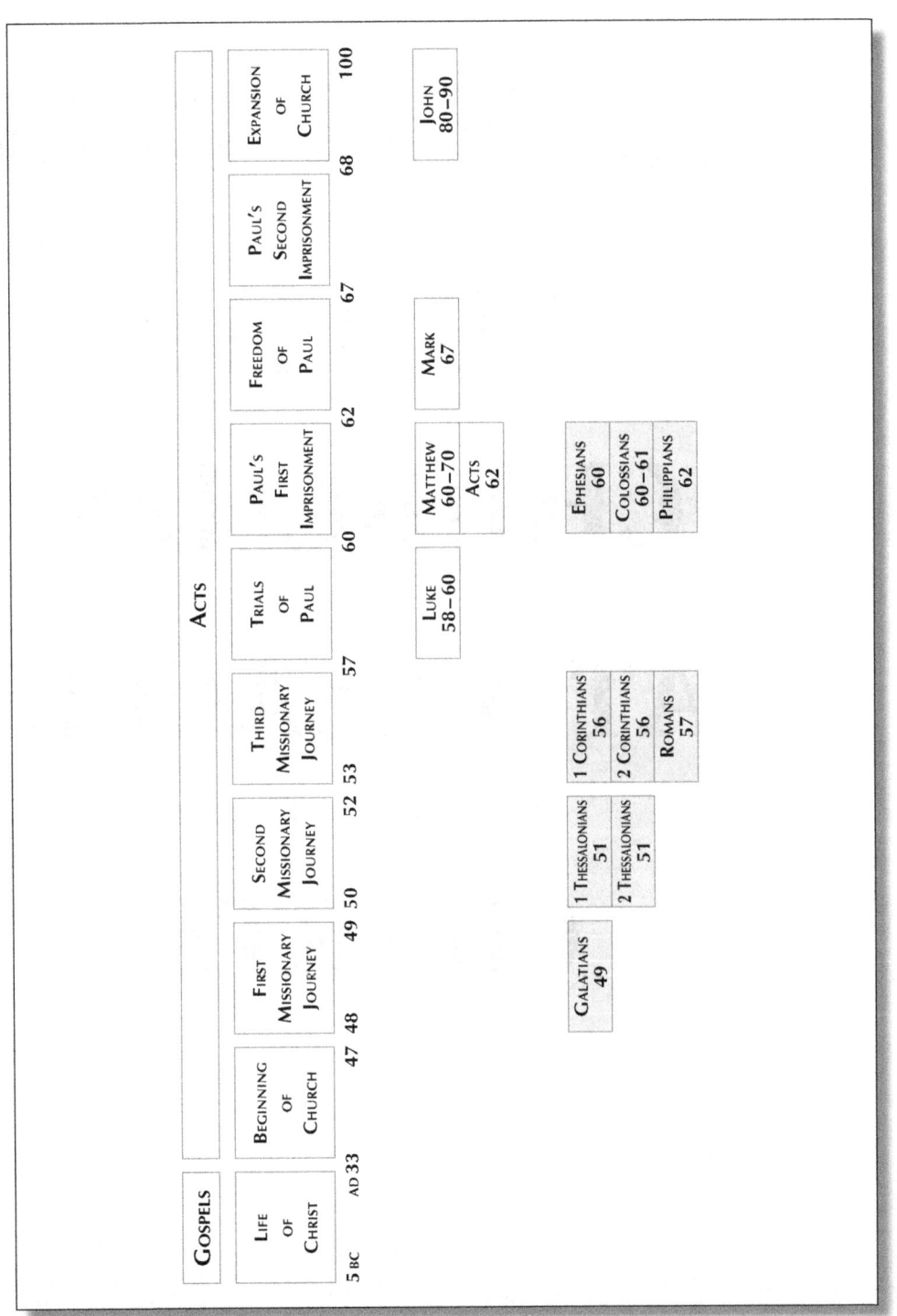

To see how these books fit into the chronology of the New Testament books as a whole, see the chart on page 246.

ROMANS

The Righteousness of God			
The NEED for It	The EXPLANATION of It	The Jews' RELATIONSHIP to It	The Practical APPLICATION of It
Man's Sin	God's Salvation	Man's Responsibility	God's Will
God's Wrath	Man's Sanctification	God's Sovereignty	Man's Transformation
1 — 3	4 — 8	9 — 11	12 — 16

Romans

Chapters 1–11	Chapters 12–16
Doctrine Belief Theology Motivation	Lifestyle Behavior Practice Action

1 Corinthians

Answer to Chloe's Report	Answer to Anonymous Report	Answer to Letter's Report
1:11	5:1	7:1; 8:1; 12:1; 16:1
Disunity in the Church	Disorder in the Church	Difficulties in the Church
Competition	Corruption	Confusion
1 — 4	5 — 6	7 — 16

2 Corinthians

1 Corinthians	2 Corinthians
Character and condition of the church	Life and character of the apostle
Objective and practical	Subjective and personal
Systematic	Unsystematic
Deliberate	Impassioned
Warns against pagan influence	Warns against Judaistic influence

2 Corinthians

Character of Paul's Ministry Explanation Personal	Collection for the Saints Exhortation Others	Defense of Paul's Apostleship Vindication Personal
1 7	8 9	10 13

GALATIANS

Paul's Gospel of Grace DEFENDED	Paul's Gospel of Grace DEFINED	Paul's Gospel of Grace APPLIED
Biographical	Doctrinal	Practical
Authenticity	Superiority	Liberty
Paul's EXASPERATION	Paul's EXPLANATION	Paul's EXHORTATION
1　　　　　　　　2	3　　　　　　　　4	5　　　　　　　　6

Galatians

BOOK	2 TIMOTHY 3:16	BELIEVER IS	AREA OF FOCUS
Romans	Teaching	Grounded	Salvation
1 and 2 Corinthians	Reproof	Guided	Sanctification
Galatians	Correction	Guarded	Salvation and Sanctification

EPHESIANS

"The calling with which you have been called"	Hinge Verses	"Walk in a manner worthy of the calling"
What God Has Done Spiritual Blessings Past Creation of the Body	His Power in Us	What We Are to Do Spiritual Behavior Present Conduct of the Body
1:1 3:19	3:20–4:1	4:2 6:24

Philippians

Christ Our LIFE 1:21	Christ Our ATTITUDE 2:5	Christ Our GOAL 3:8	Christ Our STRENGTH 4:13
Joy in Suffering	Joy in Servanthood	Joy in Salvation	Joy in Stability
1	2	3	4

Philippians

Three Instructions			Three Examples		
Look out for the interest of others	Consider the example of Jesus Christ	Work this out with fear and trembling	Paul the apostle	Timothy the kindred spirit	Epaphroditus the messenger and minister
1 4	5 11	12 16	17 18	19 24	25 30

COLOSSIANS

Supremacy of Christ	Supremacy of Christ	Supremacy of Christ	Supremacy of Christ
In His Person and Work	In the Church	Over Other Teachings	In Practical Experience
Key Verse: 1:15	Key Verse: 1:28	Key Verse: 2:8	Key Verse: 3:17
1:1 — 1:23	1:24 — 2:7	2:8 — 2:23	3:1 — 4:18

COLOSSIANS

IN CHRIST	**IN COLOSSAE OR** _____
Our spiritual home	Our physical home
It is eternal, beginning immediately	It is merely temporal
It is heavenly	It is earthly
We are citizens	We are aliens
There is power for godly living	There is pressure for ungodly living
Expectation of the fruit of the Spirit	Enticement to the works of the flesh
It cannot be physically:	It can be physically:
seen	seen
heard	heard
smelled	smelled
tasted	tasted
touched	touched

1 Thessalonians

REFLECTIONS by Paul on His Relationship with Them Personal	INSTRUCTIONS from Paul on Their Thinking About the Future Practical
1 3	4 5

2 Thessalonians

Persecution's Rewards Because of the Grace of Our Lord Jesus Christ 1:12	Paul's Instructions Regarding the Coming of Our Lord Jesus Christ 2:1	Paul's Exhortations in the Name of Our Lord Jesus Christ 3:6
Persecution Before the Day of the Lord	Misunderstanding About the Day of the Lord	Behavior in Light of the Day of the Lord
Key Verse: 1:4	Key Verse: 2:2	Key Verse: 3:10
1	2	3

New Testament Books

Chronological Relationship of the New Testament Books

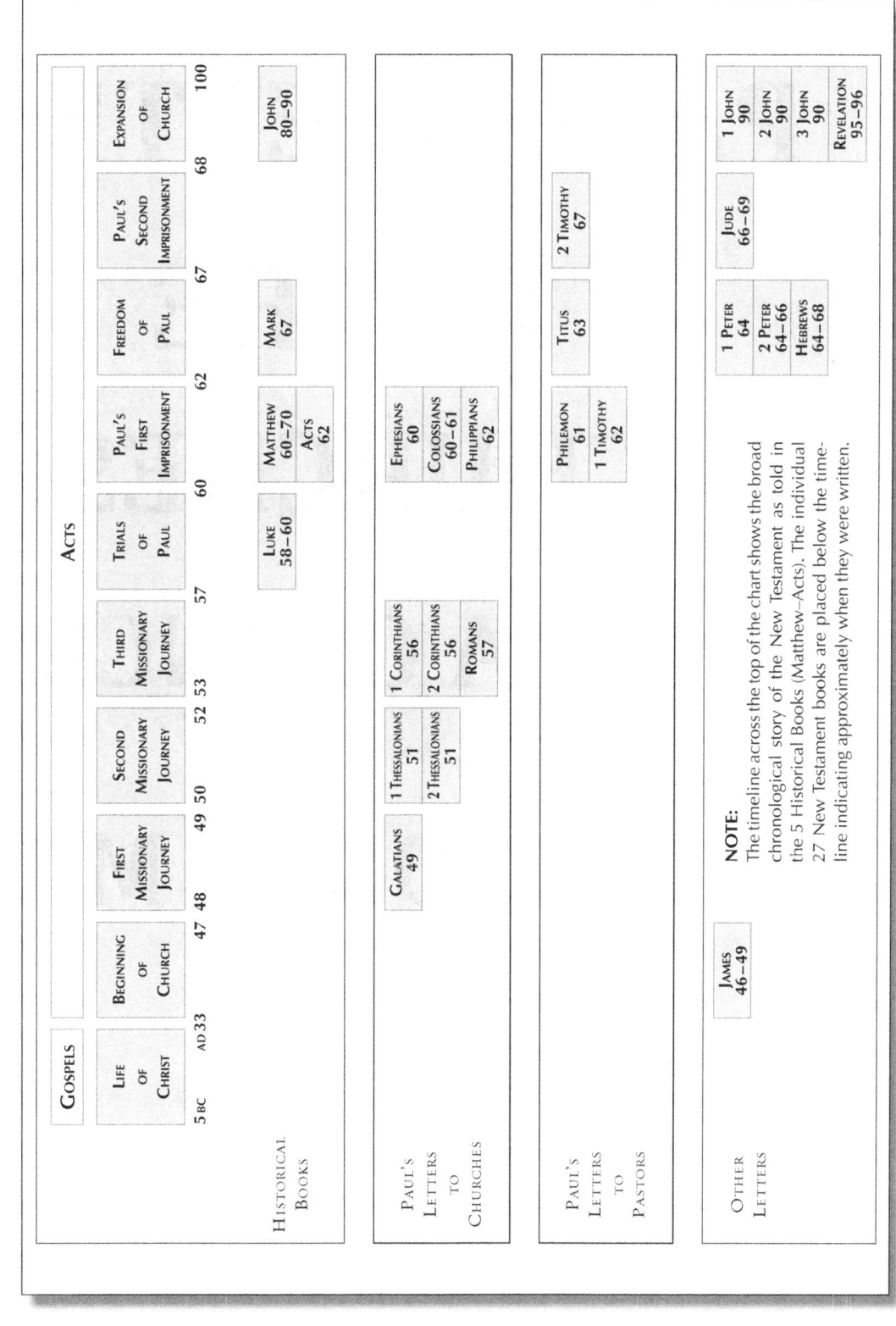

PAUL'S LETTERS TO THE CHURCHES AT A GLANCE

****

ADDITIONAL MAPS

The First Missionary Journey of Paul

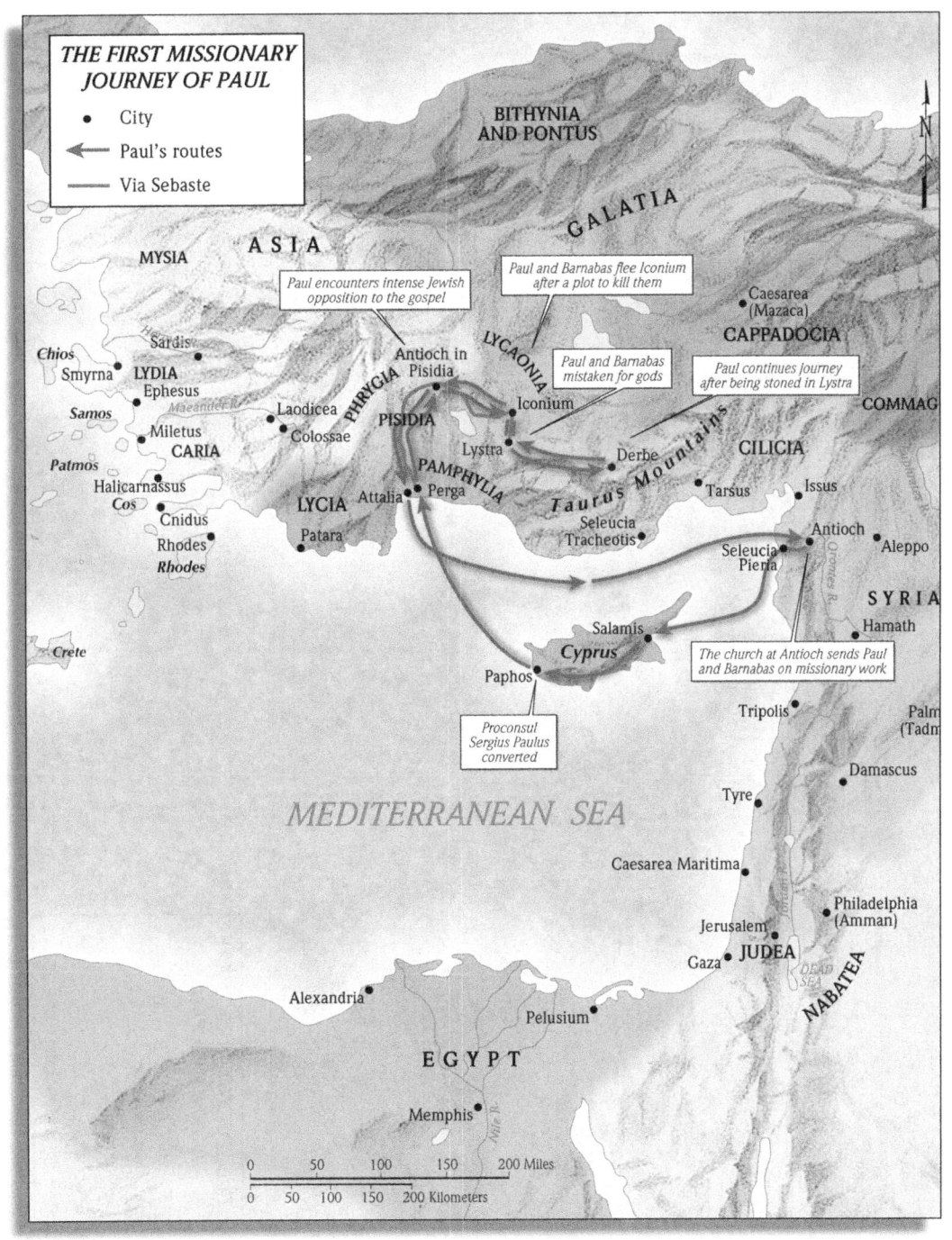

The Second Missionary Journey of Paul

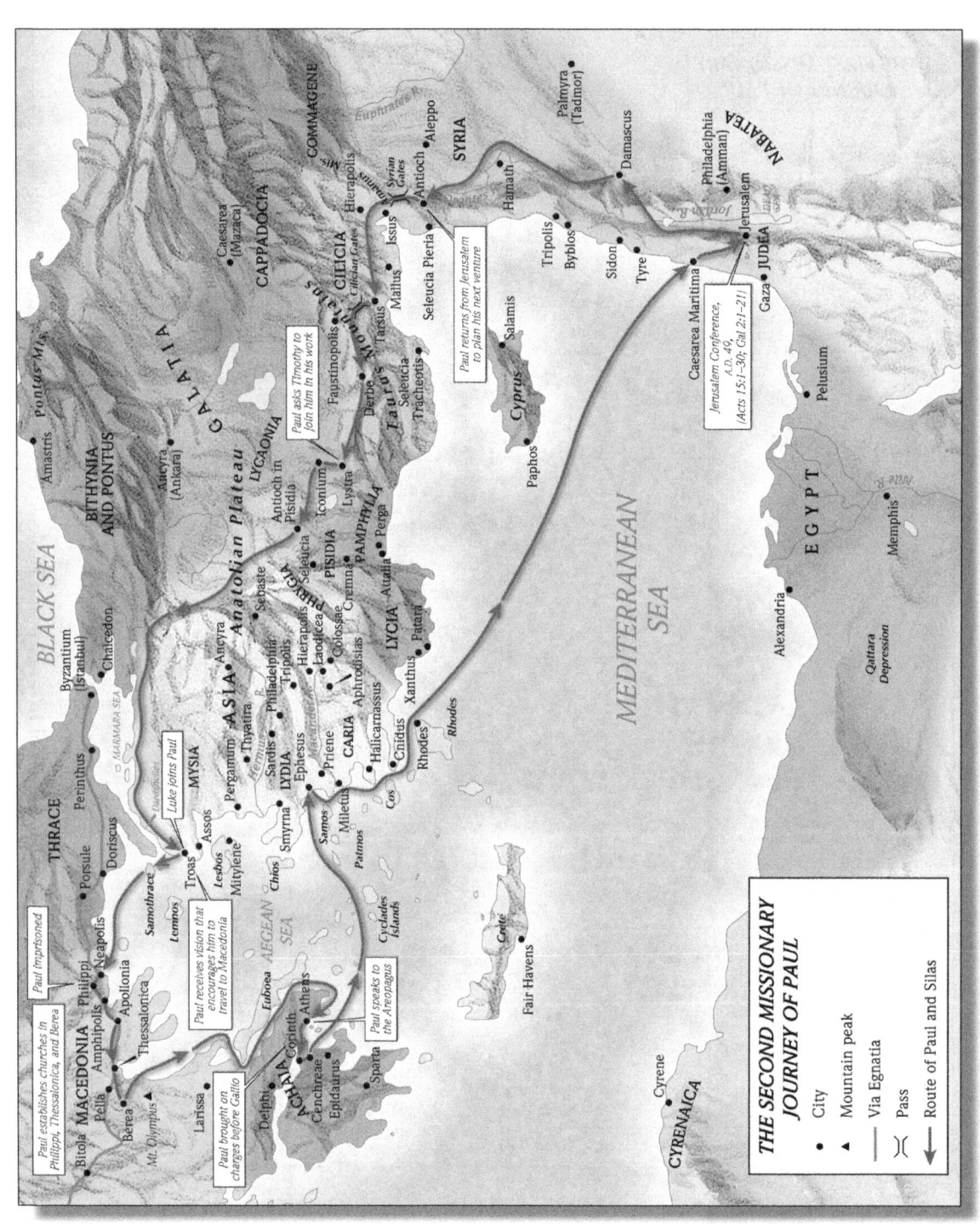

The Second Missionary Journey of Paul from Holman Bible Atlas © 1998, Holman Bible Publishers. Used by permission.

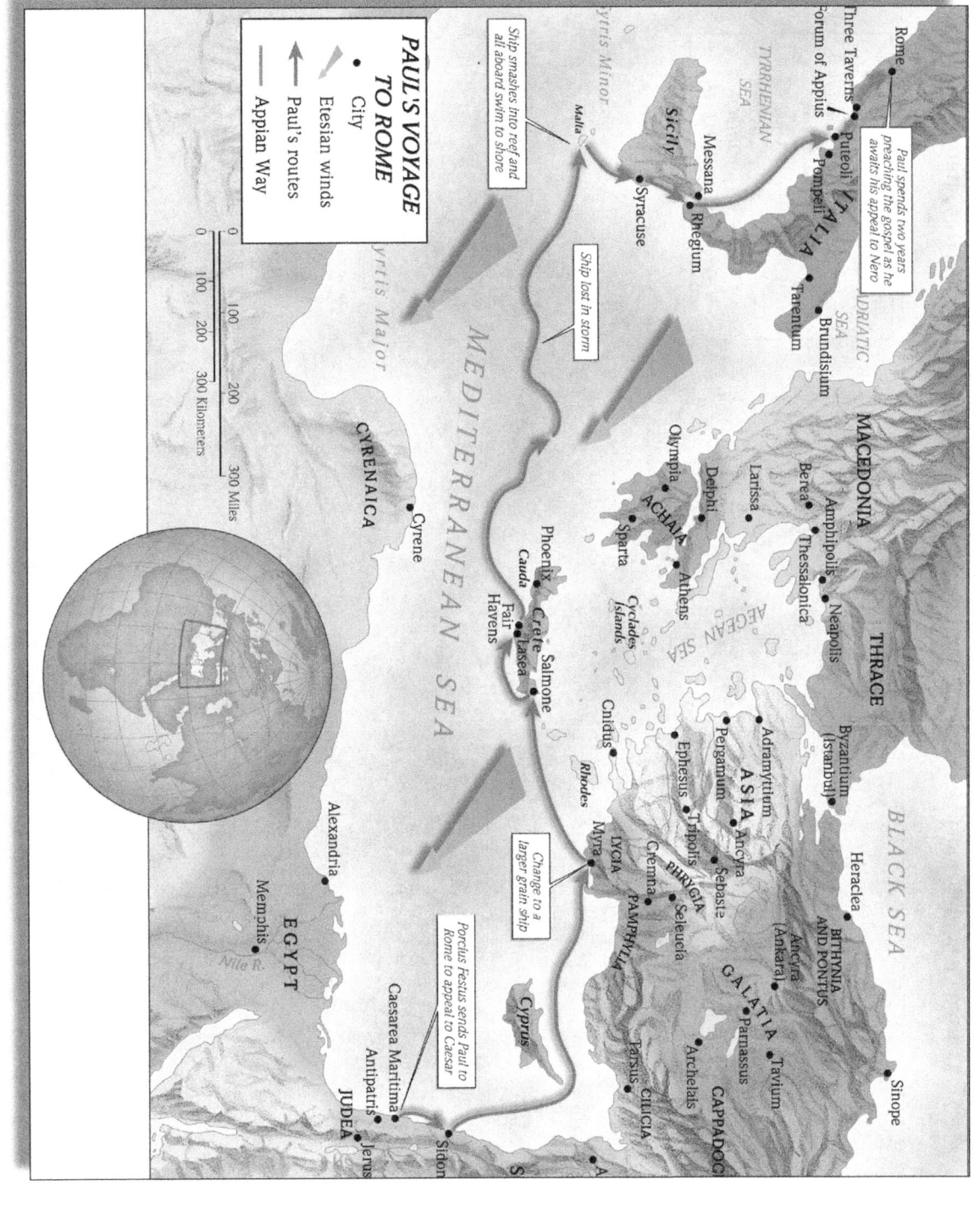

Paul's Voyage to Rome from Holman Bible Atlas © 1998, Holman Bible Publishers. Used by permission.

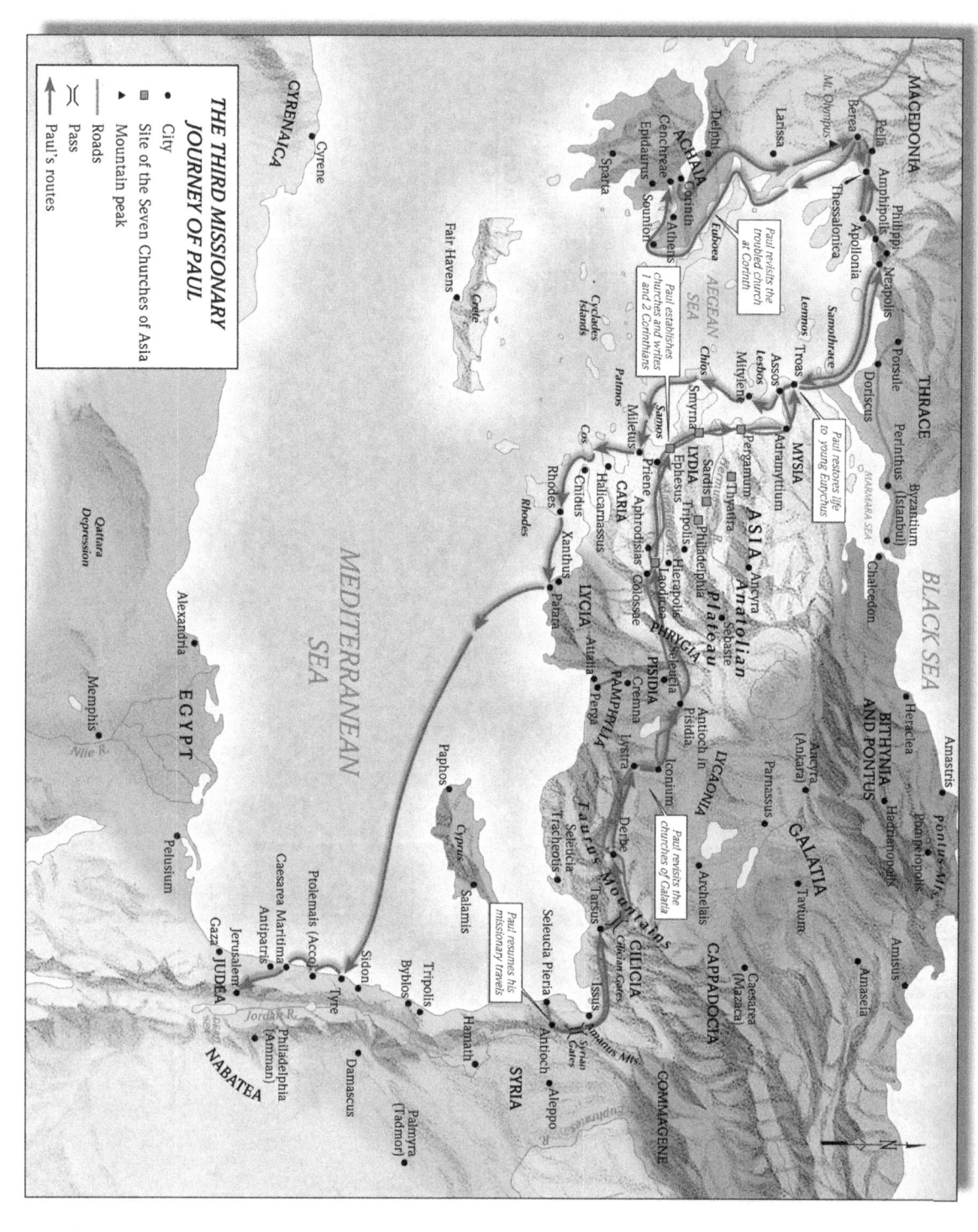

The Third Missionary Journey of Paul from Holman Bible Atlas © 1998, Holman Bible Publishers. Used by permission.

THE THIRD MISSIONARY JOURNEY OF PAUL

Made in the USA
Las Vegas, NV
07 March 2025